THROUGH WET AND DRY

Essays in honour of David Hall

Edited by
Tom Lane and John Coles

Heritage Trust of Lincolnshire
The Old School
Cameron Street
Heckington, Sleaford
Lincolnshire NG34 9RW

W.A.R.P.
Wetland Archaeology Research Project
Laver Building
North Park Road
Exeter
EX4 4QE

Lincolnshire Archaeology and Heritage Reports Series No 5
WARP Occasional Paper 17

Heritage Trust of Lincolnshire
in conjuction with
WARP and English Heritage

Series Editors : David Start and Tom Lane

British Library Cataloguing in Publication Data :
Lane, T. and Coles, J. (eds)
Through Wet and Dry: Essays in honour of David Hall
(Lincolnshire Archaeology and
Heritage Reports Series; No 5)

WARP Occasional Paper 17
ISBN 0-9540224-0-8
ISSN 0950-8244
Heritage Trust of Lincolnshire ISBN 0-948639-35-0

This volume is published with the aid of a grant from
English Heritage

Printed by:
Short Run Press Ltd.
Bittern Road, Sowton Industrial Estate,
Exeter, EX2 7LW

Designed and produced by :
Susan Unsworth
Heritage Trust of Linconshire
The Old School
Cameron Street
Heckington, Sleaford
Lincolnshire NG34 9RW

Cover Design : Susan Unsworth
Cover Illustration : With trademark scarf, clipboard and pencil, David Hall retrieves more artefacts from the desiccating Fenland

CONTENTS

CONTRIBUTORS

Bryony Coles, University of Exeter, Department of Archaeology, Laver Building, North Park Road, Exeter, EX4 4QE

John Coles, Fursdon Mill Cottage, Thorverton, Devon, EX5 5JS

Christopher Evans, Cambridge Archaeological Unit, Department of Archaeology, University of Cambridge, Downing Street, Cambridge, CB2 3DZ

John Hutchings, 6 Queens Road, Colmworth, Bedford, MK44 2LA

Tom Lane, Heritage Lincolnshire, The Old School, Heckington, Sleaford, Lincolnshire, NG34 9RW

Paul Martin, 23 Chalky Road, Broadmayne, Dorchester, Dorset, DT2 8EJ

Rog Palmer, Air Photo Services, 21 Gunhild Way, Cambridge, CB1 8QZ

Francis Pryor, Inley Drove Farm, New Fen Dyke, Sutton St James, Spalding, Lincolnshire, PE12 0LX

Stephen Rippon, University of Exeter, Department of Archaeology, Laver Building, North Park Road, Exeter, EX4 4QE

Brian K. Roberts, Department of Geography, University of Durham, Science Laboratories, South Road, Durham, DH1 3LE

Robert Silvester, Clwyd-Powys Archaeological Trust, 7a Church Street, Welshpool, Powys, SY21 7DL

Robert Van de Noort, University of Exeter, Department of Archaeology, Laver Building, North Park Road, Exeter, EX4 4QE

Preface

Seldom has one individual made more impact on a particular branch of archaeology than has David Hall on Field Survey. No-one has walked more miles over more fields or charmed more farmers. No-one has recognised more fragments of ancient landscape surviving within the modern countryside. In honour of David's completion of 40 extremely active years in archaeology, the contributors of this volume have presented a collection of papers that reflect some of David's particular interests in and his passion for the subject. Featuring prominently is the Fenland of Eastern England, where between 1978 and 1990 David surveyed and mapped tens of thousands of hectares of this bleak terrain. David's skills and academic insights opened up the Fenland to archaeologists and formed a framework on which other studies, such as those presented here, were to benefit. It says much for his dedication that during the heyday of the Fenland Survey, when his weekdays were spent walking the fens, his weekend 'relaxation' was to fieldwalk his native county of Northamptonshire - all of it. Reflected in these papers are both the wetland and dryland interests of David Hall. They serve as a small tribute to an outstanding archaeologist.

Vorwort

Selten hat eine Einzelperson einen größeren Einfluß auf einen bestimmten Zweig der Archäologie gehabt als David Hall auf den Geländesurvey. Niemand ist mehr Meilen über mehr Felder gelaufen oder hat mehr Bauern bezaubert. Niemand hat in der modernen Landschaft mehr Überbleibsel vergangener Landschaften erkannt. Aus Anlaß von Davids Vollendung von 40 äußerst aktiven Jahren in der Archäologie ehren ihn die Autor(inn)en mit dieser Aufsatzsammlung, die Davids spezielle Interessen und seine Leidenschaft für das Fach widerspiegelt. Besondere Beachtung findet das ostenglische Marschgebiet der Fenlands, wo David zwischen 1978 und 1990 zehntausende Hektare dieses kahlen Geländes beging und kartierte. Davids Fähigkeiten und akademische Einsichten eröffneten das Fenland den Archäolog(inn)en; sie bildeten ein Grundgerüst, von dem andere Studien, wie die hier vorgelegten, profitieren konnten. Es spricht für seine Hingebung, daß David während des Höhepunktes des Fenland Geländesurveys, als er seine Wochentage damit verbrachte, die Fenns zu begehen, als 'Wochenenderholung' seinen Heimatkreis Northamptonshire beging – und zwar vollständig. In den hier versammelten Aufsätzen spiegeln sich sowohl die Feuchtboden- als auch die Trockenbodeninteressen von David Hall. Sie dienen als eine kleine Anerkennung für einen hervorragenden Archäologen.

Übersetzung: Cornelius Holtorf

Préface

Peu d'individus auront eu autant d'impact sur une branche particulière de l'archéologie que David Hall sur les études de terrains. Personne n'a parcouru autant de kilomètres, à travers autant de champs, ni charmé autant d'agriculteurs. Personne n'a reconnu autant de fragments de l'ancien paysage dissimulés dans la campagne moderne. En l'honneur de l'accomplissement de 40 années d'archéologie extrèmement bien remplies, les collaborateurs de ce volume présentent un recueil d'études qui sont le reflet de certains des intérêts spécifiques de David et de sa passion pour ce sujet. Occupant une place proéminente, on y trouve les marécages des Fens dans l'est de l'Angleterre, où, entre 1978 et 1990, David a arpenté des dizaines de milliers d'hectares de ces terres inhospitalières et en a établi la cartographie. Les compétences de David et sa perspicacité intellectuelle ont ouvert les marécages des Fens aux archéologues et constituent un cadre duquel d'autres études, telles celles présentées ici, ont pu bénéficier. Ce qui en dit long sur sa dévotion, c'est le fait qu'au plus fort moment de la campagne de repérage des Fens, alors que David passait toute sa semaine à parcourir les marécages, pendant le weekend, il se "détendait" en arpentant son comté natal du Northamptonshire - dans son entier. Ces études reflètent l'intérêt de David Hall à la fois pour les terrains marécageux et les terres sèches. Elles constituent un petit hommage à un éminent archéologue.

Traduction: Annie Pritchard

Many of the papers in this volume were first presented at a conference held in Stamford Arts Centre, Stamford, Lincolnshire on Saturday May 6th, 2000, to celebrate David Hall's 40th year of fieldwork.

1. DAVID AND GOLIATH : THE FENLAND SURVEY

by John Coles

On a very hot and humid summer day about 25 years ago, a small committee met in Cambridge to discuss the priorities for state-funded research in the counties of Cambridgeshire, Essex and Hertfordshire. Designated as the Area Archaeological Advisory Committee, the representatives had before them a long list of work to be done, set out by a variety of agencies. Proposals for those projects deemed to be worthy and of high priority would be forwarded to the Inspectorate of Ancient Monuments, Department of the Environment, for consideration. The afternoon meeting dragged on, and projects were introduced, discussed, and prioritised. There was strong competition and serious debate, because it was known that funding was scarce and that only those projects at the top of the list had any hope of support.

One of the proposals on the table was for a Fenland Field Officer for the county of Cambridgeshire. The Black Fens north of Cambridge itself were known to have yielded many historic and prehistoric finds, almost all by accidental discovery through the activities of peat-cutters, drainage operators and farmers. A good deal of historic information existed and there were also traces of prehistoric occupation, well-assembled over the years by a number of authorities (*e.g.* Miller & Skertchly 1878, Phillips 1951).

But it had never been possible to establish a project, the purpose of which would be to examine in a systematic way the Fenland deposits and their contained archaeological evidence. In the 1930s a more limited effort had been made, through the efforts of Grahame Clark and Harry Godwin at Cambridge. A Fenland Research Committee was established in 1932, drawing upon the expertise of a number of University-based scientists and a few others, to explore areas where deep deposits of peat and silt could be identified. The Committee demonstrated its credentials at Shippea Hill, on the Suffolk-Cambridgeshire border, in a deep excavation where Mesolithic flints could be seen near the base, traces of Neolithic activity higher up, and a Bronze Age occupation at the top (Clark *et al.* 1935). Much other work was done by the Committee, but its geographical spread was limited in the main by the distance from Cambridge where most of the members had full-time teaching positions. The 1939-45 war virtually ended work in the fens, just at a time when agricultural requirements were at their most demanding, with drainage, land-take and deep ploughing exerting maximum pressure on the fertile and fragile soils.

In the decades after the war, Fenland research languished, and those who had driven the work forward were diverted into other fields of enquiry (Phillips 1951). The advent of radiocarbon dating allowed a satisfactory chronological framework to be established, and several small research projects dealing with environmental issues were carried out. Archaeology was noticeably absent from any of these projects. In the mid-1970s, Godwin began work on a popular book on the Fenland, bringing together some aspects of its ancient history and arguing that it had an uncertain future. When it finally appeared, the book was a very useful reminder to us all of the potential rewards that might come from a serious study of the southern Fenland (Godwin 1978). By then, however, the nettle had been firmly grasped by the Area Archaeological Advisory Committee, at the Cambridge meeting.

At the end of the meeting, and after prolonged discussion about the merits of numerous proposals, it was generally agreed that the Fenland project was very important, and it lay equal first with another project from outside the county of Cambridgeshire. The Chairman considered that he had done enough and began to close the meeting. There were two members who thought otherwise, one of them the author of this paper (JC) and the other was John Alexander (JA). JC whispered to JA – 'this is not good enough, we have to be first alone' – and JA whispered back – 'have a go!'. JC proposed that the Fenland Field Officer be first priority and the only one at the top of the list. The Chairman sighed, and wearily said to the full Committee – 'is that agreed?'. No one said a word. The Chairman then announced the new priority list and we all trooped out. JA said – 'I know just the man for this job, a chemist from Oxford'. JC said – 'never heard of him'.

The priority list, sent to the Inspectorate, was acted upon with remarkable speed, and the top proposal was accepted. Interviews were held, and David Hall, the Oxford chemist, was appointed. Little did he know what the work would entail, nor how long the Fenland would engage him – how large and resistant was Goliath.

David arrived in Cambridge in 1976 and began to think about how he would tackle the 142000 ha. of black peat. Although work in the peatfields of the Somerset Levels was already well underway, conditions there were unlike those of the Fens. In Somerset, peat was being actively cut by machines, thereby exposing hundreds of long sections through the deposits. In the Fens, the exposures were horizontal, and less dramatic, as ploughing turned the soils and the peat dried, shrank and was wind-blown away. Centimetre by centimetre the Fenland had diminished in height, and long-buried surfaces were exposed, ancient islands and peninsulas, extinct streams and river-beds, and with them the traces of long-vanished settlements and burial grounds.

In retrospect, it is easy to see that the survey work in the Fens had to be pursued in the way that David devised. At the time of initial appraisal of the conditions and the scale of work, matters were not so clear-cut. The land itself was under the ownership of many different agencies, from huge estates with offices far removed from the Fens, to small-holders still clinging on to their precious patch of soil. Permission to gain access to the land was an essential task and here it was that David's empathy with those whose lives are dominated by the reality of landscape and seasonality was a crucial element. It was one of the stones in David's sling. Another was his energy and determination to see the job through, no matter what the conditions underfoot or overhead might try to hinder and impede. But above all, the real weapon to conquer the Fenland was David's feel for the land and its ancient history. This is more easily sensed than described; it needed a calculating and evaluating eye, assessing the shape of the soil, its colour and consistency, the look and the feel of it – in effect, what it said to David as he grew more closely attached to and familiar with the black fields laid bare and the coloured fields awaiting his arrival in more revealing seasons.

The pattern of work developed over the first years of field survey is now well-known, and has been adopted by other projects. A strict regime for equal coverage of the land was not allowed to fossilise the work but had to be maintained overall, while allowing for the special circumstances of discovery, confirmation and additionality that archaeology demanded. A 30-metre walking interval proved successful for rapid assessment, with a 10-metre pattern for closer identification. By trial, and with little error, the spreads of debris – flints, potsherds, tiles and other materials – were located, evaluated, recorded, and mostly left *in situ*. Mapping by pacing and sketch-plotting was developed to a high degree of precision. Aerial photography, long practised in the Fens by Cambridge fliers, continued to augment the record and assist David in his work, principally in detecting variations in soil colours and textures, providing hints to the ancient configurations of the land. It is widely assumed that the Fenland survey was so large an undertaking that most of the area could be walked only once. But this was not the case in many areas where David could anticipate the value and the necessity of repeat visits, as soils barely exposed became more concentrated and more firmly edged over the course of a very few seasons; but this anticipates beyond the little history now being outlined.

Within a year or so, David had walked several parishes in the Cambridgeshire Fens, having decided that one way to control the coverage and satisfy the recording systems was to use parish boundaries as convenient edges for survey. This was psychologically satisfying both to him, I think, and to those who had the enviable task of managing the work – hardly a task as it managed itself. The results of the early surveys were truly staggering, and have never really received the recognition they deserve. At Littleport, a vast area of former land surface was strewn with thousands of Mesolithic flints, the residue of a once-thriving settlement that was based upon the exploitation of a rich marshland. At Swaffham Prior, David identified and collected several dozen polished stone axes and a large quantity of flints from a series of Neolithic sites, and on Borough Fen, he encountered the first Bronze Age barrow-top, just poking through the surrounding black peats that had once wholly obscured the burial monuments. Over time, David's time, the cemetery grew, as more and more barrows appeared due to the eroding shrinking Fen soils. Borough Fen was only one of a large series of barrow fields discovered by fieldwalking and aerial survey. These and other sites and scatters were sensational enough, but many will think the discovery of the tower at Stonea capped the lot. At Stonea, David walked up to an immense spread of roof tiles and rubble, fully one metre thick in places and perhaps 50 metres in diameter. The site, wholly unknown, was later excavated and interpreted as a Roman commanding tower with attached settlement, constructed to dominate the

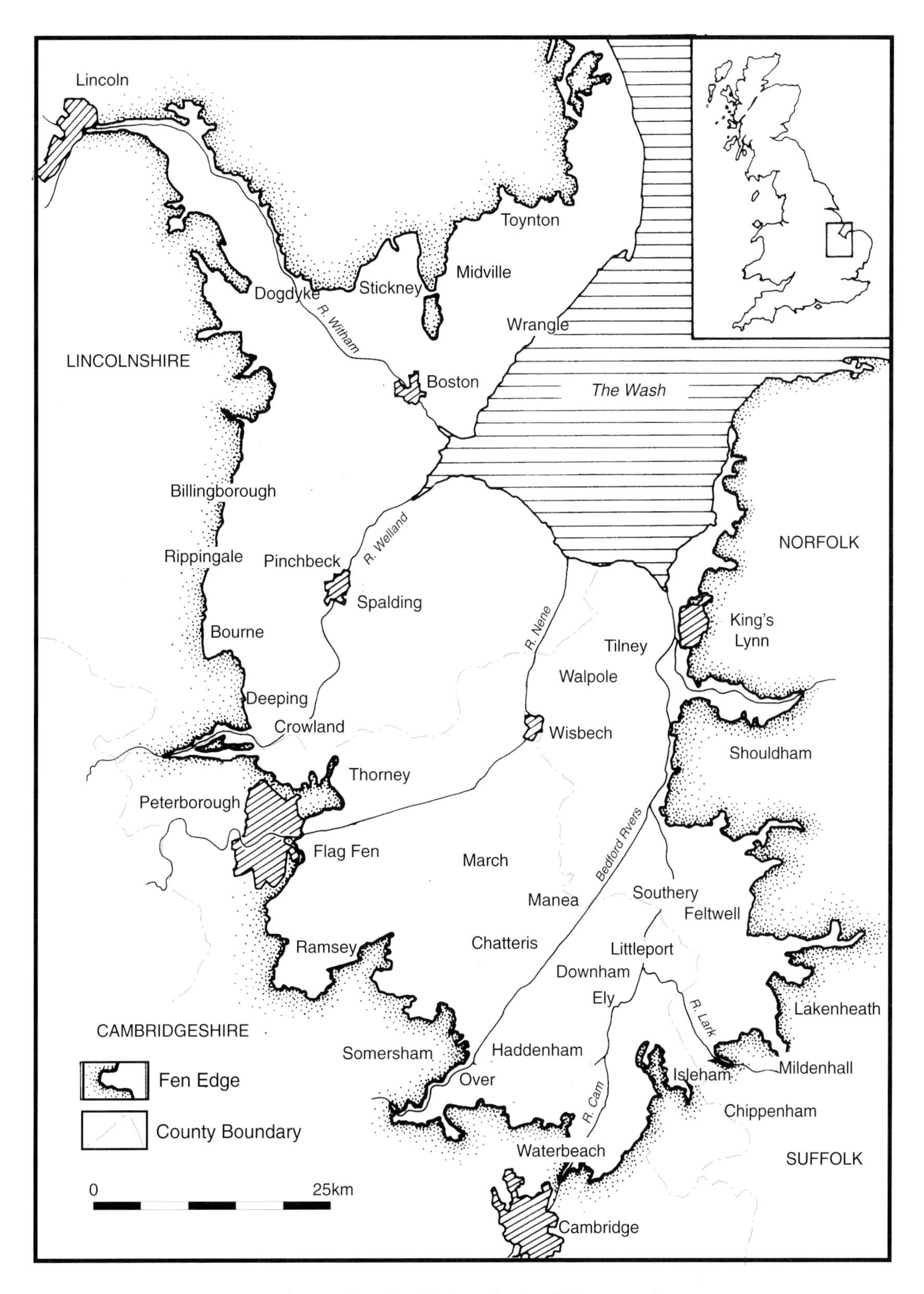

Figure 1 The Fenland with its principal rivers and some parish and other place names

Fens and provide a base from which to subjugate the natives – a difficult task at the best of times.

These discoveries in the first years of David's work were politically significant; they could hardly be ignored in the context of English archaeology of the late 1970s. In 1978, the year of publication of Godwin's book on the Fenland, funds were obtained from the Inspectorate and a more formal Fenland Project was set up to provide a structure for a wider survey of Fen soils in the counties of Lincolnshire and Norfolk, and to extend the work in Cambridgeshire. A larger committee was formed to ensure representation of national and local agencies, and what now would be called a Project Design was composed and submitted for funding. This was successful and by 1981 sufficient assurances had been made by all parties to allow the full Fenland Project to begin work (Fig. 1).

The Project was driven not by the committee but by David, who was formally secretary to the committee as well as Field Officer for the Cambridgeshire Fens, but who also acted as field advisor, sympathiser, and colleague to everyone involved. As Chairman, presiding over countless meetings and often involving matters of dispute concerning allocation of funds, time and other resources, and publication deadlines, it was reassuring to me to have David as a matter-of-fact secretary, someone who saw the survey as the only real Agenda item worthy of serious concern, and we both endeavoured, not always successfully, to keep discussions to a minimum. The Minutes were always minimalist.

As time went on, the four Field Officers (Bob Silvester for Norfolk, Tom Lane and Pete Hayes for Lincolnshire, and David for Cambridgeshire) developed their own methods of day-to-day operations but kept to the work strategy already tried and tested by David Hall. Conditions on the land were different, in Lincolnshire in particular, and soils were more varied here and there. Working with the Field Officers was Martyn Waller whose task was to construct a series of maps of the ancient Fenland at various times through its long environmental history. The simplistic models advanced on the basis of earlier work were revised and altered, as each Fenland embayment could be seen to have its own sequence. Upon the new Fenland maps could be plotted the discoveries made by the Field Officers, and patterns began to emerge. Aerial survey also played an important role in the evolution of the landscape records.

Figure 2 *solvitur ambulando* – the Fenland Project logo – often assumed to be based on David Hall

One special historic record exists in the archive, a vertical aerial photograph showing a Fenland field, with a car parked on an adjacent drove, and a tiny figure set amidst the field. A second photo, taken shortly afterwards, has the same field, the same car, but now the figure has moved along the field. That figure is, of course, David, walking his 30-metre transects, noting soils, undulations, stray finds, and any other features that deserved record. The other Field Officers were doing exactly the same. It was not for no reason that the Fenland Project acquired, by some symbiotic process, its Logo – the solitary figure plodding through the rain over boot-clinging mud, with the words 'It is solved by walking', but of course in a more classical language (Fig. 2).

In the course of the eight years of the Fenland Project, the Officers managed to survey a very large number of hectares of Fenland soils - 249000 hectares in total. This represents about 60% of the entire Fenland; for Cambridgeshire, David's responsibility, the coverage was as near 100% as was humanly possible. From the surveys came observations and records of about 2500 archaeological sites, of which over 2000 were entirely new discoveries. Considerable time was spent by the Officers in defining what the word 'site' actually meant, as opposed to a 'find'. Discrete assemblages of artefacts, concentrated in a definable area, and representing what seemed to be 'settlement', 'industry' or merely a less-defined 'activity', were generally deemed to be legitimate sites. The Officers had to make up their own minds in the field.

One of the prime requirements of the Project was the presentation of the result in monographic form, and so the annual pattern of work for all the Field Officers included post-survey analysis and preparation of reports, parish by parish. It was decided early on that the parish maps, useful as they would be with all the known archaeological sites and finds plotted upon them, could only be considered capable of analysis if they noted the quality of the recording work. A gap on a map might otherwise mean one or more of several possibilities – fieldwork not done, area obscured by buildings, conditions for observation very poor, weather terrible, Field Officer unwell, and so on. Not all these possibilities could be incorporated on the parish maps but a system of hatching was devised to show the variations in conditions of the work, from excellent to moderate to poor to not done at all. In this way, the distributions of ancient activities could be better assessed. There can be little doubt that large farm complexes still hide, if not wholly destroy, some sites, which had been on prime locations in the past just as they are at present. Stray finds adjacent to such places were of particular importance, providing hints of now-lost settlement. The parish map presentations allowed such conjecture as well as showing where future work might be directed.

One avenue of discovery in the Fenland could not be followed to its logical end. As the peat soils in particular continued to desiccate and erode, often by the famous 'Fenland blows', new levels of old landscapes were exposed. The topmost sands and gravels of an island or peninsula would thereby become visible, or be exposed more extensively and prominently. Sites on the tops would be recognised first, of course, but without field visits in subsequent years the possibility of seeing occupation scatters on the lower slopes, or on newly-exposed smaller islands, was lost. As noted above in relation to the Borough Fen barrow field, some repeat visits were possible, but a plan to re-walk the black soils was never implemented. This is a task for the future if another David can be found – not that the present holder of that name is incapable of doing it.

The first of the eagerly-awaited Fenland Survey monographs appeared in 1987 (Hall 1987), covering five parishes of the Cambridgeshire Fens. It was followed by two more volumes on that county (Hall 1992, 1996), two for Norfolk (Silvester 1988, 1991) and two for Lincolnshire (Hayes and Lane 1992 and 1993). Then came the overview of Fenland environments, a crucial volume on which all the others had relied (Waller 1994). These books are the monuments of the Fenland Project, and the basis for almost all subsequent work. It may be appropriate here to note one or two of the features of the monographs which show a remarkable uniformity in presentation, allowing for easy comparisons between parish surveys, conducted over a number of years. David carried out fieldwork on about 60 parishes in Cambridgeshire, all of them containing large or small areas of Fen soils. In the monographs, each parish receives a description of geology and soils, the archaeological survey conditions (Quality Assessment), note of previous finds, and a summary of the totality of the evidence. The simple listing of stray finds masks the fact that David collected information about countless number of objects that resided on farm mantelpieces or in dusty boxes, gathered from the fields over many years by farmers and others. All of this material could be mapped, and here the work of David's colleague, Rog Palmer, can be acknowledged; he combined an expertise in aerial survey with mapping skills.

The maps in the monographs are a major element for interpretation. They are presented in chronological order for each parish, with the degrees of environmental detail appropriate to the availability of soil identification, aerial photographs, and conditions of survey. Often we have a Prehistoric map (15 in all) and sometimes the detail is available for separate Neolithic (6), Bronze Age (10) and Iron Age (4) maps. The presence of any Iron Age maps at all is a triumph, as it had for long been believed that there was no real Iron Age presence in the southern Fenland. Maps of Roman activity are generally present in the monographs (18) and almost always there is a medieval map (29). Sometimes various periods are combined on maps (17). This makes about 100 maps that show the archaeological evidence on contemporary landscapes. Of course one of the problems of parish-based maps is that the modern, or relatively modern, boundaries may not reflect ancient environmental margins – extinct streams, woodland edges, marshland and the like – as well as long-gone social and political borders. So an individual parish, no matter how well presented on maps, cannot provide a useful guide to former settlements, or environments – a sample, perhaps, but too small for real testing. The monographs take note of this constriction and present period maps of the entire area encompassed by all the parishes surveyed in the particular book. In this way, the patterns of ancient settlement and activity begin to emerge, and, as an example, Over-Sutton-Chatteris combine to demonstrate the dynamism of Fenland occupation at particular periods in the past.

The map will need little textual explanations (Fig. 3). A submerged landscape, revealed in part by the

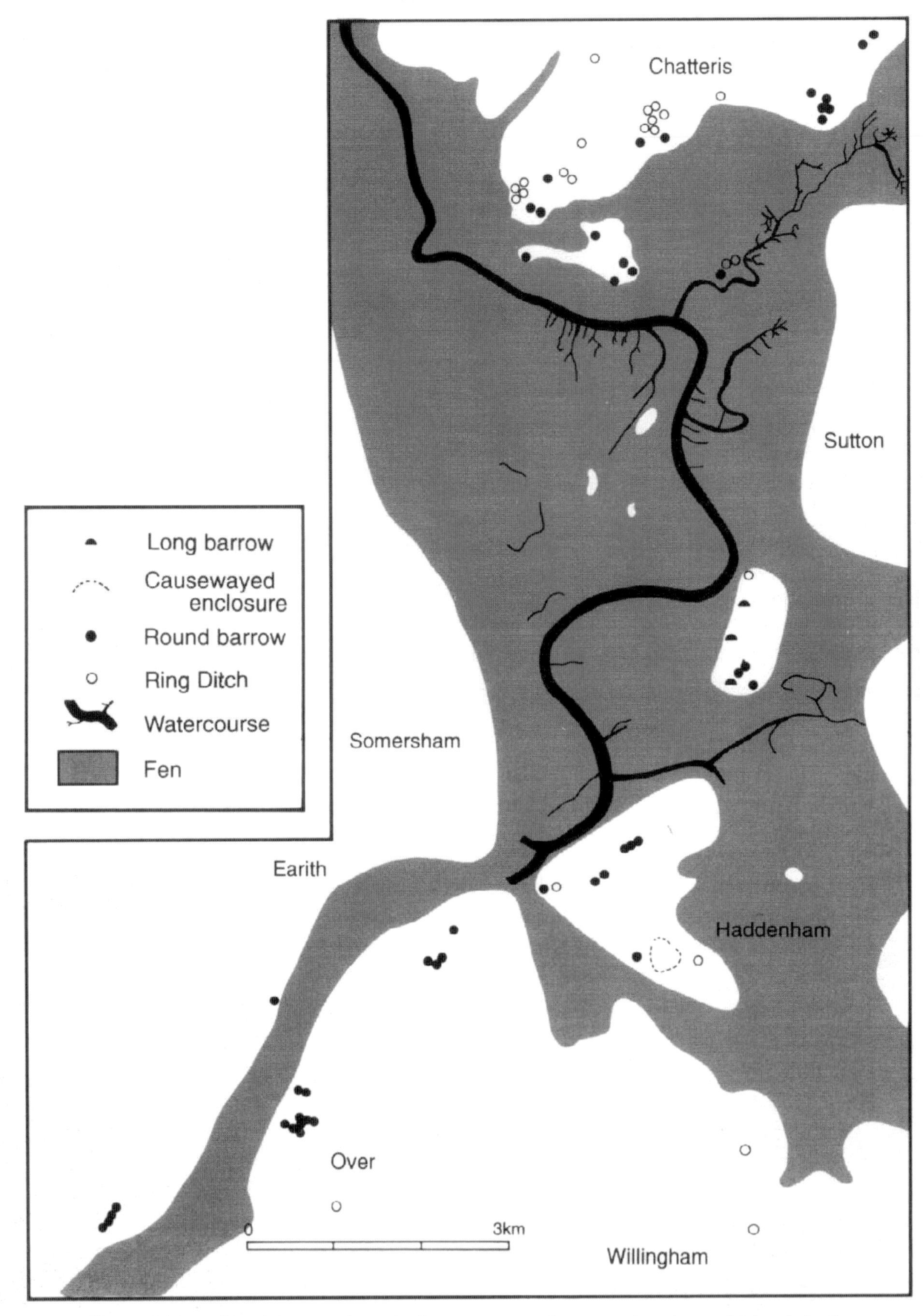

Figure 3 Map of burial mounds and other monuments on peninsulas and islands in the prehistoric Fen. The ancient river Ouse and some of its tributary streams are shown

lowering of Fen soils, by aerial reconnaissance, by environmental coring and by assiduous fieldwalking, contains a pattern of Bronze Age monuments. They are clearly positioned within a now-extinct wetland, set on slopes and heights overlooking the streams, rivers and marshlands. Even small islands can be identified, holding the burial monuments of people who were tilling the dryland, pasturing their animals on the sweet meadows, and gathering the wild plants and animals of the wetlands and waterways. The picture has some gaps, of course, in inaccessible parts of the land today, in unrecognised scatters of implements and settlement debris, in still-buried parts of the contemporary landscape, but nonetheless it is still a dynamic view of a human society long since passed into obscurity if not oblivion, until now. A depth of time is built into the picture, as the burial cemeteries represent an interest and commitment to a place over perhaps several centuries, as do our cemeteries of the present day, and a very early involvement with the rich landscape is seen on a tiny island at Haddenham, where long mounds of the Neolithic were created to house the dead in communal burial traditions. Excavation of one of these has provided unusual if not unique evidence about the rituals of death in the fourth millennium BC. Landscapes like this are archaeologically rare in the extreme, and it is difficult to find comparable preservation of vast tracts of prehistoric land surfaces anywhere else in Europe.

But David was not yet finished with the Fens and in 1989-90 he was involved in a new project, the Fenland Evaluation Project. This set out to examine all the scenes of the discoveries made by the Field Officers, and to draw out a priority list of those sites that seemed to be worthy of additional research, either by more intensive survey or by small-scale excavation, and by more environmental study. This project was to culminate in a smaller list of sites of the highest significance which English Heritage would then consider for protection, or excavation, or more limited investigations. Quite clearly, there had to be much work of liaison between the county teams, with discussions held on sites and at meetings; much of this fell upon David as secretary to the committee and as *de facto* manager of the project.

With the completion of the Evaluation Project, and with monograph preparations well underway, an opportunity arose for survey in a new region. In 1990 a new project had been established by English Heritage in the north west of England, to survey the lowland wetlands in seven counties. Groundwork had been laid by an assessment of the record of early discoveries, and work in the field was firmly based on Fenland practices. The wetlands in the seven counties were mostly

Plate 1 David Hall enjoying a site visit with Mark Leah

fragmented, unlike the great expanses of peats and silts in the Fenland, and this posed problems both for archaeological survey and for environmental sampling. Work progressed and at an early stage the wetlands of Greater Manchester were to be examined. The offer was made, and David accepted the task, knowing full well that the challenges were going to be different from those of the tranquil Fens, but equally exciting in prospect. The work was done as efficiently as expected, the wetlands were more stubborn in their release of data, and many a promising field had little or nothing to offer. But the survey was completed, analysed and published as a handsome monograph in the North West Wetlands series (Hall 1995).

By 1990, English Heritage had taken the decision to proceed with efforts to preserve a number of the Fenland sites which had been targetted in the Evaluation Project. A new Fenland Management Project was set up, David again acting as secretary to a committee, and overseeing all of the work done by teams in the three counties. Some of the prioritised sites were scheduled and thereby legally protected. Some other sites, evaluated as being seriously degraded, were abandoned to their fate. Others, however, were deemed to be significant enough in their buried potential to warrant renewed investigation. Some of the sites were only sampled for specific purposes, for the elucidation of particular deposits, parameters of occupation, or character of structures, or degree of wetness. Some sites were extensively excavated, it being accepted that preservation was not an option, and in a few cases the early results demanded an extension of work. The effect over a very few years of this project was very substantial, teams in all three counties engaged in major enterprises, with David acting as the link between the various elements, especially environmental work and English Heritage administration. In all of this, David was well aware, as we all were, of the unflagging interest and firm support of Philip Walker who had been with the Fenland Project from its earliest phase.

At the time of the Stamford Conference in David's honour, the Fenland excavations were at an end, the analytical work was mostly done, interim reports on all sites in the Management Project were assembled and published (Crowson *et al* 2000), and the work towards full publication of the entire Project – Survey, Evaluation and Management – by themes and areas, was well under way. The various authors and editors of these volumes already had an overview to set their themes and area surveys into a wider Fenland context. The overview was a book called *Fenland Survey. An essay in landscape and persistence*, written jointly by David Hall and John Coles (1994). It set out to provide a summary of the findings of the original Fenland Project,the parish surveys, bringing them all together in a chronologically-based story of the Fenland over seven thousand years. This was an opportunity to take a wide view, to look for changes in settlement patterns, to bring in the evidence of older discoveries, and to venture some comments on the historical records of Fenland lives: as one of the authors it was hugely satisfying to be able to step back and look for the broad patterns and address the major issues. The book was apolitical, tried to be factually accurate, but at the same time offer a joint opinion about the ancient Fenland. The book has been well-received, and there is a general and regular demand for it by those who live in and appreciate the Fens as a unique landscape both today and in the past. It has been succeeded, but not matched, by a smaller book by the same authors, called *Changing Landscapes. The Ancient Fenland*, which is designed to offer a more succinct and user-friendly account of the land, its evolution and its prehistoric and historic people (Coles and Hall 1998). This author has found it refreshing and stimulating to work with David on books, and their welcoming reception by archaeologists, environmentalists and the general public is due in a very large degree to the dedication, energy and understanding of David Hall.

The Fenland Project and its offshoots have been a major success for English Heritage. Internationally admired through its publications, the Project continues to excite interest through its concept - that a national agency could take a longer view, and would look for a reward that could not be anticipated in any detail or guaranteed as to quality. The Goliath of the Fens was considered by many to be too formidable, too difficult to explore, too complex to understand. Through the work of David Hall, the Fens were confronted and made to yield their many stories of ancient lives, and now it remains for us all to accept the responsibility to ensure that some parts of those stories remain for future generations to understand and enjoy. In that understanding and enjoyment our debt to David Hall will be readily acknowledged by all.

Acknowledgements

I owe a great deal to many people who have through their work contributed to the success of the Fenland

Project; and thus indirectly to this commentary. I especially thank Bob Silvester, Tom Lane and Peter Hayes (Fenland Field Officers), Rog Palmer (Fenland Research Assistant), and Philip Walker (English Heritage Inspector) for many valuable contributions over the past two decades of my involvement with Fenland matters. Geoff Wainwright (English Heritage) was instrumental in the funding of the work, and always supportive. The person to whom I owe the most is my friend and colleague, David Hall.

Bibliography

Clark, J.G.D., Godwin, H. and Clifford, M.H., 1935, 'Report on recent excavations at Peacock's Farm, Shippea Hill, Cambridgeshire', *Antiq. J.* 15, 284-319

Coles, J. and Hall, D., 1998, *Changing Landscapes: The Ancient Fenland* (Cambridgeshire County Council, Cambridge)

Crowson, A., Lane, T. and Reeve, J., (eds), 2000, *Fenland Management Project Excavations 1991-1995*, Lincolnshire Archaeology and Heritage Reports Series 3

Godwin, H., 1978, *Fenland. Its Ancient Past and Uncertain Future* (University Press, Cambridge)

Hall, D., 1987, *The Fenland Project, Number 2: Fenland Landscapes and Settlement between Peterborough and March*, East Anglian Archaeology 35

Hall, D., 1992, *The Fenland Project, Number 6: The South-Western Cambridgeshire Fenlands*, East Anglian Archaeology 56

Hall, D., 1995, *The Wetlands of Greater Manchester*, North West Wetlands Survey 2 (Lancaster)

Hall, D., 1996, *The Fenland Project, Number 10: Cambridgeshire Survey, The Isle of Ely and Wisbech*, East Anglian Archaeology 79

Hall, D. and Coles, J., 1994, *Fenland Survey. An essay in landscape and persistence*, English Heritage Archaeological Report 1 (London)

Hayes, P.P. and Lane, T.W., 1992, *The Fenland Project, Number 5: Lincolnshire Survey, the South-West Fens*, East Anglian Archaeology 55

Lane, T.W., 1993, *The Fenland Project, Number 8: Lincolnshire Survey, the Northern Fen-edge*, East Anglian Archaeology 66

Miller, S.H. and Skertchly, S.B.J., 1878, *The Fenland Past and Present* (Wisbech)

Phillips, C.W., 1951, 'The Fenland Research Committee, its past achievements and future prospects' in Grimes, W.F. (ed), *Aspects of Archaeology in Britain and Beyond. Essays presented to O. G. S. Crawford*, 258-273

Silvester, R., 1988, *The Fenland Project, Number 3: Norfolk Survey, Marshland and the Nar Valley*, East Anglian Archaeology 45

Silvester, R., 1991, *The Fenland Project, Number 4: Norfolk Survey, the Wissey Embayment and the Fen Causeway*, East Anglian Archaeology 52

Waller, M., 1994, *The Fenland Project, Number 9: Flandrian Environmental Change in Fenland*, East Anglian Archaeology 70

2. SOME EARLY MAPS OF THE FENS

by Bob Silvester

This conference, as its title indicates, is devoted largely to fieldwork, much of it inspired or led by one man whose name for many is synonymous with the landscape of the Fens and the work that has gone on there in recent years. Those of us privileged to have worked with David Hall in the Fens learnt from him not just about peat, about roddons and the recovery of artefacts from the ploughsoil, but were also inculcated with the drive and determination that were required to maintain progress in our fieldwork throughout the autumn and winter months, year after year. But I feel we should remind ourselves that David's interests and his skills are much wider than fieldwork alone. His ability to read medieval documents and utilise their contents has always impressed me. It is a skill which is manifest in his seminal work, *The open fields of Northamptonshire* (Hall 1995). When I last saw him a couple of months ago he was putting in long hours transcribing a medieval register from the Peterborough archives, and it is a comment on his abilities that he is currently the editor of the Northamptonshire Record Society journal.

Documents are not the only resource that David exploits; maps, too, have their place in his work. I started work in the Norfolk Fens late in 1982, and it was not long before I was introduced by him to the archives of Wisbech Museum. It should not be construed as a disparaging comment to suggest that Wisbech is, in many ways, a typical, small provincial museum. Yet it is one that contains a wealth of documentary and cartographic material not only for Cambridgeshire but also for the adjacent Norfolk fenlands, material which in any other part of the country would long ago have been deposited in the county record office. Included in this material are a significant number of maps, both printed and manuscript. There is a typescript catalogue of the maps which states:

"The collection of maps and plans in Wisbech Museum was catalogued in 1967-8 by B R Bailey, T G Fendick, D C Annies and A C Carter. In 1978 David Hall and Ruth Harding re-ordered and labelled the [rolled maps], checking their contents, adding much more detail to the catalogue, and compiled an index of places."

I am not sure whether I need a pretext here for examining something other than the results of fieldwork but, in the event that some justification is needed, that statement provides it. And there is another point that I should make here, one which really only occurred to me as I was preparing this presentation. I now spend a fair proportion of my professional life undertaking fieldwork and survey in the uplands of central Wales, a region very different from the Fens. But my colleagues and I use techniques that were in use and were to some extent developed during the Fenland Survey: 30m-transect walking, the use of vertical aerial photographs for site, vegetation and land-use mapping in the field (Silvester 1991), and the like. We use, too, early cartography where it is available. There is, however, a fundamental difference between Wales and eastern England. A tradition of property or estate mapping did not materialise in Wales much before the second half of the eighteenth century (Thomas 1992, 4), and our research into such topics as deserted rural settlement and the exploitation of the uplands is the poorer because of it. In eastern England that mapping tradition emerged nearly two hundred years earlier (Delano-Smith and Kain 1999, 118), and it can be used to inform and, on occasions, complement the results of fieldwork. It is this that I want to touch upon this morning.

There is a long history of compiling maps in the Fenland and the area immediately surrounding it. Professor Paul Harvey noted some years ago that in the medieval centuries it was the only region of England to witness the emergence of anything like a tradition of local map production (Skelton and Harvey 1986, 34). It is unlikely that many more medieval English maps remain to be identified, yet occasionally a new one is discovered, or a known one re-assessed. This is the case with the Pinchbeck Fen map, previously attributed to the middle of the sixteenth century (Lynam 1936, 304). Through the work of Rose Mitchell at the Public Record Office, this map can now be assigned to the mid-fifteenth century. It shows among other things twenty-eight churches and chapels, eight of which have now disappeared, and it does seem that many if not all of these buildings were drawn from life, interesting for such places as the priories of Sempringham and Spalding for which there are no other known contemporary representations (Mitchell and Crook 1999, 43).

But it is with a later phase of mapping that I am primarily concerned this morning. A significant proportion of the medieval maps in this country were probably drawn up in relation to land disputes. But by the end of the sixteenth century, the objectives in mapping tracts of land had expanded to take in both drainage proposals and the depiction of estates. As both were of importance in and around the Fens it is not surprising to find a sizeable number of maps of the area for the period extending from the later part of Elizabeth's reign through to the Civil War. Thus the mapping tradition that emerged in the medieval fenland may be said to have continued into the seventeenth century — a period of particular significance in the history of the Fens because of the first stages in a comprehensive drainage programme; and it was important too for the cartography which was, in no little way, led by the whole drainage question.

The study of early cartography can follow several paths. It may attempt to analyse the sequence of mapping, determining the patterns, the borrowings and the traditions that influenced the preparation of a particular map or group of maps. It may utilise maps to unravel the contemporary landscape and, in so doing, isolate both earlier and more recent features of that landscape. And thirdly it may address the symbolism and meanings of the map, and this as an integral part of cartographic study has become increasingly significant in recent years (see in particular the later works of Brian Harley [Woodward 1992]). As an archaeologist I am particularly concerned with the second of these approaches, that of interpreting the landscape. But the nature of fenland maps is such that the maps themselves and their sequence has increasingly come to the fore in my studies.

In the seventeenth century the copying of printed maps became a commonplace. Thus Christopher Saxton's county maps drawn up in the 1570s were copied and improved by John Speed in the first decade of the seventeenth century (Delano-Smith and Kain 1999, 72). In turn others such as the Dutch mapmakers Blaeu and Jansson used Speed's maps, as did Robert Morden at the end of the century — cartographic plagiarism, but seemingly an accepted part of the process which did not draw any opprobrium. Fenland mapping witnessed this process at work, but exceptionally it was not in the realm of printed maps of which there were relatively few, but in their manuscript counterparts.

To effect some degree of perspective to the seventeenth century maps of the fens, we can distinguish three groups: firstly, small-scale maps covering relatively large areas of land and conversely depicting little in the way of landscape detail, and here it may be a good idea to clarify one point immediately. The mapping of the Fens as an entity – for Cambridgeshire, Lincolnshire, Norfolk and Suffolk – is a relatively recent phenomenon, as far as I can ascertain no earlier than the mid-nineteenth century. Prior to this when writers refer to general maps of the Fens these are usually of the Bedford Level, that is the peat fens of Cambridgeshire, Norfolk and Suffolk, but not extending into the Lincolnshire fenland. Maps of the more northerly, Lincolnshire portion were always drawn separately. Secondly at the opposite end of the range are the large-scale estate and occasionally drainage maps that depict considerable detail. And between the two groups are maps of intermediate scale, though these are rare.

Several late sixteenth century maps of the southern Fens are either extant or feature in contemporary references. Around 1588 John Hexham and Ralph Agas, his more famous contemporary, were appointed to produce a map of the south Holland fens of Lincolnshire (Skelton and Summerson 1971, 53). This map has not come down to us, though it is known that Agas had completed his portion of it by the middle of 1589. There is, however, another map by Hexham, this one signed, which is in the Hatfield House archives. Thought to date to about 1590, it shows with a modicum of detail Cambridgeshire's western fens between Crowland and Whittlesey Mere, and depicts an area of fen disputed by Whittlesey and Wisbech for which Hexham had been appointed a special commissioner in the years 1577-79 (Skelton and Summerson 1971, 52). A second map in the same collection, showing the same area of Cambridgeshire but extending too across southern Holland, has the appearance of a slightly earlier map, though Skelton and Summerson (1971, 54) argued that it might have supported a drainage initiative put to the Privy Council in 1590-1. Little more can be said in the absence of a detailed analysis of this map.

One small-scale map of the southern fens has drawn more frequent comment. Prepared by William Haiwarde in 1604, and accompanying a written survey submitted in the following year (and which was reproduced by Sir William Dugdale in 1662 in the first edition of his *History of Imbanking and Drayning.....*), its whereabouts are unknown and it is presumed to have been destroyed. Many years ago Edward Lynam – superintendent of the British Museum map room between the two World Wars, and with Sir Herbert Fordham one of the two distinguished commentators on early fenland cartography – pointed out that this was the earliest map of the whole Fens; in that it extended over the whole of the black fens in Cambridgeshire, Huntingdonshire, Norfolk and Suffolk, he was almost certainly correct (Lynam 1934, 420). He drew attention to two copies of Haiwarde's masterpiece, one prepared by the surveyor Thomas Badeslade for inclusion in his volume on the Port of King's Lynn (1725), and the other in manuscript by Payler Smyth who in 1727 was paid by the Fen Commissioners to produce "an exact copy " of Haiwarde's map. However, as Lynam astutely demonstrated, Payler Smyth used the wrong map for his model, copying a rather inexact replica of the original that had been drawn in 1618.

There are, however, at least two other manuscript copies of the Haiwarde map in existence. One is in the British Library (*Cotton Augustus I.i.78*), having been liberated by that inveterate collector of manuscripts, Sir Robert Cotton, prior to his downfall in 1629: his autograph can be detected in the bottom right-hand corner of the map. Lynam thought that this map was by Haiwarde himself, perhaps a precursor of the lost map (1934, 422). This, however, seems unlikely. In 1934 Lynam was able to call on only three other maps drawn by Haiwarde. Now the number of maps assignable to Haiwarde is around thirty of which perhaps half are signed, permitting us a much clearer idea of his style and also his use of colour (Silvester 1989). On the basis of both, it is evident that the British Library map was not drawn by him. Yet in its details the Cotton map reveals enough points in common with those by Badeslade and Payler Smyth to signify a common source which must have been Haiwarde's original. Large numbers of names are inscribed on the Cotton map, and in attempting to establish the purpose of the map we should look to the south-western Cambridgeshire Fens where numerous names are included around Whittlesey Mere and where, exceptionally, three colours have been used to outline various blocks of fen bordering on the lake (Fig. 1). Here too the frequent references to the land of Ramsey, one of the three monasteries (together with Thorney and Peterborough) that in the medieval era had rights on Whittlesey Mere (VCH 1936, 186), imply that this map may have had a role in defining landholdings in that localised area of the fen.

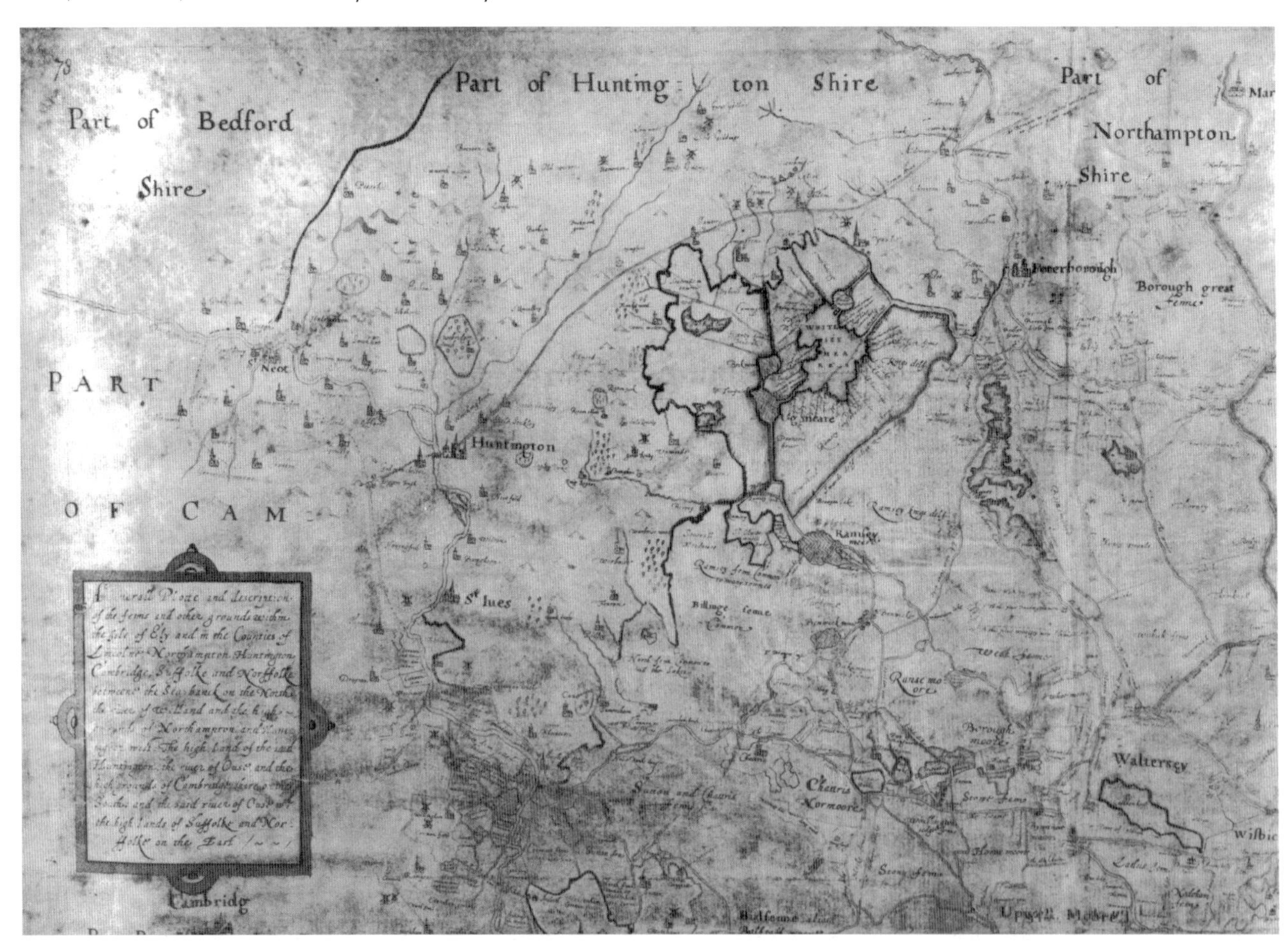

Figure 1 Early seventeenth century manuscript map of the Fens: detail around Whittlesey Mere
Reproduced by permission of The British Library

A specific purpose can also be assigned to the second manuscript map which is much less well-known. Outside the catalogues of the Public Record Office (*MPB 9*), where it is held, the only reference that I have encountered is in the magazine *Country Life* (Croft 1983) where, in familiar fashion, it was claimed as Haiwarde's original map. But what we are witnessing is another copy, one very much sparser on detail than the Cotton, Badeslade and Payler Smith maps. Two different hands of late sixteenth/early seventeenth century date are visible on the map (Rose Mitchell, *pers comm.*), the second confined to the addition of further minor topographical names in the peat fen area of west Norfolk and also the definition of the boundary between Norfolk and Cambridgeshire, both in name and by colour. As Croft pointed out the map was presented to the Privy Council in 1611 by several Commissioners of Sewers whose signatures appear on the back of the map.

There is a fifth map, this one in the University Library in Cambridge (*MS Plans 598*). It survives in a later copy, perhaps by Thomas Badeslade from the early eighteenth century, but in its detail it depicts the Fens at the beginning of the seventeenth century. Though it may be another derivative of the Haiwarde survey, in contrast to the previous maps it appears to be focused more on the road network than on the waterways and drainage pattern in the Fens. How this fits into the overall picture has yet to be resolved.

There are, then, a number of maps that collectively might enable the form of the lost Haiwarde archetype to be established with reasonable precision. This is of more than minor interest, for Lynam claimed that the Cotton map was utilised by Henricus Hondicus in 1632 as the basis for the first engraved map of the Fens (1934, 422). Regardless of whether the Cotton map or Haiwarde's original was the model, Hondicus' engraving was copied by later Dutch mapmakers as well as by Sir William Dugdale, and thus this lost map stands at the head of a series of Fenland maps produced during the seventeenth century. But what information these small-scale maps yield about the fenland landscape of the late sixteenth century is a rather different matter; for this larger-scale depictions are required.

Sub-regional maps of the Fens covering smaller areas at a larger scale are not common, but do occur occasionally. The manuscript map of Wisbech Hundred, now in Wisbech Museum, has Latin legends and in its present form was prepared by Thomas Watts in 1657, a copy of a lost map by John Johnson from 1597 who in turn seems to have copied an earlier sixteenth century example (Lynam 1934, 299). Some years ago Arthur Owen suggested that it was originally derived from a late fourteenth century map of the Cambridgeshire and south Lincolnshire fens now housed in the Public Record Office (Owen 1986, 97). But as a statement of the sixteenth century Fenland landscape it has remained under-researched since the Wisbech historian, G M G Woodgate, wrote about it nearly seventy years ago (Woodgate 1934).

This, however, is not the case with William Haiwarde's map of Marshland. Compiled in 1591 (and I use the word 'compiled' advisedly), it has come down to us only in a copy, now in the Cambridge University Library (*MS Plans 599*), which is dated to between 1680 and 1700 on the basis of the paper on which it was drawn (Silvester 1988, pls II and III). But in its general appearance it conforms to Haiwarde's works and it is only the minutiae of the style of lettering as well as the paper that give it away.

This map was used extensively during the research on Marshland (Silvester 1988) in the belief that it was an original ground survey by Haiwarde from the end of the sixteenth century, the earliest dated example of many accurate surveys by him. It provides a wealth of detail about the landscape of Marshland, the name attributed to much of the Norfolk siltland edging the Wash which was registered as one of the most prosperous regions of the country in the Middle Ages (Glasscock 1975, map I). Amongst other features it illustrates the layout of the primary villages; the greens near those villages, all of which have now disappeared but which can be traced, if only intermittently, on the ground; the great droves that led from the villages to the common pastures of Marshland Smeeth and West Fen, again long gone but still discernible as great linear depressions; and the sea bank which retained its integrity from late Saxon times, and in contrast to the Lincolnshire siltlands appears not to have been superseded by further sea banks encompassing new intakes from the salt marshes in the medieval period. In practice the map serves to reinforce and develop the landscape pattern of Marshland built up through years of fieldwork, and it explains or at least confirms some of the anomalies in features such as the greens and droves that puzzled this writer during the ground survey.

The map in fact depicts in large part the medieval landscape of Marshland, one that had but little changed by the end of the sixteenth century. And

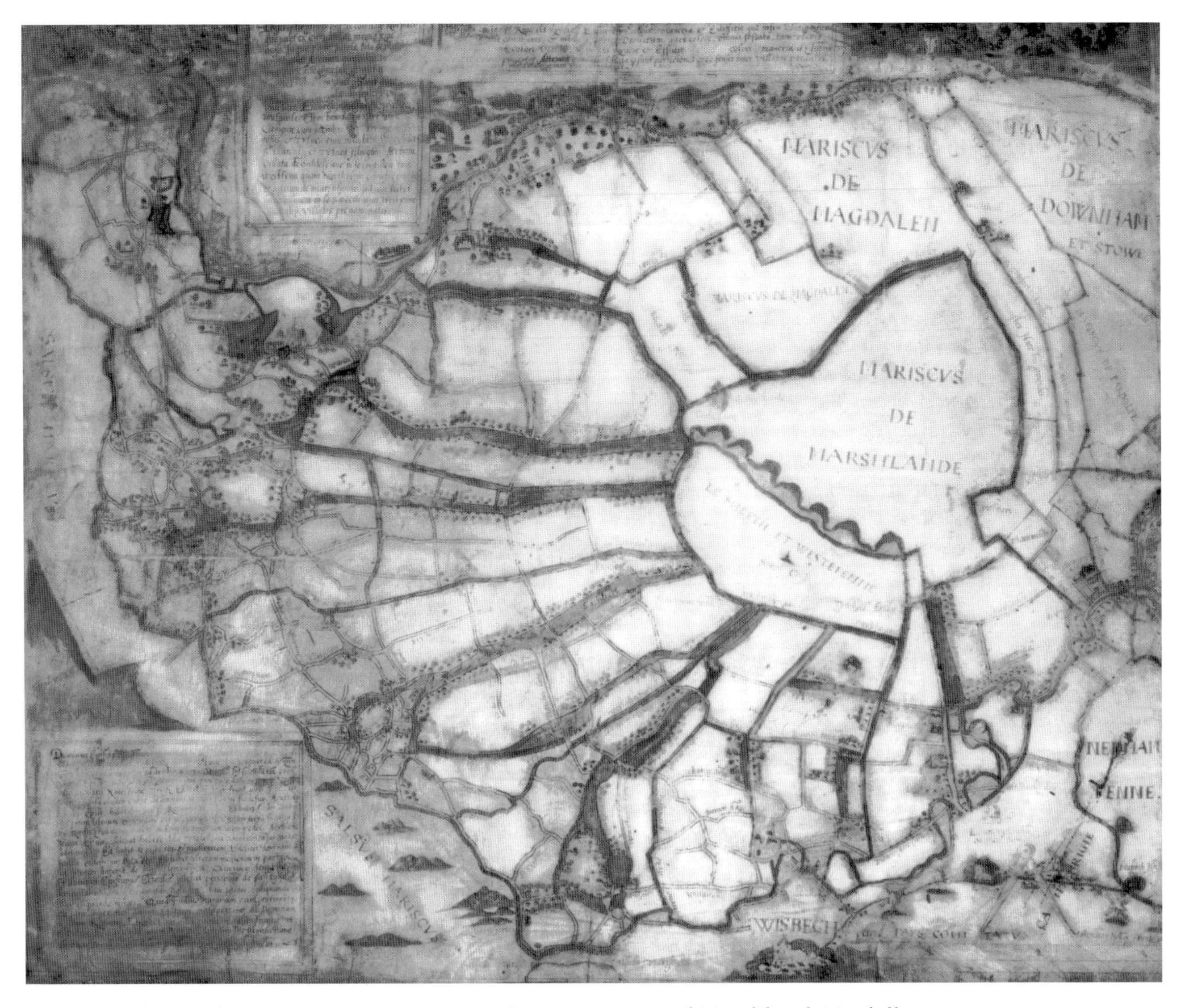

Figure 2 Late sixteenth-century map of Marshland, Norfolk
Reproduced by permission of The British Library

because of its perceived accuracy and the fact that we were able to overlay it satisfactorily on a modern map, it played a significant role in informing the map of the complete medieval landscape between the rivers Ouse and Nene which has achieved some currency beyond the Fenland Project volumes (Wade Martins 1995, fig 25; Silvester 1999, fig 9.3; Rippon 2000, fig 60).

Yet in assuming that this was an original ground survey by William Haiwarde, even though in later copy, I made a fundamental error. In 1992 the British Library purchased at auction a manuscript map of Marshland which had been in a private collection in Wisbech (*BL MS Add 71126l*; Fig. 2). A careful examination of the two maps together with a third manuscript map archived in Wisbech Museum demonstrates that they all derive from an archetype, presumed to be lost. This lost map was drawn in or soon after 1580 when the Bishop of Ely's estates were appropriated by the Crown. That much is clear from the legend in the cartouches of both the British Library and Wisbech Museum maps. The reason why there must have been an earlier map that belonged to the Crown focuses on an incongruity in what is depicted at the top of the map. Here a country house is shown as prominently as the town of Downham Market. Stow Hall was situated in Stow Bardolph – the church too is depicted on the British Library and Wisbech Museum maps – and was the home of Nicholas Hare, a London lawyer, who around 1582 inherited the large Stow estate on the edge of the Fens. But Stow Hall lay three kilometres to the east of the Great Ouse, well outside the geographical range of the map. So the draughtsman deliberately distorted the map in depicting it, and I think we must assume that this would only have been done at the request of the client who commissioned the map, namely Nicholas Hare, who as far as can be ascertained had absolutely no involvement with either the Ely or Crown lands. Hare did have the ownership of much of Bardolph Fen and thus, unusually, his name is recorded on these manuscript maps, though we can be fairly certain that the attribution would not have appeared on the original map prepared for the Crown (Silvester, forthcoming).

The emergence of a sequence of maps of Marshland all ultimately derived from a single original is only the first part of the story. There is another manuscript map from Sir Robert Cotton's collection in the British Library (*Cotton Augustus I, vol I*, 79) which was based either on that lost original or on Haiwarde's copy, I think probably the former. Sir William Dugdale who had access to Cotton's library copied this map to illustrate *Imbanking and Draining* ... (1662). This map in turn was copied several times including one that was used in Blomefield's late eighteenth century county history of Norfolk, while Haiwarde's map was used as the basis of at least two eighteenth century manuscript maps of Marshland now in the Norfolk Record Office, the latest being of 1796.

In its essential characteristics the Marshland map of the 1580s was still being copied, with some relatively minor amendments, more than two centuries later, and thus the maps of late eighteenth century date are depicting a landscape which by then was already more than two hundred years old. This has significant implications, particularly for any study of the contemporary landscape that utilises such maps.

Property or estate maps offer the largest scale of mapping and, therefore, to the landscape historian the greatest degree of detail. The earliest scaled examples in this country date to the mid-1570s and while estate mapping continued well into the nineteenth century until superseded by large-scale Ordnance Survey maps, it was in the early decades, up to the end of the seventeenth century, that saw the greatest emphasis on incidental detail which go to make the maps stylistically diverse and interesting (Harvey 1996, 36).

Two property maps from the decades on either side of 1600 have been used effectively to elucidate the siltland landscape of Lincolnshire. In *Medieval England: an aerial survey*, Beresford and St Joseph (1979, 262) employed a map of 1595 by William Haiwarde (*BL 3365* (5)) which depicted the whole parish of Fulstow with Marshchapel, a few miles to the south-east of Grimsby, then divided largely between the two manors of Westhall and Northhall. The map shows in great detail the open fields of Fulstow (and there was a field book that accompanied the map though whether this still survives has not been ascertained); beyond these were the reclaimed salt marshes and further seaward, in Haiwarde's own words, '...the round groundes at the east ende of Marsh Chapell are called maures and are first framed by layinge together a great quantity of moulde for the making of salte. When the maures grow greate, the salt-makers remove more easte and come nearer to the sea, and then the former maures become in some fewe yeares good pasture grounds. Those that have the Cotages nowe upon them are at this presente in use for salte'.

This is perhaps a unique contemporary representation of salt manufacture along the Lincolnshire Coast at the end of the sixteenth century, a time when the industry was in terminal decline (Darby 1983, 52). There is nothing comparable as far as I am aware from the Norfolk or Cambridgeshire siltlands. Haiwarde drew and described a dying industry, one that St Joseph was able to photograph the remains of nearly four hundred years later (Beresford and St Joseph 1979, fig 111B). But what he and Beresford did not show on their plan derived from the map were the cottages or cotes used by the salt makers. Haiwarde referred to them in his description, showing them too on his map. The presence of the cotes on the Lincolnshire salt hills goes a long way to explaining the concentrations of pottery that I found on some of the saltern mounds in the Norfolk Marshland (Silvester 1988, 40). But other aspects of the sixteenth century landscape mapped by Haiwarde remain to be explored.

More recently an early manuscript map of Wrangle (*PRO MPC* 81) was adopted as a good illustration of the various environmental zones along the Lincolnshire coast, the drawing embellished with a number of cameo sketches depicting animals grazing on the salt marshes, ships out to sea and the like (Lane 1993, 109). Drawn in 1606 by an unknown cartographer to show the coastal landholdings of the King and William Hanbeye, but showing too tofts belonging to other landowners, which suggests that it was primarily concerned with a dispute over land, the map was subsequently annotated, probably within a fairly short time. It was signed by John Malyn and Richard Smith, the surveyors acting on behalf of the two estates which were in dispute over a relatively narrow wedge across the salt marshes and a sand bank, Herring Hill, out to sea. The disputed land was defined on the map and a lengthy description was added, on a piece of paper pasted over an earlier description in a cartouche. Interesting though the circumstances under which the map was drawn and later modified may be as a visual record of a local dispute, what is arguably more significant is the portrayal of the local topography: the successive zones of farming on reclaimed silts, the salt-marshes used for grazing animals, the tidal flats and the sandbar called Herring Hill which from the nets shown across it was attractive for fishing (Lane 1993, 110). Indeed as the disputed wedge of land was at its widest over the sand bank and that a further pasted modification had been made to Herring Hill, it is probable that this resource was the main cause of contention.

My final example is another map by William Haiwarde, but one that has been considered only in a most cursory way (Silvester 1994, 8). It depicts a part of Stow Bardolph fen and the adjacent portion of Outwell parish on the border of Norfolk and Cambridgeshire and was drawn in 1605, though once again it is not Haiwarde's original drawing – both the colouring and the lettering are wrong – but in what it depicts there is no reason to doubt

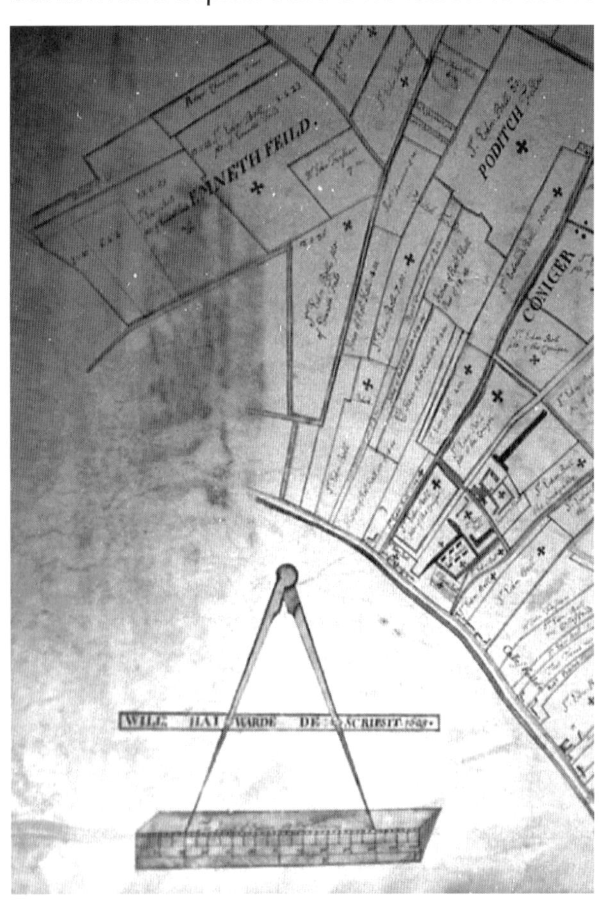

Figure 3 Copy of William Haiwarde's map of Outwell, Norfolk: detail of the village area
Reproduced by permission of
The Wisbech and Fenland Museum

that it is an accurate copy of the original. It shows the lands of Sir Edmund Bell (each distinguished by a small cross) who owned much though by no means all of Outwell, yet it also displays the strip fields and unenclosed fens of his neighbours, one of whom is named as William Haiwarde. Whether or not the surveyor and the owner of those few acres of land in Outwell were one and the same remains to be established. Topographical detail is limited to the lanes and dykes that demarcated the fields, houses along the Well Creek, and the moated site associated with Beaupre Hall, a manor house now demolished and the earthworks of the moats levelled and in places built over (Fig. 3). It is evident from the map, however, that the earthworks were considerably more complex than nineteenth century Ordnance Survey maps would indicate. Stow Bardolph Fen, some of which was owned by Sir Edmund Bell, is shown as divided up into regular parcels, 85 of them, together with droves, and the way that this enclosure is depicted suggests that in 1605 it was at the planning stage rather than a functioning system. Comparison with a modern map shows an almost precise correlation with the present pattern of fields. Evidently Sir Edmund Bell's outline plans were put into practice, and the map seems to provide a date at which this occurred.

There are other manuscript maps of the Fens from this period though in the absence of a comprehensive catalogue the complete number of such maps could only be gauged by consulting a number of archives, some of them relatively obscure. Haiwarde prepared estate maps of the adjacent Cambridgeshire parishes of Fordham and Soham, the former in 1626, the latter probably of much the same date; the remaining portion of Stow Bardolph Fen was surveyed by him in 1625, and there is a map of the Thorney region in the Huntingdon Record office, unsigned but almost certainly a Haiwarde product. There is a large-scale plan of the Nene Estuary outfall and the adjacent marshes by Richard Smith from 1636. None of these has been studied in any detail yet each provides a snapshot of a particular landscape at a specific point in time, and thus offers the opportunity for the better understanding of the development of the particular landscape that is displayed. But as with the depictions of Marshland, each requires a careful analytical assessment to ensure its integrity. We might remind ourselves that fieldwork can be conducted in isolation – indeed for the centuries prior to the Middle Ages it has by necessity to stand alone – but from the end of the sixteenth century and in rare instances even for the late medieval era in the Fens, maps can offer complementary evidence, which should not be ignored by the landscape historian.

Acknowledgements

The writer wishes to thank the British Library and the Wisbech and Fenland Museum for the provision of the photographs used here for illustrations.

Bibliography

Badeslade, T., 1725, *The history of the ancient and present state of the navigation of the port of King's Lyn, and of Cambridge* (London)

Beresford, M.W. and St Joseph, J.K.S., 1979, *Medieval England: an aerial survey* (Cambridge)

Croft, G A., 1983, An early map of Cambridgeshire, *Country Life* 30 June 1983, 18-29

Darby, H.C., 1983, *The Changing Fenland* (Cambridge)

Delano-Smith, C. and Kain, R.J.P., 1999, *English maps: a history* (London)

Dugdale, W., 1662, *History of imbanking and draining of divers fens and marshes....*, (London)

Glasscock, R.E., 1975, *The Lay Subsidy Role of 1334* (London)

Hall, D., 1995, *The open fields of Northamptonshire*, Northampton Record Society Vol. 38 (Northampton)

Harvey, P.D.A., 1996, 'English estate maps: their early history and their use as historical evidence', in Buisseret, D. (ed), *Rural images. Estate maps in the Old and New Worlds* (Chicago), 27-61.

Lane, T.W., 1993, *The Fenland Project, Number 8: Lincolnshire survey, the northern fen-edge*, East Anglian Archaeology 66

Lynam, E., 1934, 'Early maps of the Fen district', *Geographical Journal* 84, 420-3

Lynam, E., 1936, 'Maps of the Fenland', in *Victoria History of the Counties of England: Huntingdonshire, III*, London, 291-306

Mitchell, R. and Crook, D., 1999, 'The Pinchbeck Fen map: a fifteenth century map of the Lincolnshire fenland', *Imago Mundi* 51, 40-50

Owen, A.E.B., 1986, 'Isle of Ely, Cambridgeshire and Holland, Lincolnshire, late 14th century', in Skelton, R.A. and Harvey, P.D.A. (eds), *Local maps and plans from medieval England* (Oxford), 89-98

Rippon, S., 2000, *The transformation of coastal wetlands* (Oxford)

Silvester, R.J., 1988, *The Fenland Project, Number 3: Norfolk survey; Marshland and the Nar Valley*, East Anglian Archaeology 45

Silvester, R.J., 1989, 'William Haiwarde and the Fens', *Fenland Research* 6, 38-42

Silvester, R.J., 1991, 'Aerial photography and the Fenland Survey', *Aerial Archaeology* 12, 20-5

Silvester, R.J., 1994, 'Some early fenland maps in Wisbech Museum', *The Wisbech Society 55th Annual Report*, 7-9

Silvester, R.J., 1999, 'Medieval reclamation of marsh and fen', in Cook, H and Williamson, T. (eds), *Water management in the English landscape* (Edinburgh) 122-140

Silvester, R.J., forthcoming, *The early mapping of Marshland*

Skelton, R.A. and Harvey, P.D.A. (eds), 1986, *Local maps and plans from medieval England* (Oxford)

Skelton, R.A. and Summerson, J., 1971, *A description of maps and architectural drawings in the collection made by William Cecil, first baron Burghley, now at Hatfield House* (Oxford)

Thomas, H.M., 1992, *A catalogue of Glamorgan estate maps* (Cardiff)

VCH 1936, *Victoria History of the Counties of England: Huntingdonshire, III* (London)

Wade Martins, S., 1995, *Farms and fields* (London)

Woodgate, G.M.G., 1934, The Hundred map of Wisbech, *Printed lecture*

Woodward, D., 1992, 'J.B. Harley (1932-1991)', *Imago Mundi* 44, 120-5

3. THE WELLAND VALLEY AS A CULTURAL BOUNDARY ZONE: AN EXAMPLE OF LONG-TERM HISTORY

by Francis Pryor

Introduction

David Hall resembles television's Doctor Who in many significant respects. Both are tall, and lean; they also favour long and rather improbable knitted scarves (see cover plate). But that is not all: they are also Masters of Time. The Doctor merely surfs the chronological web, and has rather silly adventures with Daleks and other strange apparitions. David, on the other hand, goes far deeper: he is profoundly knowledgeable on many periods and themes. He is just as at home on a Bronze Age barrow protruding through the peat in the Fens, as in a field of medieval ridge-and-furrow in his favourite county, Northamptonshire. Few archaeologists share his extraordinary time-depth of knowledge. And I most certainly don't. I can't span the historical periods with David's ease, but I can provide a prehistoric case-study of long-term history, which I offer as a warm tribute to my old friend and colleague.

It is nothing new to suggest that archaeology is a very good way – if not the only way – of examining the long-term processes of cultural change. Indeed, for several decades many books have been specifically devoted to the subject (*e.g.* Hodder 1987; Plog 1974; Steward 1955). But in England we still tend to view archaeology synchronically, as a series of slices through time, often of quite short duration – like for example that of the Beaker presence. This no doubt reflects the way our subject is both organised and taught. And then of course there is that impenetrable obstacle to what the current government would call 'joined-up' archaeological thinking, known as the Roman Period (or Interlude, as I would prefer), which in turn is followed by the Early Saxon Period (or post-Roman Iron Age, as I would also prefer). Flippancy aside, the recent spate of PPG-16 contract excavations has accidentally helped to foster a longer-term, or diachronic view of our past, if only because there is now *so* much undigested data available that it is possible to take an in-depth view without necessarily having to organise a large-scale landscape-based research project to do so. That assuredly makes life much simpler and less hard work; in fact, I find the armchair now positively beckons.

In this case-study I will try to explain the presence of a number of ritual and other unusual sites which are distributed along the Welland Valley and extend out into the Fens along the Crowland 'Peninsula' (Fig. 1). I will also examine evidence for settlement and land-use on either side of this area. By the end, I hope I will have made a case for a significant, long-term cultural boundary that may have begun life by the fifth millennium BC and which continued throughout the Bronze and Iron Ages.

Upstream

David Hall and John Coles have given us some remarkable insights into the Fens in their *Essay in Landscape and Persistence* – the masterly summary of the Fenland Project's main findings – but I was both surprised and delighted to discover that they, like me, believed (and I think we are all agreed that it still has to be a matter of faith rather than of absolute hard-and-fast proof) that the earliest Neolithic inhabitants of the Fens were essentially the same people as their Mesolithic hunter-gatherer forebears (Hall and Coles 1994, 45-7). If ever there was an incursion of new settlers, then it was very small and was soon assimilated into the 'native' culture.

If there was indeed a degree of cultural continuity between the Neolithic and Mesolithic periods, then it follows that any major cultural divisions observable in the fourth millennium BC and subsequently, may well have origins that go back very much earlier. I have argued elsewhere that the largely livestock-based economy of the Fen margins was ultimately a development from earlier hunting practices where game was carefully husbanded as an essential economic resource (Pryor 1998a, 35). Of course we cannot be at all certain, but it seems probable that many significant earlier Neolithic ritual monuments – and I am thinking particularly of causewayed enclosures here – were placed at points in the landscape that had long been important to local Mesolithic communities, as they moved through the land, following the cyclical rise and fall of seasonal resources.

In many instances these places would have been naturally striking in some way: perhaps they dominated the surrounding countryside, like, for

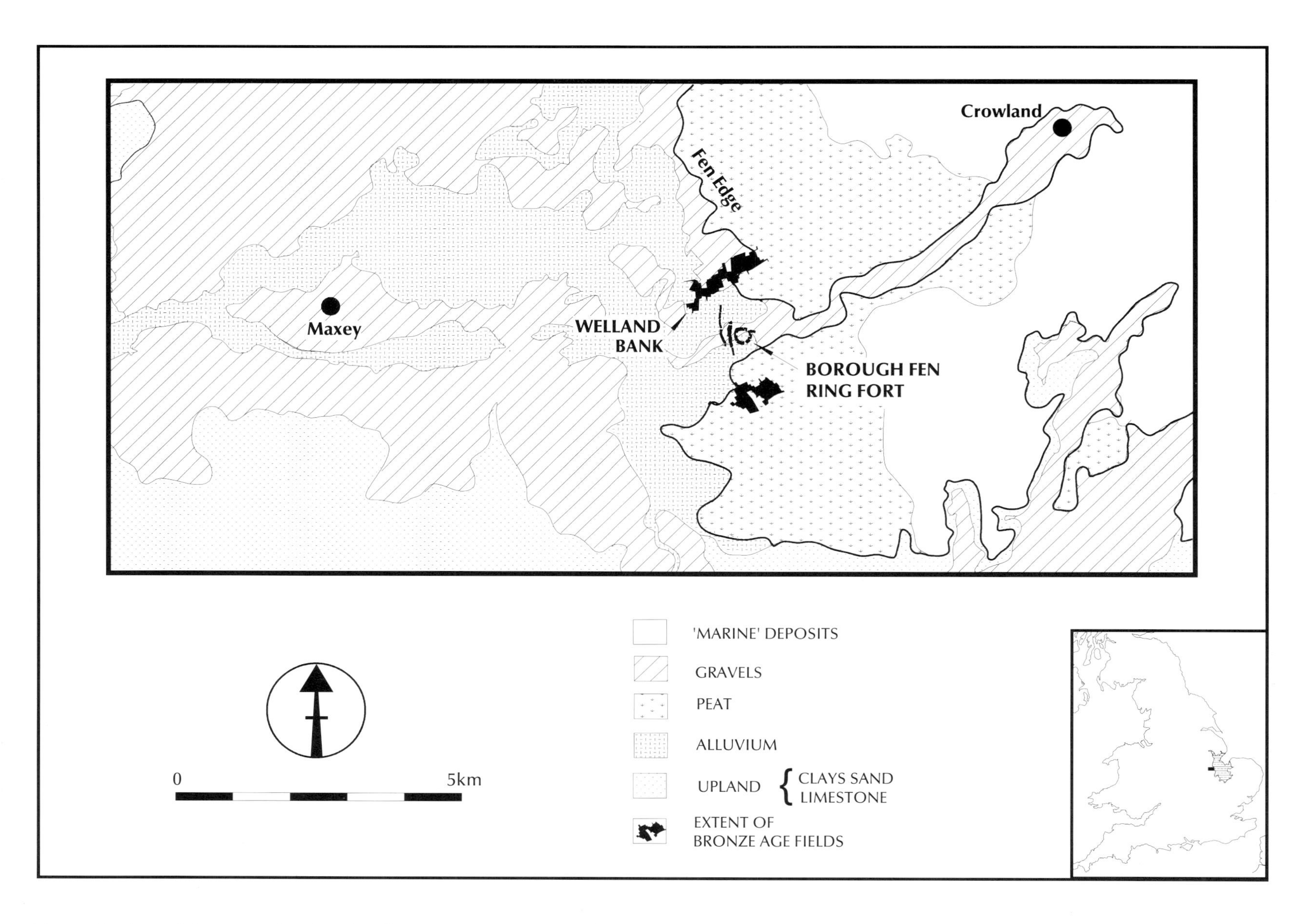

Figure 1 Map of the lower Welland Valley and Fen margins, showing the Crowland 'Peninsula' and principal sites mentioned in the text

example, Briar or Hambledon Hills (Bamford 1985; Bradley 2000; Mercer 1980). In some cases, such as Windmill Hill, there is evidence for Mesolithic activity in the area; at Stonehenge (where the outer ditch may be seen as a form of causewayed enclosure) a row of very large pine posts which yielded Mesolithic radiocarbon dates were found in the car park nearby (Cleal *et al.* 1995, 43-8; Smith 1965; Whittle *et al.* 1999). It seems absurd not to assume that these posts were associated with a ritual structure – which may or may not have been a much earlier precursor to the stones.

Windmill Hill could have been placed on the crown of the hill, but it wasn't (Whittle *et al.* 1999, fig 14). Similarly, Etton could have been placed at the centre of the relict ox-bow meander which surrounded it (Pryor 1998b, fig 4). In each instance it is as if the new site was located within an area – a space – that was already special, and in the process it allowed people to create a very much more rich and complex symbolic arena in which special ceremonies could take place (Bradley 2000, 103-110).

The remarkable concentration of causewayed enclosures in the lower Welland valley was first noted by Rog Palmer in 1976. This group was made even more remarkable following the discovery of Etton later that year, and more recently by the discovery of another, by Jim Pickering in 1996, at Northborough; this example is defined by four interrupted ditches, arranged in two tightly parallel pairs which together define a roughly oval shape (RCHM 1997). Oval causewayed enclosures are not common in Britain and the Royal Commission report points out the close resemblance of Northborough to neighbouring oval-shaped enclosures in the Welland Valley at Etton, Barholm and Uffington; a fourth is known at Southwick, in the Nene valley nearby; so on the basis of simple morphology, it would appear that the group are inter-related in some way, or ways.

Two closely parallel (*i.e.* paired) causewayed ditches have been observed on air photos near the Car Dyke a kilometre southeast of Glinton (Palmer 2000a); another, smaller (but also roughly oval) enclosure has been noted immediately west of Etton village (Palmer 1998). These are both very probable candidates, although sadly the former has largely been covered by housing (built, alas, in pre-PPG-16 times). Large ditched enclosures are also known north of Etton at two locations: EL3 and close to the course of the A15 Glinton By-Pass some 500 metres northeast of the published Etton causewayed enclosure; both are shown in the Etton Report (Pryor 1998b, fig 4). Of these two candidates, the latter now seems very much more promising, being roughly oval-shaped and more obviously segmented than EL3, whose ditch appears to be continuous and does not define a complete enclosure. With hindsight, I should have made more of the enclosure close to the A15 in the Etton Report.

So to sum up, this extraordinarily dense concentration of seven known, one very probable and one possible causewayed enclosures in the lower Welland/Nene region is probably unique in Britain, even surpassing the group around Avebury, which is also being progressively enlarged by continuing research (Gillings *et al.* 2000). Palmer (1976, fig 9) used the then much smaller group of Welland/Nene sites to mark the northern limit of his Midland group of causewayed enclosures, which also includes East Anglia. In marked contrast to the situation south of the Welland, there was a clear blank on Palmer's distribution map north of the Welland. To this day that area remains blank.

During recent (1999) discussions which have taken place as part of the English Heritage-sponsored initiative to produce regional research agendas, it became clear that there was a distinct difference in character between the prehistoric sequence of Neolithic Lincolnshire, and that encountered further south and west. The absence of causewayed enclosures was notable, but so also was the presence of many substantial and well-known long barrows and of course a massive concentration of Group VI axes (May 1976). The Trent was seen as a possible western boundary to this area. As the discussant on the day, Mike Parker Pearson put it, Lindsey was in effect a physical and perhaps a cultural 'island'.

It would be a mistake to think of the possible cultural boundary represented by the Welland Valley as being a thin line, analogous to the Berlin Wall. More likely it was a wide boundary zone or area which would have been considered both actually and ideologically liminal – at the very edges of the day-to-day domestic world. It would have been a special place visited on very special occasions. Although I shall argue later for stability, it is also quite possible that the boundary flexed and moved through time. Remember, we are talking here about some four (or more) millennia, so a state of complete stasis seems inherently improbable. We will see shortly that a kin-group or family pattern of land tenure in the Bronze Age might be seen as characteristic of East Anglia, and that another, more centralised system existed north of our posited boundary zone. The West Deeping fields undoubtedly belong with those of East Anglia, yet they are located just north of Maxey (*i.e.* on the 'wrong' side of the valley), albeit it well within the Welland Valley floodplain. Maybe this position might partly be explained by the late date of the field system – or maybe it is the exception that proves (or disproves!) the rule. Doubtless time will tell one way or another.

Northamptonshire Archaeology, under the direction of Ian Meadows, are currently excavating the landscape of braided stream channels immediately south of the Etton causewayed enclosure (NCC 1999). Although fieldwork is still in progress it is already clear that the slightly raised parts of this wet world were far from abandoned. There is much evidence for the digging and filling of numerous pits – many undoubtedly of ritual significance – during Neolithic and Bronze Age times (Ian Meadows, *pers comm.*). It is a pattern of activity which suggests that regular visits were made to the area, presumably during the drier months of the year. In such circumstances it is difficult to decide where ritual stops and settlement starts – even if there is a hard-and-fast distinction between the two (which I doubt); but so far there is no solid evidence, in the form, for example, of permanent structures to suggest anything approaching long-term occupation by a significant number of people. The activity would seem to be episodic, if repetitive, which would fit well with such a flood-prone and watery environment.

North of Etton, on the higher ground of Maxey 'island', is the well known ritual landscape at whose centre lies the so-called Great Henge. This is a complex monument, which was linked to the Etton causewayed enclosure by the Maxey Cursus. In actual fact it probably was never a henge, *sensu stricto*, and possesses far more in common with a class of 'great barrows', which were funerary-cum-ceremonial sites, such as Willie Howe or Duggleby Howe (Richard Bradley, *pers comm.*; Manby 1988, 85-6). Certainly this would fit better with what is known of the site's date, size and complex development (Pryor and French 1985). Around the Great Henge, and distributed across most of the 'island' and the countryside around, were the dozens of henges and barrows that together comprised the Maxey ritual landscape (Fig. 2).

Barrows, henges and other smaller shrines form an important component of the Neolithic and very early Bronze Age farmed landscape. Essentially this was an open landscape, given over to livestock, but it was parcelled-up into individual holdings by these monuments, which were usually regularly spaced throughout the countryside, and often in rows that acknowledged the 'grain' of the landscape. In the full Bronze Age, fields were laid-out in a manner that respected these earlier monuments which were frequently re-used, presumably by the communities who laid-out and farmed the fields. In other words, there was no significant cultural change: the new fields signify the intensification of a pattern of land-use and tenure that had already been in existence for some time. Boundaries of family land holdings within the fields were not only marked by monuments: single burials, small filled pits or just offerings in field ditches were frequently placed at important points in the landscape. Incidentally, the small area of burnt limestone at the northern edge of the central zone of Bronze Age fields at Fengate, described in the Third Report as the 'Industrial Area', might well represent the plough-flattened remains of a burnt mound (Richard Bradley, *pers comm.*; Pryor 1980, 70-4). Certainly such a feature would be entirely appropriate at the edge of a significant part of a field system (Bradley 1984, 163). Smaller monuments, such as burnt mounds, barrows and isolated pits and burials might be seen as the physical evidence for, or perhaps the cultural residue of, processes whereby the powers of the ancestors were invoked to control the behaviour of the different families and kin-groups who were actually farming the fields round about them.

It is interesting that, despite massive evidence for Neolithic and Bronze Age ritual activity in and around Maxey, a system of Bronze Age fields never developed there. For a start, the individual ritual features – the henges and barrows – do not appear ever to have been positioned across the landscape at regular intervals. If anything, they tend to cluster. Nearby, at West Deeping, the picture is very different: here, although somewhat later (probably later Bronze Age to Early Iron Age) than the Maxey ritual landscape, we encounter the familiar pattern of spaced-out barrows and ring-ditches that seem to anticipate the location of the subsequent double-ditched droveways (Fig. 3). As if to emphasise the contrast, the Maxey Cursus cuts a diagonal swathe across the landscape. This is a path that completely ignores the anticipated orientation or 'grain' of the usual domestic landscape. In this regard it is interesting that the medieval 'broad rig' fields were laid out in the expected fashion; they follow the 'grain', at right-angles to the common wetland pasture surrounding the 'island'. Put another way, the evidence now suggests that this prehistoric ritual landscape was never parcelled-up into practical, easily farmed, family holdings.

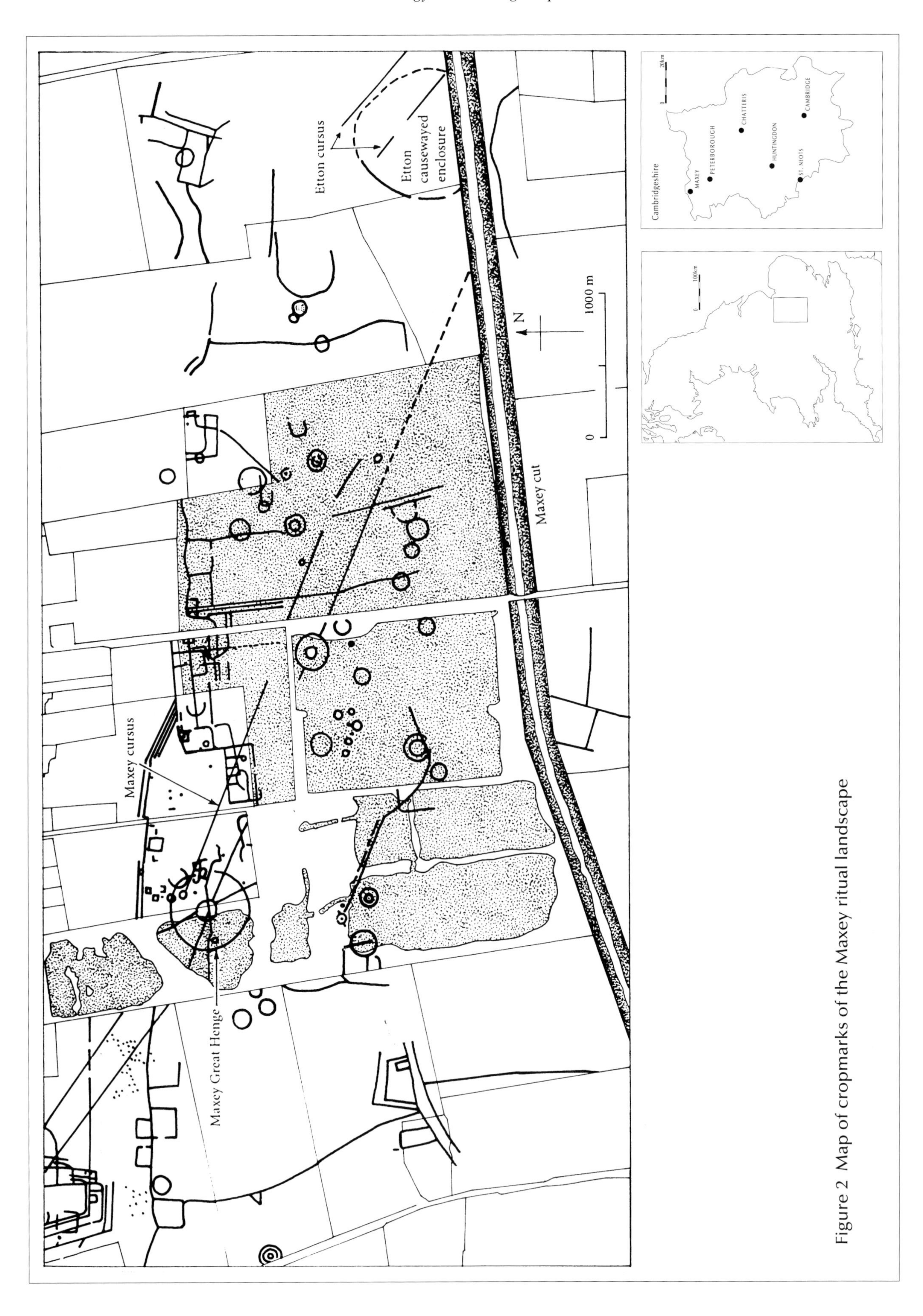

Figure 2 Map of cropmarks of the Maxey ritual landscape

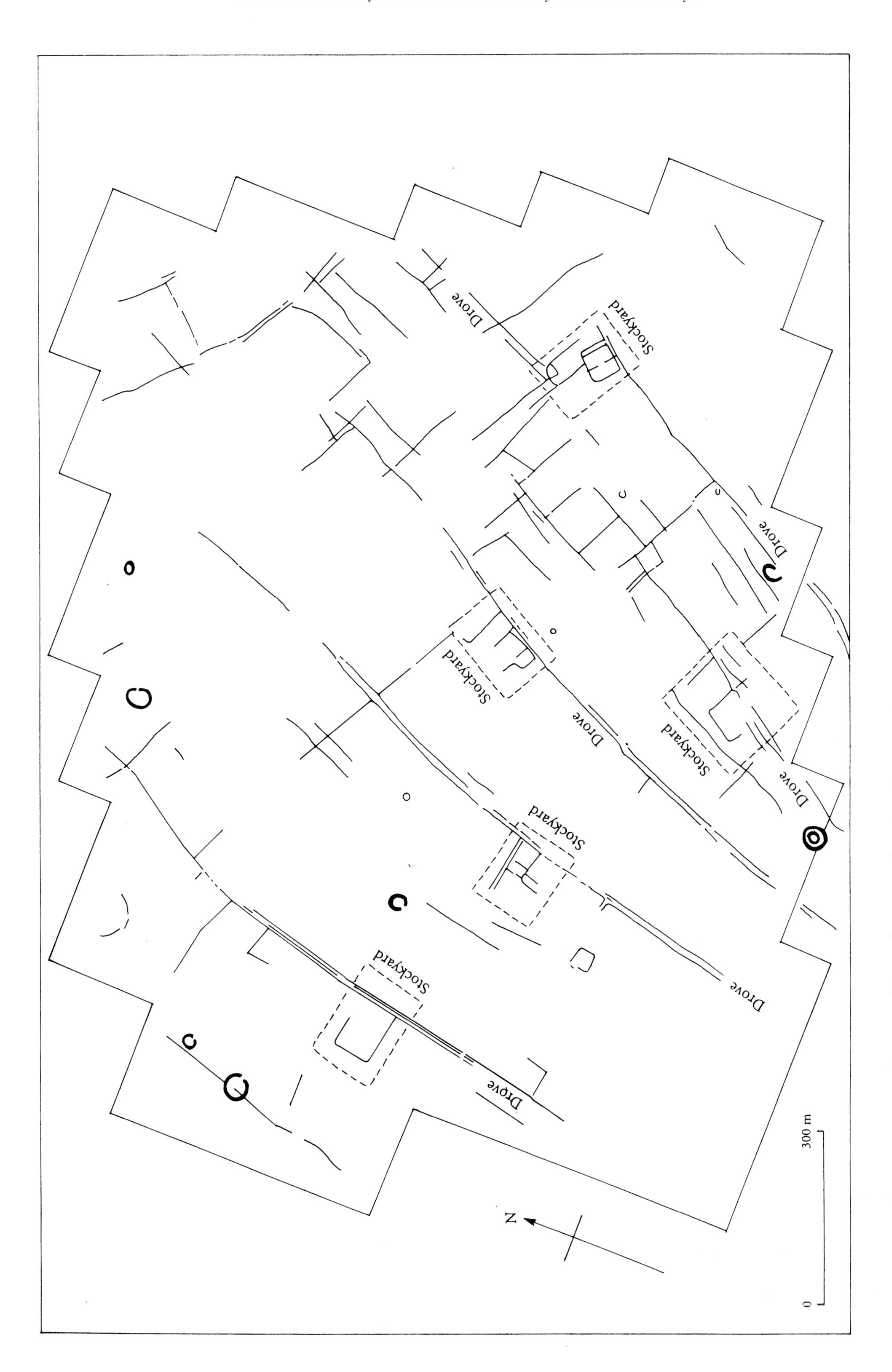

Figure 3 Map of cropmarks of prehistoric fields and barrows (in bold) near West Deeping

We know from palaeoenvironmental evidence that the Maxey Neolithic and Bronze Age ritual landscape was grazed (French 1985), but there is no archaeological evidence (in the form of fields or droveways) to indicate that this was as intense as elsewhere in the region. At Maxey patterns of land tenure, if they existed at all, were very different indeed. One cannot be certain of such things, but it is tempting to suggest that this was an open, deliberately unbounded, liminal landscape held in common by people on one or both sides of the boundary. To breach that boundary was, therefore, to incur the hostility of more than one single community. An incursion into or across such an unbounded liminal landscape could have had serious consequences, because everyone on the 'other' side would believe they had been affected by such a breach of their common security – as symbolised by common land. This may well help to explain the longevity of the phenomenon.

Downstream

The landscape between Maxey and the Fen edge at Welland Bank has not been studied in great detail, but it does include at least one authenticated causewayed enclosure, at Northborough. It would however be a mistake to view the modern course of the Welland as being necessarily that of the hypothetical prehistoric boundary. The landscape is essentially flat and the various streams of the Welland would have followed multiple, braided courses. Indeed it is impossible to detect, when driving for example from Peterborough to Market Deeping, at what point one is crossing the interfluve between the Nene and Welland. So for present purposes we will return to our boundary zone at the point where the narrow Crowland 'peninsula' joins the gravel plain of the lower Welland Valley, just east of Deeping St James (Fig. 4).

This is where we encounter one of the lowest-lying 'hillforts' in Britain: the ringwork at Borough Fen which in the Fenland Survey was dubbed site BoF 7 (Hall 1987, fig 11 and pl V). Recent aerial survey has shown this ringwork to have been more complex than the plan offered here would suggest. There are indications of another, narrower, external ditch or palisade and the north-south ditches to the west, which seem to resemble some form of defence-in-depth against horses, or even wheeled vehicles, are remarkably elaborate and extensive (Palmer 2000b).

The interior of the ringfort contains a deposit of 'dark earth', sealed beneath alluvium; this 'dark earth' revealed sherds of Middle Iron Age 'scored ware' (French and Pryor 1993, 68-76). This material however was taken from a very small sample exposure and may only date to a later phase of the monument's use. Taken as a whole, the monument bears a striking resemblance to a group of later Bronze Age ringworks found in Essex and Kent (Bond 1988; Champion 1980; Couchman 1980). A foundation date for the Borough Fen ringwork early in the first, or late in the second millennium BC, would not cause surprise.

The ringwork undoubtedly catches the eye and tends to draw attention away from the field systems, to north and south, which it separates. They are very different. The system to the south is laid-out in the manner characteristic of East Anglia. There are droves and the linear parcels of land run down to the seasonally flooded land, at right angles. Barrows occur, but often in rows, again running at right angles to the wetter ground. These surely are 'internal' partitions or boundaries and can be closely paralleled by recent excavations carried out at King's Dyke West, Whittlesey by the Cambridge Archaeological Unit (Knight 2000). This site features at least one row of barrows laid out at right-angles to the fen nearby. Were it not for the presence of the modern bank of the river Nene, these barrows would have had a clear view of the Flag Fen post alignment. Using evidence from sites such as West Deeping I have suggested that these linear strip-like holdings of land were held by, or the property of, individual families or kin-groups (Pryor 1998a, 109-23). The barrows located at key points within the system would have celebrated the ancestors of the various kin-groups. They would also have served to solemnise the boundaries against trespassers. They would not have 'worked' in this way against strangers from outside; everyone involved, both within and outside the various kin-groups, must have possessed detailed knowledge of what the different barrows represented.

The fields north of the ringwork, around the Welland Bank Quarry, are altogether different (Fig. 5). For a start, barrows seem to be absent and the nearest group is close to the modern town of Crowland, several kilometres distant. The fields do not share the same common alignment and partitioning droves are absent. Although clearly part of an overall system, the fields are less formally aligned and appear to be more 'organic' in plan. Maybe this layout might suggest that the Welland Bank field system grew up piecemeal, whereas that to the south was laid out more formally with major

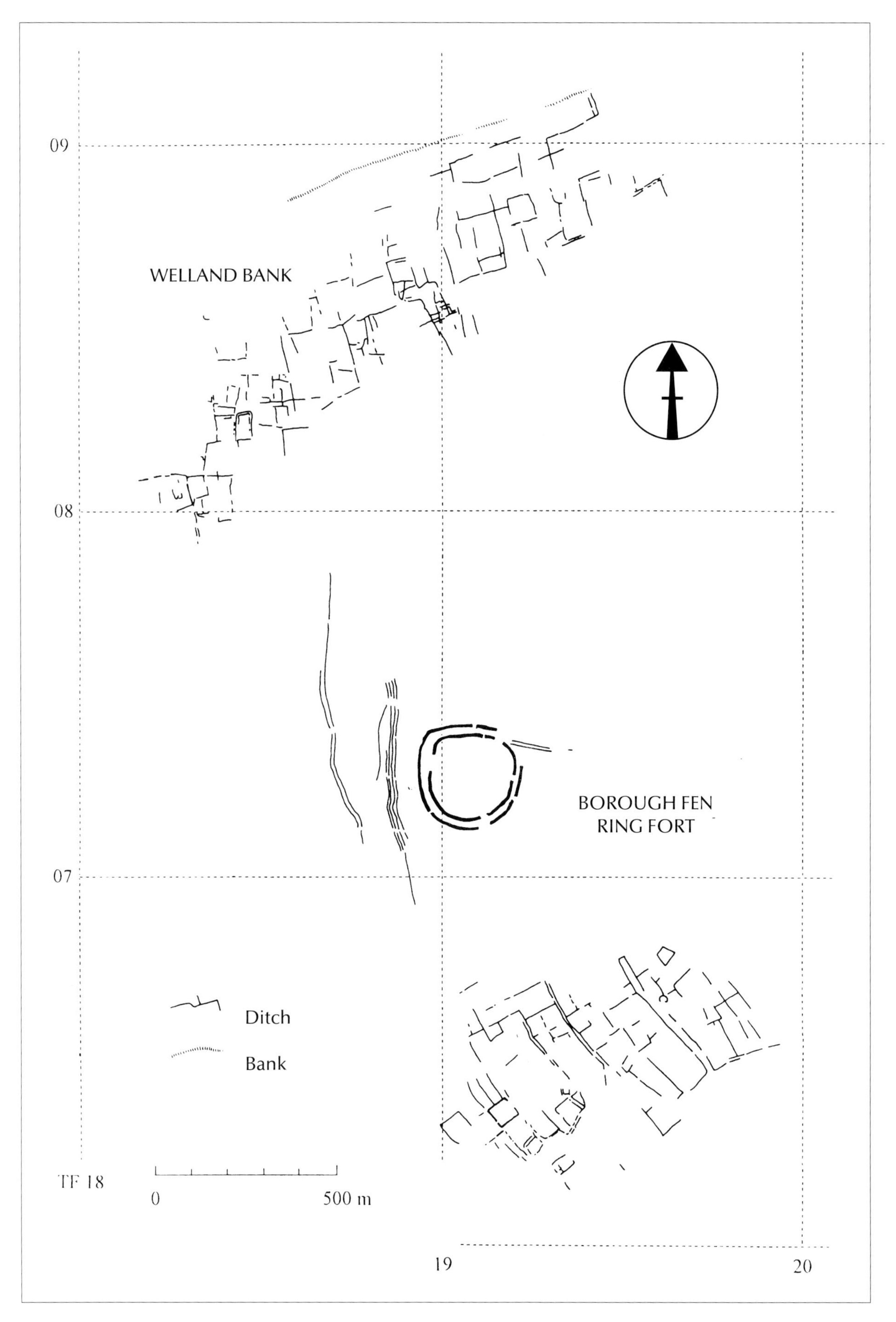

Figure 4 Map of cropmarks and other features north of Newborough (after Rog Palmer)

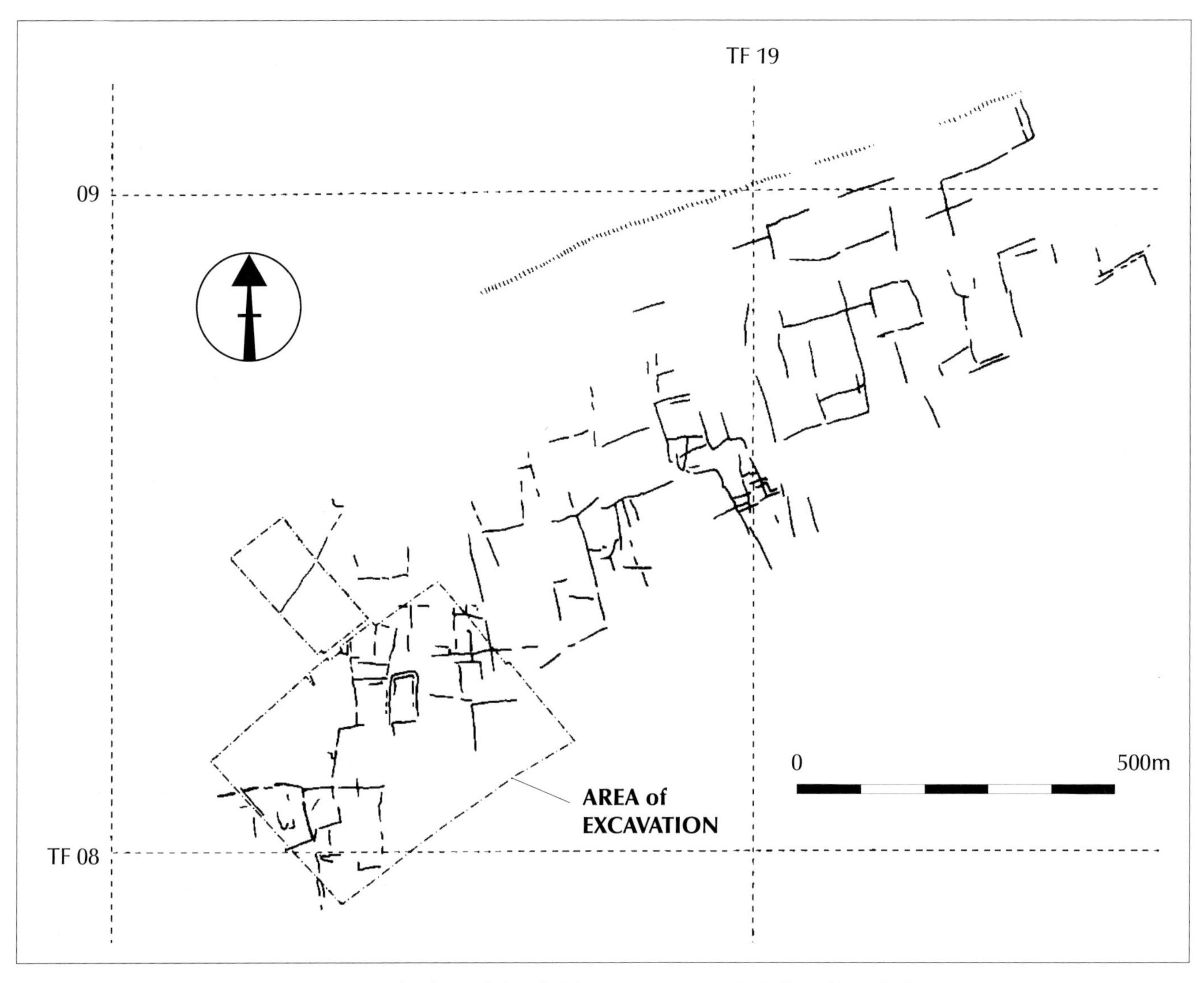

Figure 5 Cropmark plan of the field system around Welland Bank Quarry

divisions being marked-out well in advance of actual construction. Certainly this pattern of marking-out in advance would appear to be what happened at Fengate, where the latest evidence suggests that whole segments of the fields there had gone out of use while others – laid out on essentially the same alignment – were just coming into being (Pryor 2001a).

The settlement pattern that goes with the East Anglian style of aligned fields consists of single farmsteads or small hamlets that were spread in an extensive pattern, throughout the field system. This pattern of settlement is seen, for example, at Fengate, Barleycroft Farm and perhaps also at Whittlesey King's Dyke West; by and large these farmsteads appear to be short-lived (Knight 2000; Evans and Knight 1997; Pryor forthcoming [a]). Rebuilding is rarely encountered, and if the reconstructions at Flag Fen are anything to go by, we must suppose the life-span of the houses was short – maybe ten to twenty years, but probably no more. Then settlement moved elsewhere, but probably within the same holding. This would appear to contrast with the much longer use-life of buildings on the southern chalkland proposed by Peter Reynolds (1979, 29-45). At present the chronology is not altogether clear, but it would seem that it is not until sometime after the Middle Bronze Age that the dispersed pattern of settlement gives way to true nucleated settlement. At Fengate the Late Bronze and Early Iron Age pits, made famous by Hawkes and Fell (1945) are now believed to have been associated with the earliest manifestation of truly nucleated settlement located at the Tower Works site; this site included at least one rectangular hall-like building (Lucas 1997). The Tower Works settlement went with a late manifestation of the Fengate Bronze Age ditched fields (Pryor 2001a).

The Welland Bank fields are generally quite large and where droveways are encountered they are wide. At face value this might indicate that they were laid-out for cattle, although sheep could also have used the system. Incidentally the keeping of cattle and sheep together is good practice: the cattle take-off the top growth of the longer grass and the sheep crop lower and keep the sward in good order. In recent times, however, the occurrence of cross-communicable diseases has led many farmers to abandon the keeping of the two species together. Further evidence that cattle played an important role in the contemporary economy at Welland Bank is provided by the rectangular ditched and banked enclosure that formed the principal feature of the southerly part of the excavations. This large rectangular enclosure showed-up clearly on aerial photographs and was thought to be associated with human settlement. When excavated (and despite excellent preservation below a layer of protective alluvium) it revealed no buildings and very little domestic debris of any sort. The north-east corner held an oval pen-like wooden structure built of massive square-dressed timbers set edge-to-edge and the accompanying bank and ditch bent to accommodate it, so it was clearly a feature of some importance (Fig. 6). It is probably best seen as a holding pen for concentrating and inspecting livestock that had been driven into the larger enclosure by way of the four corner entranceways. These entranceways show much evidence for modification, as one might expect on a working livestock-handling system.

The south and east sides of the enclosure are approached by droveways that significantly stop just short of the enclosure, thereby allowing animals to be diverted (either using drovers or hurdles) around the outside of the enclosure to an appropriate entranceway. The scale of the droves and the size and depth of the bedding trenches around the oval pen suggest that large animals, such as cattle, were being handled. Certainly sheep alone would not need anything so substantial. The over-lapping and outward deflection of ditches evident in the smaller droveway that ran towards the south-west part of the enclosure is also very characteristic of the type of measure one would expect to encounter on a stockyard. By any standards this is a large, elaborate and well thought-out livestock-handling facility. It is sufficiently large to handle hundreds, rather than dozens of beasts, if required. The size and complexity of the feeder droveways suggests, too that they could have held animals before they were needed inside the enclosure. All the evidence therefore points to batch-handling, which is characteristic of farms where animals have to be checked, confined, sorted and inspected *in large numbers*.

The settlement at Welland Bank Quarry was located north and west of the stockyard. We are still working-out the precise phasing of the settlement, but it included many round houses and at least two hall-like buildings, reminiscent of Barleycroft Farm and Tower Works, Fengate. The available evidence (Deverel-Rimbury pottery) suggests that the settlement began in the Middle Bronze Age and extended throughout the Late Bronze Age and even into the Early Iron Age. There is also evidence for Early Bronze Age activity to the south of the main settlement. Mindful of the fact that the relevant analyses have yet to be done, it is tempting to suggest that the rectangular cattle enclosure held the animals that belonged to the people of the nearby settlement. It is quite possible that these beasts were held in common, as no efforts seem to have been made to keep the various elements of the herd separate, either in the stockyard or in the surrounding fields.

So we appear to have an altogether different pattern of settlement and land-use at Welland Bank, that cannot simply be explained by chronology alone. To the south of the Borough Fen ring-fort the landscape was organised by family holdings in a manner that we are now beginning to recognise as typical of East Anglia. To the north, people lived in more closely-knit and larger communities and held their livestock in common. We do not yet know to what extent the Welland Bank pattern was typical of the northern region as a whole, and the full publication of key sites such as Billingborough might provide us with clues. But whatever future research turns up, these are fundamental cultural differences – and they appear on either side of our postulated boundary zone.

Conclusion and Summary

I have suggested that the Welland Valley was a possible cultural boundary zone from Mesolithic/ Neolithic times, until at least the Iron Age. I have also looked at the 'solemnisation' of smaller or subsidiary boundaries within the territory south of this zone and I have concluded that many ephemeral features such as groups or isolated filled pits and solitary burials (of humans or animals), as well as larger more permanent monuments, such as barrows, mortuary structures and smaller henges served to provide an ideological dimension to the partition of the landscape. Put more simply,

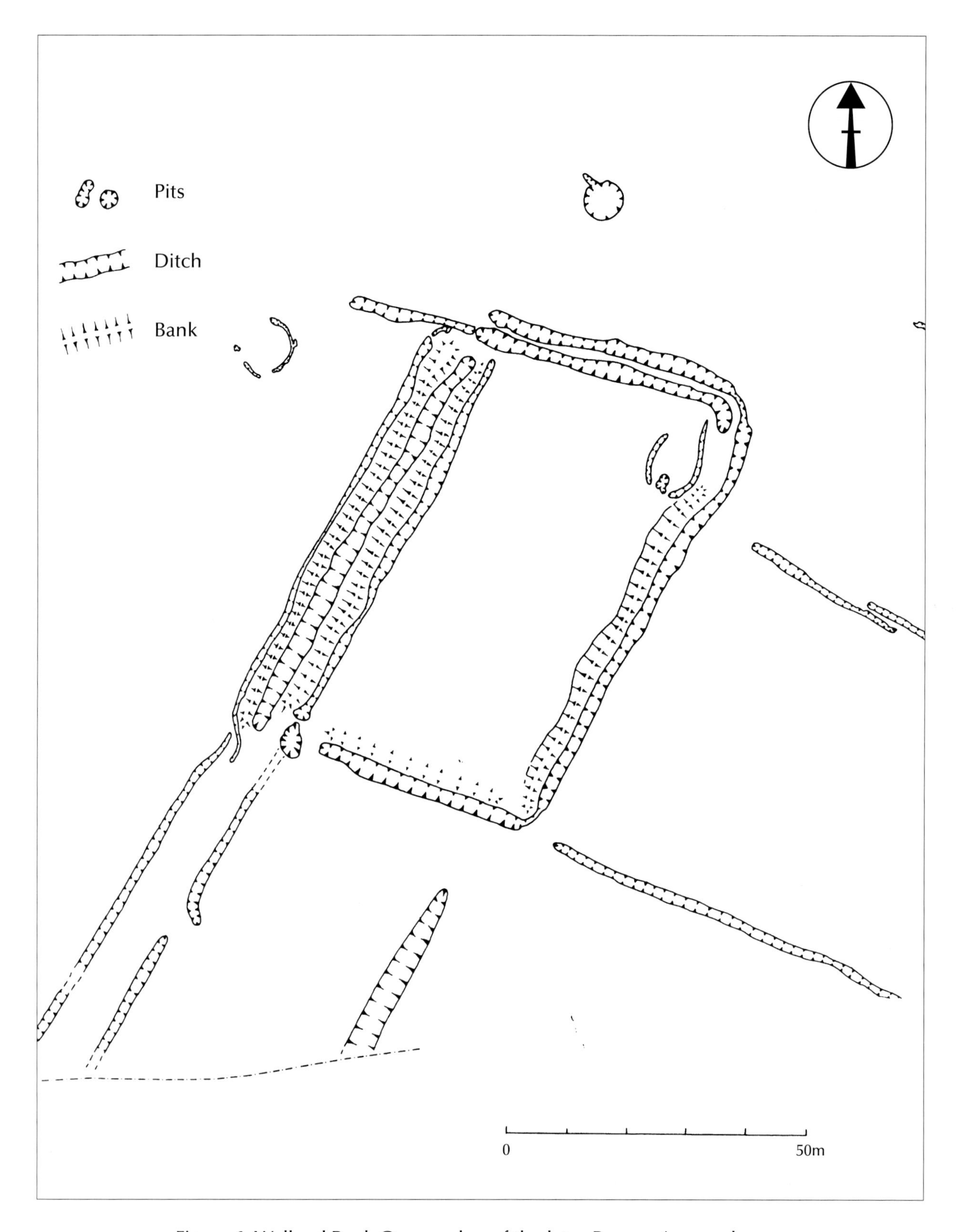

Figure 6 Welland Bank Quarry plan of the later Bronze Age enclosure

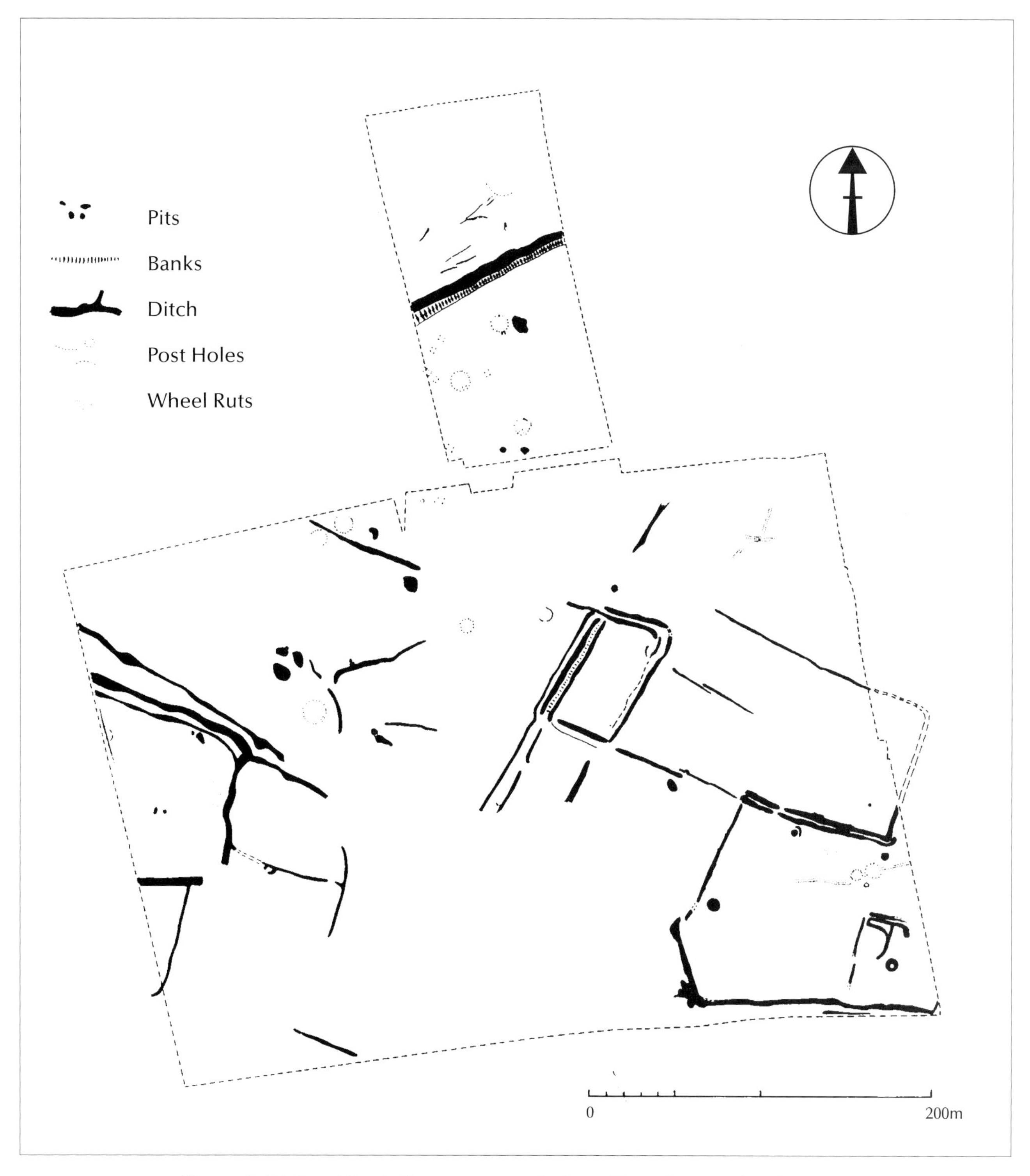

Figure 7 Welland Bank Quarry: general plan of later Bronze Age features

the forces controlled by their ancestors could be invoked to assert a particular kin-group's right to a certain parcel of land. But like all boundaries existing within the day-to-day domestic landscape, they required constant reiteration and were subject to testing, to rationalisation, modification and amalgamation. This was why so many of the features marking them were visited and re-visited over several centuries.

The implied association between ancient fields and such isolated features as pits and burials is potentially of very considerable importance. For long I have been convinced that archaeologists have consistently under-estimated the true age and longevity of field boundary ditches – and thereby of entire field systems. This is because material only begins to accumulate in such ditches after their abandonment. During their active life they would have been cleaned out more or less regularly, because they served a practical purpose as a physical boundary and as a drain for surface water. A partially silted-up field ditch is of little use to anyone. In certain instances boundary-marking burials, or other offerings, were actually placed in field ditches and were presumably marked in some way, so as not to be disturbed during subsequent maintenance operations. Twigs from below the skeleton of a female in one of the ditches of the Newark Road sub-site at Fengate yielded a date of cal BC 3030-2500 (HAR-780; 4190±90BP), at 95% confidence (Bayliss in Pryor 2001a). This is notably earlier than other post-abandonment samples, but it is by no means at variance with what was found in many seemingly unassociated pits, placed near significant boundary ditches, and filled with Late Neolithic and Beaker material, elsewhere at Fengate. Clearly caution should be exercised before every isolated pit is linked to a field system in this way, but if a consistent pattern can be established the case becomes somewhat easier to argue.

There was also a second, or 'higher' category of boundary where a different set of 'rules' apply. In this paper I have suggested that one is to be found running along the lower Welland Valley and up along the Crowland 'peninsula' into the Fens. This land was never parcelled-up like the domestic landscapes on either side of it. Indeed, monuments such as the Etton and Maxey cursuses seem to have been deliberately laid-out to defy or counter the logic of normal landscape partition in wet regions, where farms extend (usually at right-angles) from flood-free to seasonally flooded and very wet ground. This leads to a characteristic pattern of strip-like or radiating holdings, each one of which embraces a selection of land ranging, as we have seen, from wet to dry. By far the best Fenland example is the Marshland landscape southwest of King's Lynn where William Haiward's map of 1591 shows fields and droveways radiating from 'Marshlande Fenne' (Silvester 1988, pls II and III). Within the ritual landscape, however, it would seem that other, ideological influences are paramount: small monuments tend to cluster together, but not in rows, as we so often see in the domestic landscape.

Large monuments, such as the Etton causewayed enclosure or the Maxey Great 'Henge' provide a focus for such groups. Whatever else was going on, this arrangement takes no account whatsoever of the farmed landscape – nor even of a landscape that had the potential to be farmed – and it is tempting to suggest that the contrast was deliberately intended. For whatever reason, this was land that (had always?) stood aside from the mundane. The arrangement of the various barrows, ring-ditches and henges that accumulated there may have reflected social groupings and perceived hierarchies of power and influence, in both this and the next worlds. But it was most definitely not to do with practical considerations of tenure and land-management. What is now also clear is that a ritual landscape was relevant to a *far* larger cultural group than, for example, a causewayed enclosure on its own.

Given the recent proliferation of discoveries in the Maxey-Etton-Northborough area, it is apparent that the paired enclosures of Fornham All Saints are by no means unique (Palmer 1976). So the ritual landscapes that grew up from middle/later Neolithic to Early Bronze Age times must be seen as a reflection of a broader social change whereby the previously more isolated communities of the fourth millennium BC began the process of drawing together into larger, more united polities. This change would probably also have been attended by a slowing-down of cyclical movements. Maybe cursuses, which so often accompany causewayed enclosures played an important role in diffusing the power, influence and ideological 'magic' found within causewayed enclosures across the embryonic ritual landscape and thereby from one community, or group of communities, to others.

If this view has any validity at all, then the ritual landscape we have been considering must actually have been a place of stability. It was on an *agreed* boundary of great antiquity and it was not until very much later that there was any hint of fortification – and again, this was probably more symbolic than military. The Welland ritual landscape provided symbols of cultural identity and, as at Flag Fen, these were positioned at the edge and not at the centre, where identity was not an active issue. But there was also another aspect to this extraordinary landscape, and that, of course, concerns its ideological liminality. This was the appropriate landscape where members of different kin-groups and communities could come together to communicate with the world of their ancestors. Perhaps we are witnessing something similar at the Holme-next-the-Sea timber circle, which is now seen to have been part of a coastal ritual landscape, of unknown extent (Brennand and Taylor 2000; Pryor 2001b). Here the boundary was not between different cultural groups, but between land and sea: this world and the next. At Holme ideological liminality played a greater role than inter-cultural liminality.

So, making the huge assumption that what applies to the lower Welland might also apply elsewhere, how should we regard ritual landscapes in the future: were they centres of ancient cultural and ideological life, or were they an edge-effect – albeit an important one? I think the answer lies somewhere between the two. They were positioned at the boundary, but they expressed the identity of the centre. In the familiar symbolic language of modern England, it is as if Westminster Abbey had been built atop the White Cliffs of Dover.

Acknowledgments

I would particularly like to thank Ben Robinson, Development Control Archaeologist for the City Council at Peterborough Museum, who kindly provided me with detailed and up-to-date information on recent aerial reconnaissance in the Peterborough area, especially as regards actual and possible causewayed enclosures. Richard Bradley, as part of his recent national 'grand tour' of archaeological colleagues, has discussed many of the ideas with me, and I am particularly grateful for his thoughts on the Maxey 'Great Henge' and the Fengate 'industrial area'. Neither Ben nor Richard, however, can be blamed for what I have done to their contributions.

Bibliography

Bamford, H.M., 1985, *Briar Hill Excavations 1974-1978*, Northampton Development Corporation Monograph 3 (Northampton)

Bond, D., 1988, *Excavation at the North Ring, Mucking, Essex: a Late Bronze Age enclosure*, East Anglian Archaeology 43

Bradley, R.J., 1984, *The Social Foundations of Prehistoric* Britain (London, Longman)

Bradley, R.J., 2000, *An Archaeology of Natural Places* (London, Routledge)

Brennand, M. and Taylor, M., 2000, 'Seahenge', *Current Archaeology* 167, 417-424

Champion, T., 1980, 'Settlement and environment in later Bronze Age Kent', in Barrett J. and Bradley R.J. (eds), 'The British Later Bronze Age', 223-46, *Brit. Archaeol. Reps.* 83(i) (Oxford)

Cleal, R.M.J., Walker, K.E. and Montague, R., 1995, *Stonehenge in its landscape*, English Heritage Archaeological Report 10 (London)

Couchman, C.R., 1980, 'The Bronze Age in Essex', in Buckley, D.G. (ed), *Archaeology in Essex to AD 1500*, Council for British Archaeology Research Report 34, 40-6

Evans, C. and Knight, M., 1997, *The Barleycroft Paddocks Excavations, Cambridgeshire* (Unpublished Report, Cambridge Univ. Archaeol. Unit Rep.)

French, C.A.I., 1985, 'Soil, Sediment and Molluscan Analyses of Excavated Features', in Pryor, F. and French, C.A.I., *Archaeology and Environment in the Lower Welland Valley*, East Anglian Archaeology 27, 205-216

French, C.A.I. and Pryor, F.M.M., 1993, *The South-West Fen Dyke Survey Project 1982-86*, East Anglian Archaeology 59

Gillings, M., Pollard, J. and Wheatley, D., 2000, 'Avebury and the Beckhampton Avenue', *Current Archaeology* 167, 428-33

Hall, D., 1987, *The Fenland Project, Number 2: Cambridgeshire Survey, Peterborough to March*, East Anglian Archaeology 35

Hall, D. and Coles, J., 1994, *Fenland Survey: an essay in landscape and persistence*, English Heritage Archaeological Report 1 (London)

Hawkes, C.F.C. and Fell, C.I., 1945, 'The Early Iron Age Settlement at Fengate, Peterborough', *Arch. Journal* 100, 188-223

Hodder, I. (ed), 1987, *Archaeology as long-term history* (Cambridge University Press)

Knight, M., 2000, 'Henge to House – post-circles in a Neolithic and Bronze Age landscape at King's Dyke West, Whittlesey, Cambridgeshire', *Past (Newsletter of the Prehist. Soc.)* 34, 3-4

Lucas, G., 1997, *An archaeological evaluation at the Tower Works, Fengate, Peterborough* (Unpublished Report. Cambridge Univ. Archaeol. Unit Rep. 206)

Manby T.G., 1988, 'The Neolithic in Eastern Yorkshire', in Manby, T.G. (ed), *Archaeology in Eastern Yorkshire*, 35-88 (Sheffield University)

May, J., 1976, *Prehistoric Lincolnshire*, History of Lincolnshire Series Volume I (Lincoln)

Mercer, R.J., 1980, *Hambledon Hill: a Neolithic Landscape* (Edinburgh University Press)

NCC, 1999, *Proposed Quarry extension at Maxey, Cambridgeshire, Archaeological Assessment* (Northamptonshire County Council, Northampton)

Palmer, R., 1976, 'Interrupted ditch enclosures in Britain: the use of aerial photography for comparative studies', *Proc. Prehist. Soc.* 42, 161-86

Palmer, R., 1998, *Maxey Quarry, Area TF1306, Maxey-Etton Cambridgeshire: Aerial Photographic Assessment*, Unpublished Air Photo Services Report 1998/18

Palmer, R., 2000a, *Car Dyke, Deeping Gate to Stanground, Cambridgeshire: aerial photographic interpretation*, Unpublished Air Photo Services Report 2000/05

Palmer, R., 2000b, *Aerial Photographic Interpretation and Mapping. Project 1: Peakirk Area, Cambridgeshire*, Unpublished Air Photo Services Report

Plog, F.T., 1974, *The Study of Prehistoric Change* (New York, Academic Press)

Pryor, F.M.M., 1980, *Excavation at Fengate, Peterborough, England: The Third Report*, Northants. Arch. Soc. Monograph 1 / Royal Ontario Museum Monograph 6

Pryor, F.M.M., 1998a, *Farmers in Prehistoric Britain* (Stroud, Tempus Books)

Pryor, F.M.M., 1998b, *Etton: excavations at a Neolithic causewayed enclosure near Maxey Cambridgeshire, 1982-87*, English Heritage Archaeology Report 18 (London)

Pryor, F.M.M., 1998c, 'Welland Bank Quarry, South Lincolnshire – a tale of a sausage sandwich', *Current Archaeology* 160, 139-45

Pryor, F.M.M., 2001a, *The Flag Fen Basin: Archaeology and environment of a Fenland landscape*, English Heritage Archaeology Report (London)

Pryor, F.M.M., 2001b, *Seahenge: New Discoveries in Prehistoric Britain* (London, Harper Collins)

Pryor, F.M.M. and French, C.A.I., 1985, *Archaeology and Environment in the Lower Welland Valley*, East Anglian Archaeology 27

RCHM, 1997, *A Neolithic Causewayed Enclosure at Northborough, Peterborough, Cambridgeshire: aerial transcription and analysis (by Carolyn Dyer)*, Royal Commission on the Historical Monuments of England (Swindon)

Reynolds, P.J., 1979, *Iron Age Farm – the Butser Experiment* (Colonnade Books, British Museum, London)

Smith, I.F., 1965, *Windmill Hill and Avebury: Excavations by Alexander Keiller 1925-1939* (Oxford University Press)

Steward, J.H., 1955, *Theory of Culture Change, the methodology of multilinear evolution*, University of Illinois Press (Urbana)

Silvester, R.J., 1988, *Fenland Project, Number 3: Norfolk Survey, Marshland and the Nar Valley, Norfolk*, East Anglian Archaeology 45

Whittle, A., Pollard, J. and Grigson, C., 1999, *The Harmony of Symbols – the Windmill Hill causewayed enclosure* (Oxford, Oxbow)

4. METALWORK AND 'COLD CLAYLANDS': PRE-IRON AGE OCCUPATION ON THE ISLE of ELY

by Christopher Evans

The recovery of a rapier fragment from a multi-period settlement recently excavated on the west side of Ely, and, too, the recognition of substantive later Bronze Age occupation at the site of the Wardy Hill Ringwork in Coveney, provides the impetus of this paper. What links these, apart from chronology and David Hall's participation in both projects (discovering the Wardy Hill complex in the course of the Fenland Survey and responsible for the analysis of post-Roman ceramics from the two sites), is their relationship to the island's marshes and its heavy clay sub-soils. These factors frame the central theme of this contribution, that is the nature of Ely's pre-Iron Age usage, particularly during the Bronze Age given the wealth of metalwork of that period known from its environs. As such, this study also raises key questions concerning low density register within the archaeological record, the caricature of landscape and the context of ritual deposition.

Extending over 91sq km (excluding its low embayments) and projecting up to 30m OD, Ely remains a land-locked island amid the flat lowlands of the southern peat fens. Surrounded by marsh prior to drainage in post-Medieval times, it was isolated by 3-4km from fen-edge villages to the south and by 5-10km to those in the east. It is essentially a great clay rise and its geology largely consists of Kimmeridge beds with localised deposits of Ampthill and Boulder Clay (Gallois 1988). Aside from swathes of lower Greensand along its southern side and west around the town itself, the island's interior has only very localised gravel terraces. While glacial sands and gravels cap the rises of Downham and Littleport, together these light sub-soils amount to less than 15% of its land-mass. At *c.* 12.5sq km, though not an inconsiderable area, these light sub-soils are largely distributed in narrow seams and, limiting their 'use-value', it is questionable whether they would have been readily, or at least superficially, apparent in prehistory. Therefore, the scale of Ely's surrounding, peat-sealed skirtlands becomes critical, as these areas would have been an obvious locale of early settlement. Like all of its low gravel beds, these are probably more extensive than has been mapped (especially to the north of Wardy Hill). Nevertheless, it is only around the island's southern flanks that these extend widely and there First Terrace gravels continue for 2-3km across Setchel Fen and the 'Cuts' to meet the clay plain north of Cottenham.

Conjured in the popular imagination as if some manner of marshland fortress and/or refuge, as a place Ely has a remarkably strong sense of itself and its past. This rests in a series of key historical figures and an ethos of rebelliousness, to which the fact that it is a major island – a remote place with well-defined borders and a substantial population – obviously contributes. The 'rootedness' of this identity and the evidence of the island's apparent colonisation during the later Iron Age are issues explored at length in the forthcoming Wardy Hill volume. In this capacity, and in the light of the area's later prehistoric metalwork distributions, the extent and character of its usage during the Bronze Age becomes crucial. While it was the region's metalwork that first drew attention to the Fenland archaeology, with the 'modern' phase of investigation there has been little integration of these earlier findings. This neglect becomes all the more telling in the case of Ely – how do we mesh its many bronzes with the island's clays? – as heavy sub-soils have long been deemed unsuitable for pre-Iron Age settlement (*e.g.* Fox 1923).

Lost Lands – Creating Places

Second only to the Thames valley in England, the southern Fenland is renowned for its quantity of later Bronze Age metalwork, especially its weaponry (*e.g.* Rowlands 1976; Bradley 1990). Therefore, the recovery of still another rapier from the Ely area is not itself particularly surprising. It adds to the island's corpus; five from its interior marshes and a further seven from the Great Ouse valley between Ely and Littleport. This cluster outlies their main distribution which extends along the southeastern fen-edge from Cambridge and the lower reaches of the Cam to West Row, Suffolk and north to Methwold and the river Wissey. The Ely grouping is all the more distinct given that, whereas three have been recovered from the central Fenland islands, none is known on the lower reaches of the Ouse valley (Fig 1; Trump 1968; Burgess & Gerloff 1981). (**1**)

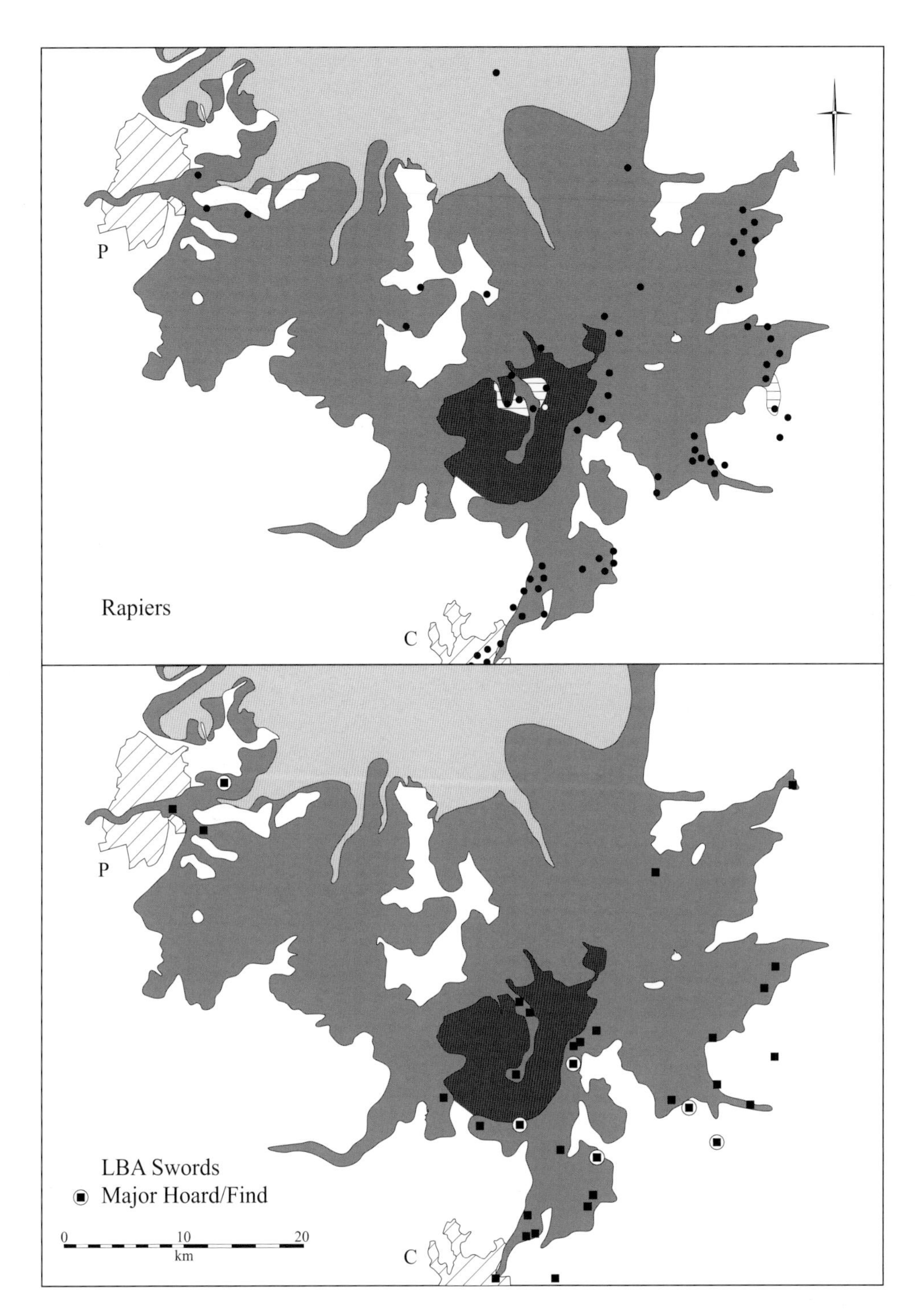

Figure 1 Bronze Age metalwork distributions superimposed upon Waller's reconstruction of the southern Fenland *c.* 3,000BP (1994: fig 5.20): Top – Trump's 1968 rapier plot (fig 52) shows a remarkable 'closeness of fit' to the environmental evidence and, aside from the addition of the subsequent Peterborough and Ely finds, no amendment whatsoever has been made to it (the rogue finding in the marine silts at Wisbech can only be explained as either through re-deposition or 'boat-loss'). The only points of discrepancy between her distributions and Waller's map are in the potential scale/chronology of the Coveney and Lakenheath embayments (indicated by horizontal hachure; the Isle of Ely is shown blackened; *P* – Peterborough and *C* – Cambridge). Bottom – Largely based on Burgess and Colquhoun's 1988 plot (pl. 117; augmented by Fox's 1923 and Hall's 1996 mapping), the Later Bronze Age sword plot has required much 'adjustment'; due to the general provenancing of many of the finds their locations can only be considered approximate (for both Figures see Healy's detailed plotting of the Wissey Embayment metalwork; 1996, fig 24 & 25)

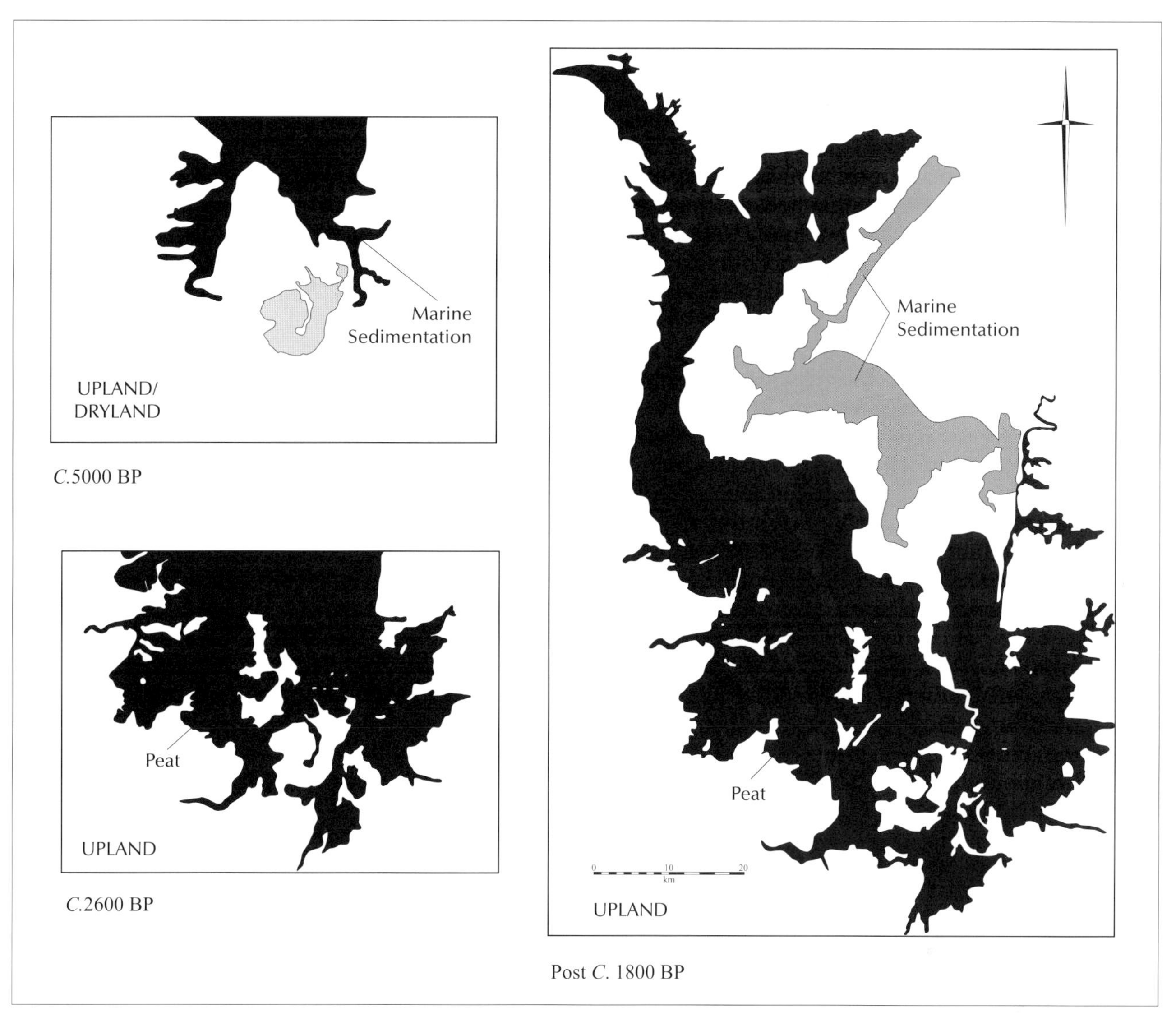

Figure 2 *Creating Places* – The successive loss of land (based on Waller 1994: fig 5.16 – with subsequent area of Ely shaded – 5.21 & 5.23)

Swords of the later Bronze Age period again show a marked concentration along the adjacent portion of the southeastern fen-edge (extending to the lower reaches of the Cam). Aside from the more than twenty fragments from the Wilburton hoard, nine are reported from the immediate Ely environs including two from Coveney Fen itself (Fig. 1; Burgess & Colquhoun 1988, pl. 117; Fox 1923, pl. IX.2 &.3); none is recorded from the central Fenland islands (there is also a cluster in the Peterborough area). (**2**) Equally localised is the recovery of two later Bronze Age shields from Coveney's marshes (Hall & Coles 1994, fig 54). Apart from another at Langwood, Chatteris (Fox 1923, pl. VIII.1), these are the only examples known from the Fenland (Wait, Coles 1962, No. 8-10).

It is imperative that these metalwork distributions be integrated with Waller's palaeo-environmental sequence for the region (1994). Only by the end of the first millennium BC was Ely completely isolated as a island (Fig. 2). Prior to the later fourth millennium BC (c. 5,000 BP) Ely and the central Fenland islands interconnected as a great peninsula that joined with the 'mainland' between the river valleys of the Ouse and Cam. In the southeast its divide was only then marked by the narrow corridor of the Cam system. It was over the course of the next c. 3,000 years that this land-mass fractured, separating into the islands of the historical landscape with Ely's division from the Chatteris/ March 'archipelago' occurring over the first half of the second millennium (Waller 1994, fig 5.16-22). Generating new 'wet-edges', during this time there would have been a 60% loss in the land-mass of the peninsula. Much of this, quite critically, would have been its lighter skirtland deposits. Effectively 'sculpting' landscape by accentuating contour and resulting in a much more marked definition of elevated *places*, the extent of land loss must have resulted in a considerable disruption to settlement patterns. (**3**)

Postulating a direct linkage between environmental succession and metalwork deposition, it could be argued that the latter reflects a 'stress-related' response to inundation and the employment of ritual to 'stop the waters'. Certainly arguments that the majority of these bronzes result from the erosion of settlement sites can be dismissed from the outset, if for no other reason than such pieces are almost never found in domestic contexts. (**4**) Yet, though such activities may well have found a particularly local resonance, the deposition of metalwork in watery contexts was then a widespread phenomenon (*e.g.* Bradley 1990) and by no means can it only be mechanically tied to a regional environmental sequence. Nevertheless, these factors would have brought pressure to bear on local settlement and have impacted upon its cultural geography.

The most substantial single loss of land at this time occurred within Block Fen, Chatteris where some 14 sq km of gravel terrace was inundated, resulting in the abandonment of its extensive later Bronze Age field system (Hunn 1993) and the barrows dotting its plain (Hall 1992). Block Fen was the one area of the central fens to also see significant metalwork deposition and land-use thereafter evidently shifted up to the upper slopes of Chatteris island and the Langwood Ridge. Discovered in the course of the Fenland Surveys and investigated during the FMP, a vast, primarily Early, Iron Age complex extends over some 10ha on Langwood Ridge and it is one of the largest settlements recorded from that time (Evans 2000c and forthcoming b). This seems not so much a matter of centralisation/nucleation as 'clustering' born out of the necessity of low ground retreat. (**5**)

These environmental changes and their socio-cultural consequences must be seen in both the context of short- and long-term change. The former involves the immediate 'tragedy' of land loss, entailing the abandonment of holdings and patterns of land-use; the latter, that the sequence of Ely and the central Fenland islands would come to markedly differ. So separated, in the later Iron Age the latter clearly were subject to eastward, Icenian influence. While Ely, situated at the northern fringe of 'core' Aylesford-Swarling distributions, seems to have been southwardly oriented (Hill *et al.* 1999; Evans forthcoming a).

Geologically the Isle of Ely relates to the north Cambridge clay plain, to which its southern 'land bridge' at Aldreth would have provided connection until the late second/early first millennium BC (Fig. 2; Waller 1994: fig 5.21 & .22). (**6**) However, the later Bronze Age metalwork distributions suggest that Ely lay within the sphere of more easterly communities along the southeastern fen-edge, and this should caution against confusing physical and cultural geography. Yet, at least at first glance, even the depositional context of this metalwork within these two areas appears to vary. Whereas those which dot the fen-edge between Soham and Methwold occur in areas of light soils which evidently attracted a high density of contemporary settlement, little pre-later Iron Age settlement is known from Ely and the island's predominately heavy clays. Unless admitting that the latter saw some extraordinary mechanism involving the long distance transportation of material specifically for the purposes of watery deposition – and, if so, this requires exploration – then a missing settlement dimension must be acknowledged for Ely itself.

Whilst noting the occurrence of 'background' flints on Ely's claylands (and its sprinkling of axes of various periods), within the Fenland Survey only four Bronze Age scatters were identified upon the island; only one, and that very minor, occurred on its clays (Wentworth Site 2). (**7**) Drawing upon Hall's

	Ely	**Fen-edge**
Neo.	5	48
BA	4 (+1)	30
IA	10 (+4)	8
R-B	13 (+3)	39

Table 1 *Site density: Isle of Ely and southeast fen-edge* Post-Fenland Survey discoveries on Ely are indicated in brackets; whilst Wardy Hill's Bronze Age occupation is thus indicated, given the ambiguities of definition, the Trinity Lands hollow, for example, is not. For the sake of consistency, the Littleport 'rise' sites – though not those on its northern 'in-fen' riverside – are included in Ely's tallies for the IA/R-B, despite that it was then a separate island. Note that it is only the density of the Romano-British sites that seems to be proportional between the two areas (no./sq km)

Figure 3 *Wardy Hill* - Location plans

distribution maps, Table 1 compares the frequency of sites on the island to the adjacent portion of the southeastern, Cambridgeshire fen-edge alone (*i.e.* excluding Suffolk and Norfolk data; Hall 1996, fig 87 & 88; *cf.* Hall & Coles 1994, fig 35) and clearly attests to their discrepancy during the Neolithic and Bronze Ages. Given that the area of the fen-edge involved is just less than three times that of the Isle of Ely, also in contrast is the greater density of the island's later Iron Age sites. It is this, and the paucity of 'earlier' Iron Age settlements on Ely, that suggests its possible colonisation in the later first millennium BC (*i.e.* to date there seems no obvious evidence of immediate post-Bronze Age retreat onto the island).

The dismissal of clays as supporting pre-Iron Age settlement essentially derives from arable-dominated models of agriculture and the presumption that these communities would have been incapable of tillage on heavy soils. What this overlooks is the crucial role of pastoralism within earlier agrarian systems (*e.g.* Pryor 1996; 1998) and, certainly for pre-later Bronze Age communities, the degree of settlement mobility which must have involved regular excursions onto heavy woodland soils for hunting, foraging and leaf fodder. Equally, aside from that much of the Neolithic and Bronze Age settlement on the Continent actually occurred on clays, 'typical' later Bronze Age settlement – in other words, roundhouse accompanied and, seemingly, permanent – has now been documented on clays in Essex and the East Midlands (*e.g.* Brooks 1993; Liddle 1982; Tura 1982; Cooper 1994). Whilst obviously not a sub-soil of preference, clays clearly could be tolerated.

The implications of the paucity of Bronze Age occupation on Ely (*viz.* its metalwork) can only really be considered a 'problem' in the light of recent recovery rates of settlement of the period elsewhere in the region and this adds a historiographic dimension to this study. Whereas eighty years ago in Fox's time so little contemporary settlement was known that the distribution of stray find bronzes and hoards could/had to be read as effectively equating with usage-*cum*-settlement, the same is not true today. Aside from the evidence of aerial photography and fieldwalking survey (leading to the excavations at Fengate/Flag Fen and Block Fen, Chatteris), more recent development-related initiatives have variously fostered the discovery of major Bronze Age field systems and settlements in the lower Ouse and Cam valleys, and the islands of Ely and Whittlesey (*e.g.* Evans & Knight 2000a; Gibson & Knight forthcoming). 'Unannounced' by aerial and surface survey techniques, from this we can begin to appreciate the extent and density of the period's settlement and, perhaps as important, start to recognise where it does not seem to be forthcoming within the region.

Wardy Hill – Causeways and Embankments

As the first substantive investigation of a major lithics site on the Isle of Ely, it is appropriate to review the evidence of early occupation at Wardy Hill, Coveney. Its recovery was unexpected and only arose through the excavation of the later Iron Age Ringwork by the Cambridge Archaeological Unit (CAU) during 1991 and 1992 as part of the Fenland Management Project (FMP) programme. The site is situated on the lower fenward flanks of the hill, which rising to 6-10m OD is a spur of Ampthill clay (its crown capped by Kimmeridge deposits) which dominates the eastern side of the Coveney embayment (Fig. 1 and 7). Given the site's interim and ensuing reportage (Evans 1992, 2000b and forthcoming a), there is no need here to rehearse the details of its Iron Age defensive occupation. What does warrant emphasis is that although only the *c.* 1ha of the ringwork proper was excavated, this subsequently proved to be only a part of a much more extensive, quasi-linear system. Aerial photographic appraisal indicates that a major ditch boundary arcs off from its northern perimeter and geophysical survey, aside from locating further 'roundhouse settlement' to the south (its Iron Age date confirmed by further fieldwalking), demonstrated that the enclosure system continues up over the crown of the Wardy Hill spur (Fig. 3). There its main axis appears to conjoin with a pair of parallel ditches which run down off the hill to the fen-edge in the southeast. Appearing to flank a great droveway, arguably these approached a causeway crossing the Cove's marshes and it was the commanding of this putative route that provided the *raison d'être* of the enclosure system in the first place.

The excavations were thorough and all phases of the FMP's surface sampling techniques – grid fieldwalking, test pitting and chemical survey (see Evans 2000a for project methodology) – were applied prior to machine stripping. It was in the course of these topsoil investigations that the site's pre-Iron Age utilisation first came to attention, most notably the traces of a ploughed-out burnt flint mound in its northeastern sector. Implying *en masse* importation of lithics, though this seems remarkable given the site's clay sub-strata, a seam

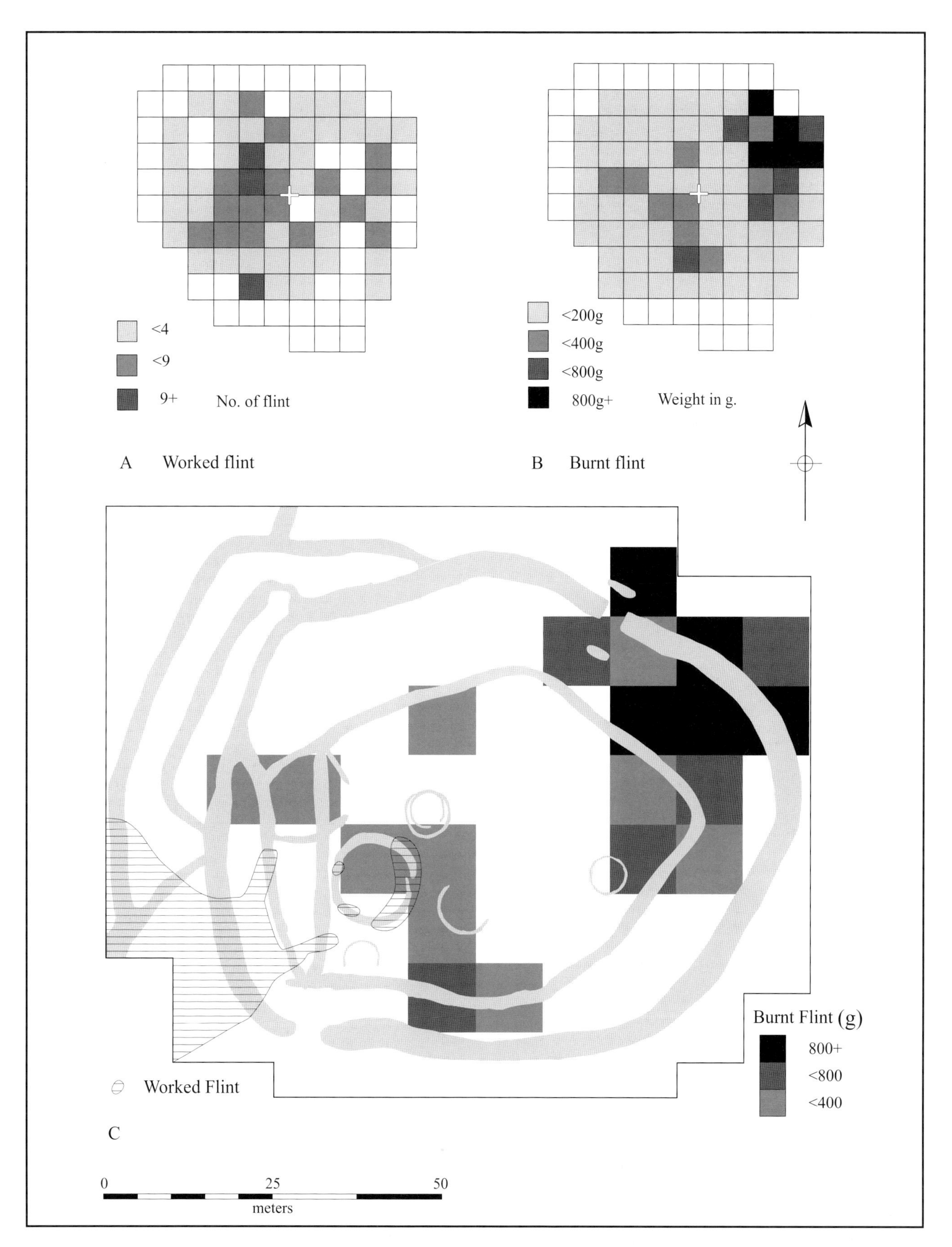

Figure 4 *Wardy Hill* – A & B) 10m grid square plot of surface-collected worked and burnt flint; C) Composite Figure showing fieldwalking burnt flint 'highs' and southwestern concentrations of residual worked flint in excavated contexts (>2 pieces per metre segment) superimposed upon Iron Age ringwork features

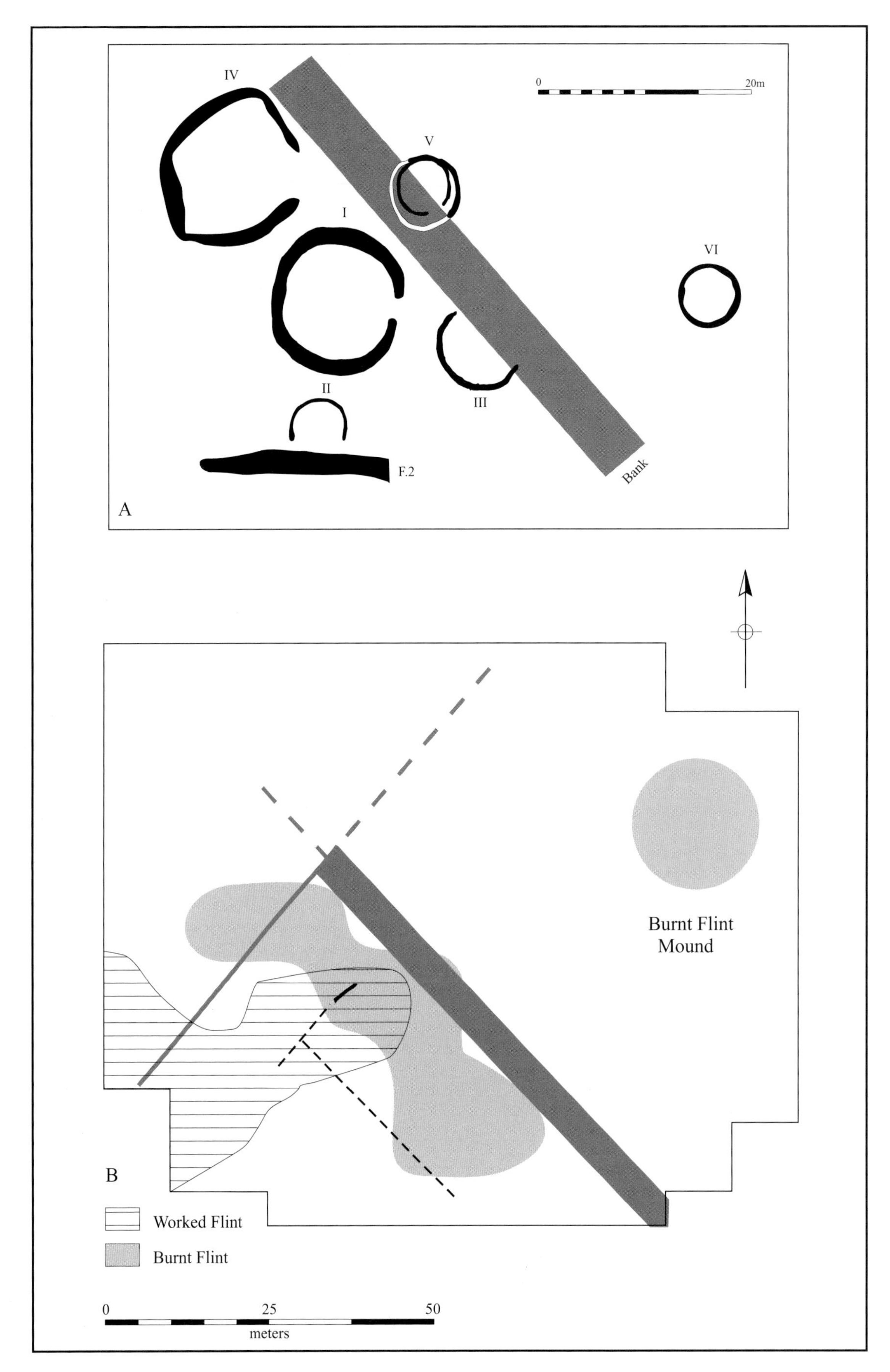

Figure 5 *Wardy Hill* – A) Shows postulated location of main pre-ringwork bank-line based on layout of Iron Age roundhouses; B) Reconstruction Figure showing southwestern lithics site in relationship to the putative bank system with pot boiler mound lying at northeastern margins of the grid

of Pleistocene gravels is known to fringe the southeast side of the hill-top and lies at a distance of *c.* 300m (site-related coring demonstrated a localised outcropping of gravel only some 100m to the southeast of the excavations).

The traces of the 'lithic site' were largely confined to the site's ploughsoil and as residual artefacts within later contexts. In total 676 pieces of worked flint were recovered from the fieldwork, of which 258 were collected during fieldwalking and test pitting. The ploughsoil density of worked flint varied from 0-12 pieces per 10m collection unit (2.9 mean; Fig. 4.A). At first there seems little obvious patterning or even a 'site' as such, aside from the fact that higher densities (5+ pieces) tend to occur in an east-west band across the middle of the collection grid. However, even this swathe is punctuated with nil values and the more consistent pattern could be read as only attesting to a distinct western central 'high'. While definition of the latter perhaps acquires greater credibility through the occurrence of locally higher burnt flint values in the same area, this immediate spread also corresponds with the main high in Iron Age pottery and bone. This may well mark the location of enclosure-contemporary middens and, therefore, the high flint values could equally relate to material scraped up and re-deposited during its Iron Age occupation. Yet the distribution of this material continues further southwest than the main extent of the middening spreads and clearly correlates with an increase of worked flint re-deposited within Iron Age features that does not directly correspond with the main focus of Ringwork-associated deposition. Therefore, taken as a whole, the evidence suggests a distinct distributional 'high' in the southwestern-central quarter of the grid.

Not surprisingly, the lithics assemblage reflects diverse usage. Studied by Mark Edmonds, it includes microliths likely to date to the later Mesolithic, and a core recovered during fieldwalking may be of similar attribution. Neolithic artefacts also form a component, including a burnt end scraper and a fine leaf-shaped arrowhead (Fig. 9.1) – both probably of earlier Neolithic date – other artefacts of the period include a flake from a polished axe and an end scraper with invasive retouch along both sides. A crude thumbnail scraper would be broadly contemporary with the few scraps of probable Beaker that were recovered from tree-throw hollows in the northwestern quarter of the site.

Artefacts attributable to the Bronze Age form the largest component of the assemblage. A limited number, such as a multi-platform core, probably date to the Early Bronze Age. However, many of the crude notches, scrapers and retouched flakes belong to the later phase of the period, as could also be crude cores and worked pebbles which show no signs of consistent platform preparation and maintenance. In addition, there is evidence on a number for the reworking of discarded pieces by the patina that had formed on the original flaked surfaces. While the relatively small number of Mesolithic and earlier Neolithic pieces represent little more than the usual 'background noise', the scale and character of Bronze Age lithics suggest some form of sustained settlement activity. Given that raw material does not occur naturally in the immediate area, it is certainly difficult to understand their densities as a simple product of 'off-site' discard.

Here, other finds categories provide insight. Across the fieldwalking grid the density of burnt flint ranged from 0-612 pieces per 10m unit or 0 to 5020g (22.6 pieces/283.4g mean). Aside from a swathe of locally increased values in the western centre of the grid which fringe the worked flint high in that quarter, it is the concentration in the northeastern sector that is most apparent (Fig. 4.B). There, over an area of *c.* 30 x 30m, values greater than 500g consistently occurred, averaging 1.68kg per 10m unit (Fig. 4.C). Given these densities, this must reflect the location of a burnt flint mound comparable to other 'pot boiler' sites in the region (Edmonds *et al.* 1999, Table 5). A metre square test pit dug in the approximate centre of this spread (producing more than 5kg of burnt lithics) indicated that the putative mound had been entirely ploughed out and its soil sequence was 'structureless'. Upon machine stripping a number of shallow, burnt flint-filled hollows were found scattered over 5 x 5m within the area of the core densities (traces of burnt flint lay impressed in the surface of the natural over an area of 12 x 14m). These proved to be natural groundsurface depressions and the products of tree-rooting filled with a black soil matrix characteristic of pot boiler mounds, largely reduced charred material.

Obviously not of later Iron Age attribution, a quantity of small, burnt flint tempered sherds were also recovered in the excavation. Occurring in residual context within later features, their distribution is dispersed and displays no obvious patterning. They are assigned to the Late Bronze Age (*c.* 1,200-800BC; see Hill in Evans forthcoming a) and, consistent with the vast majority of the site's lithics, probably date the 'pot-boiler' activity.

The lithic assemblage clearly suggests a palimpsest of episodic usage ranging from the later Mesolithic, earlier Neolithic and the Late Neolithic/Early Bronze Ages, with the vast majority of the material being of later Bronze Age attribution. Although by any measure this activity at Wardy Hill can only be accounted as a low density lithics site, as in the case of the Soham scatters (Edmonds *et al.* 1999) this must be qualified by the volume of worked flint that had evidently later been burnt and subsequently re-deposited in the pot boiler mound. Edmonds estimates 30-40% of the burnt material had previously been worked. Extrapolating from the test pit-to-fieldwalking densities, if assuming an average weight of 10g per flint then upwards of 15,000-20,000 worked flints may have been bound up in its matrix. Even if halving this figure, this still must represent a considerable 'erasure' of the original lithics site. Of course, one cannot be certain that all this material was generated by the immediate occupation and some, if not most, may derive from the larger Wardy Hill complex.

While such burnt flint mounds were not an uncommon feature of the cultural landscape of the second millennium BC along the southeastern fen-edge, none has previously been found on the region's clays. Concerning their character and interrelationship with monuments, it has been argued that it is erroneous to see them strictly in a context of quasi-industrial refuse (Edmonds *et al* 1999). The regularity of their mounding, on a comparable scale to barrows, would not have been a 'natural' way to dispose of such mineral waste. Instead, whatever their functional derivation, by the regular heaping of what would have been their brilliant white matrix (previous to plough dispersion) they probably served as some manner of cairns, marking settlement and/or seasonal territory. This demarcation of the spur suggests its early distinction as a locale. There is, however, no argument to suggest direct continuity between the site's Bronze Age and Iron Age usage. Given that the outer ringwork circuit evidently cut through the mound without deflection (despite that it would presumably still then have been without plough damage and, therefore, apparent) indicates that this was not a relationship of obvious respect.

Amongst the more intriguing aspects of the ringwork's occupation is that, by the alignment of minor ditch-lines both within and exterior to its circuits, and from the arrangement of three of its interior buildings, the existence of a northwest-southeast oriented bank system can be inferred (Fig. 5.A). Evidently pre-dating the ringwork, this would have had to have been substantial, probably upwards of some 4-5m across. The main basis for its identification is the layout of subsequent roundhouses: the straight northeastern arm of the eaves-gully of that in the northwestern quarter (IV) and the two small, central round structures (III & V). The construction sequence of the northern of the latter two indicates that, like the southern, its gully was also originally 'C'-shaped. Unlike the layout of the definite 'half building' in the southwestern corner of the enclosure, whose gully clearly terminated in relationship to the interior ringwork circuit (or at least its interior upcast bank), in the case of structures III and V this seems rather to have been determined by differential survival and that their remainder lay upon the surface of this putative bank (see Evans 1997a concerning 'half' and bankside-elevated buildings).

Superimposing the line of this feature onto the lithics plots suggests that it influenced site activities (Fig. 5.B). The bulk of the worked flint is confined to its southwestern side where it is ringed by a swathe of increased burnt flint densities, possibly attesting to middening against the side of the bank; whereas the pot boiler mound lies isolated to the northeast. Apart from one slight ditch, given the otherwise paucity of contemporary features by no means can this be accounted as intense later Bronze Age occupation. Nevertheless from the quantity of material present and its apparent structure, its seems to mark something more than just short-lived 'visitation' or camp episodes. By the south-westward distribution of the worked material it appears that the site saw only the fringes of a larger settlement spread that extends up onto the crown of Wardy Hill. Effectively, spilling out across the area of excavation, what is surprising is that the evidence suggests that the core of this occupation lies on the hill-top's clay and not down towards the lighter skirtland sub-soils.

Perhaps attesting to its lingering landscape presence, the line of the pre-ringwork bank appears to have influenced the later alignment of the enclosure's northeastern perimeter. Yet, even more telling, it also falls at a right-angle to the ditch that extends southwest from the ringwork and continues across the crown of the Wardy Hill-top (Fig. 6). It is from the latter's axis that the droveway flanking ditches ran down the putative trans-marsh causeway. Although many suppositions underlie these arguments and certainty is not possible, it is reasonable therefore to propose that this bank system probably both related to a larger system of pre-ringwork land division and other embankments across the Wardy Hill-top.

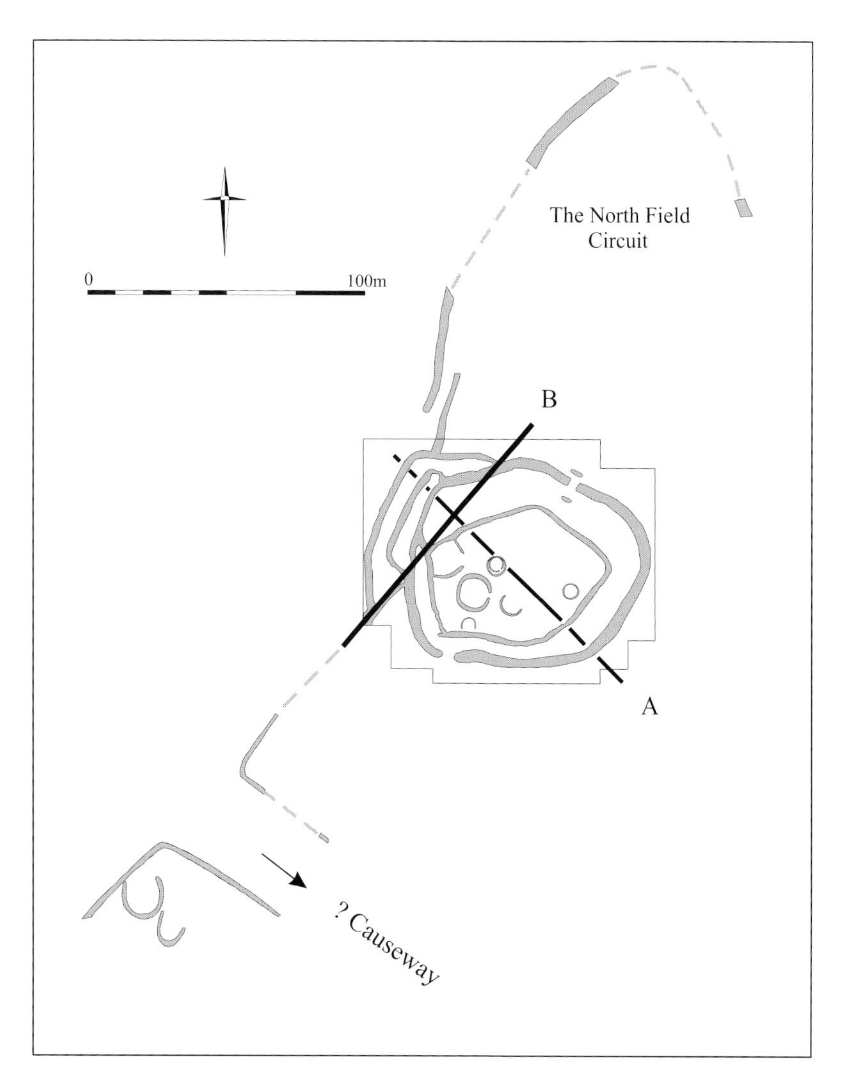

Figure 6 *Wardy Hill* – Showing line of pre-ringwork bank (A) in relationship to the main axis of the hill-top system (B) linked to droveway ditches running down to the putative causeway crossing

Presumably regulating access to the causeway crossing, further credence would here be gained by the fact that the later Bronze Age attribution of the site's pre-Iron Age settlement would broadly coincide with the establishment of the two other causeways investigated in the southern Fenlands – that at Flag Fen, Peterborough (Pryor 1991 & forthcoming) and, nearer at hand, at Stuntney, Little Thetford (Lethbridge 1933 & 1936; Malim 2000). Of course, by these arguments Wardy Hill would itself have then been a distinct place in the later Bronze Age cultural landscape of the island. By this determination the recovery of settlement from this period, though unanticipated, cannot then constitute any manner of unbiased landscape sample typical of Ely's clays as a whole; for this we must rely upon more recent area-wide excavation exposures.

Off-Site Reconnaissance

Subsequent to the Wardy Hill investigations, three substantial later Iron Age settlements have been discovered and excavated in the course of development-led fieldwork alongside the 'Cove' and Ely's western ridge (Fig. 7 & 8.A). Two of these occur on clays. Complementing the pattern of Fenland Survey-recovered sites of this period along the south side the Cove and north of Ely itself (Hall 1996), and located at a distance of c. 0.5km from each other, this suggests a high local density of late Iron Age settlement. Given their recovery and consistency of date, this seems to mark a major 'arrival' and suggests colonisation of the island with little, if any, relationship to what went before.

From the recovery of 'early' occupation at Wardy Hill and in reference to Ely's later prehistoric

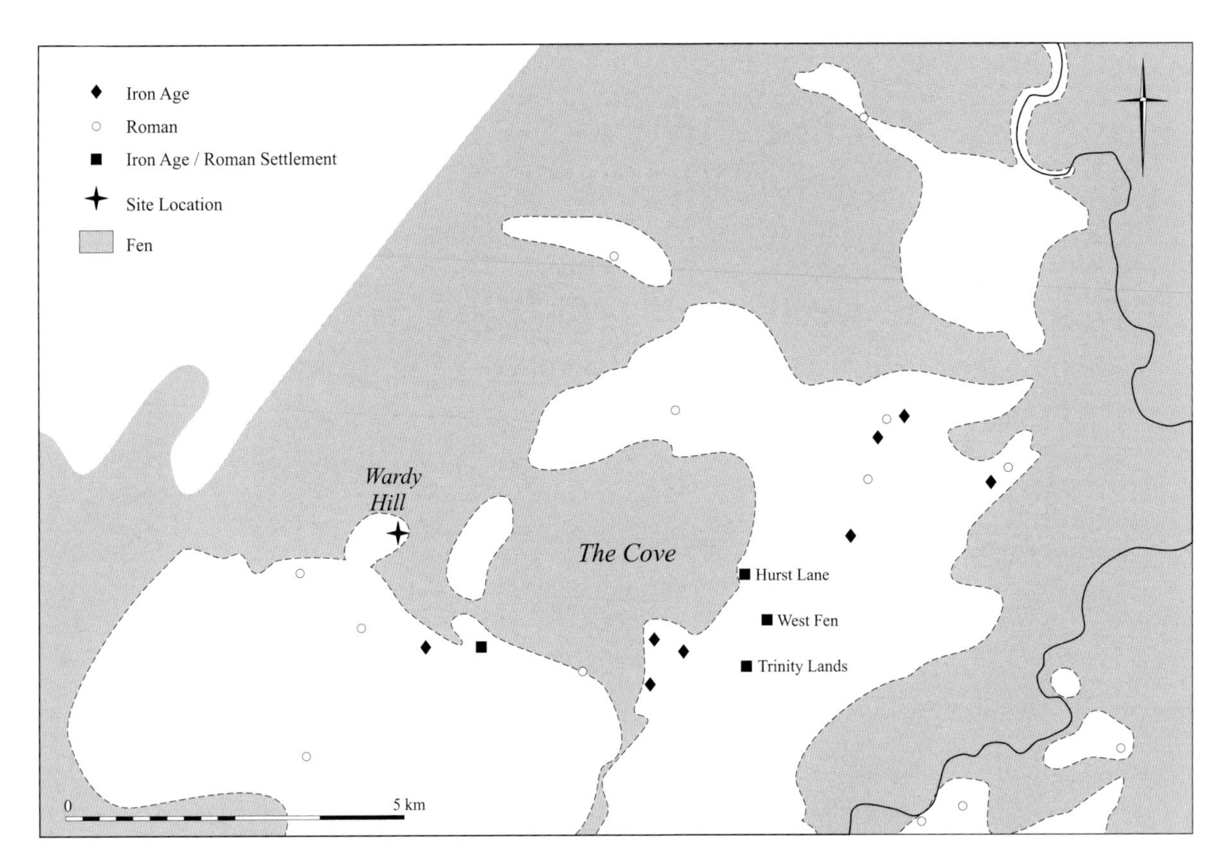

Figure 7 Recent sites investigated around The Cove Embayment, Ely

metalwork distributions, it could be anticipated that the island's few gravel beds constituted micro-environments attracting dense pre-Iron Age settlement. Therefore, it is rather surprising that the one recent substantial exposure of the Cove's skirtland gravels at the Hurst Lane Reservoir failed to register more intensive usage (Evans & Knight 2000b). (**8**) Stripped over *c.* 2.8ha to expose the Iron Age settlement – despite that the overall excavation sample of its thirty roundhouses was, by necessity, low – the fieldwork only generated 43 worked flints. All of these occurred within residual contexts, there being no contemporary features. Few diagnostic pieces were present – a Late Neolithic transverse arrowhead and two later Bronze Age denticulate scrapers. Nevertheless, the knapping debris indicates the presence of two distinct technologies: the use of multi-platform cores and hard hammers in the Bronze Age to produce squat flakes and a Mesolithic/Neolithic blade-based industry. Of the 520g of burnt flint recovered, only one piece showed signs of previous work suggesting an 'incidental' source for most. (**9**)

Extending, in total, over 22ha, the multi-period West Fen Road excavations have seen the largest exposure to date of Ely's clays (Mortimer 2000; Regan 2001). With evidence of Iron Age to Medieval settlement (continuous apart from a substantive Early Saxon component), the situation of this evidently long-term 'place' on the west side of the saddleback ridge immediately opposite Ely itself – which from its Roman occupation onwards was clearly bounded by a drove-/roadway along its southern side – could suggest that it was sited at the eastern end of another cross-fen causeway, perhaps one inter-connecting with that from Wardy Hill *via* Coveney island. Otherwise, the relevance of these excavations to this paper not so much relates to any specific pre-Iron Age component of its long settlement sequence, but the scale of its stripping and the extraordinary density of its subsequent cut features, especially those of later Saxon and earlier Medieval date. These, effectively, act as a sample grid 'catching' residual lithic distributions and, in Figure 8.C. their distribution has been expressed as if surface data. Subject as it is to different intensities of excavation, it is impossible directly to compare uniform, surface grid-collected/controlled material with that retrieved in this manner. Nevertheless, varying between 0-8 flints per 10m^2 unit, the CAU's West Fen Road densities are low and, over *c.* 3ha, only 213 worked flints were recovered in total (*c.* 0.7 per 10m^2 avge.). Their distribution was, moreover, sporadic and occurred in only *c.* 35% of the excavation grid squares. Though no discrete 'sites' as such are identifiable a degree of clustering is apparent. This is most obvious in the central

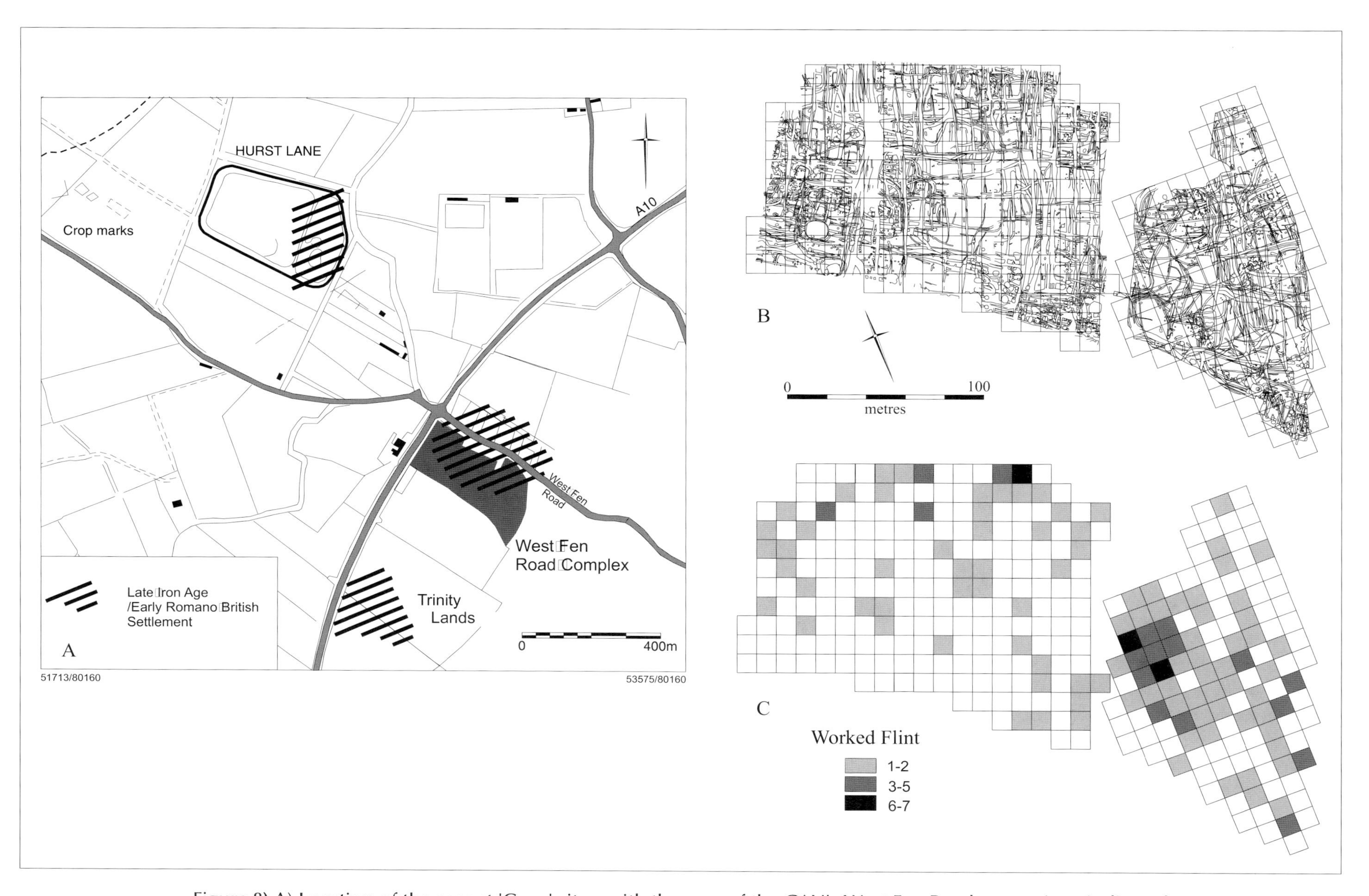

Figure 8) A) Location of the recent 'Cove' sites, with the area of the CAU's West Fen Road excavations indicated; B) Feature base-plan (all periods); C) The distribution of worked flint (as recovered by feature-excavation) expressed by 10m grid square

eastern quarter of the site where densities greater than four flints per 10m occurred consistently across an area of $600m^2$.

Studied by Chantel Conneller, the same three main 'horizons' as identified at Wardy Hill are present within its lithic assemblage (those proverbially distinguished in 'landscape' collections). While a scraper, crude flakes and multi-platform and denticulated cores attest to a later Bronze Age presence, most of the material would seem to be of later Neolithic/Early Bronze Age attribution. The latter includes a variety of knife-types, and both an oblique and barbed-and-tanged arrowhead (Fig. 9.2). Debitage characteristic of this period would, moreover, point to 'on-site' core reduction and tool manufacture. Later Mesolithic/Early Neolithic activity is also evident. While the recovery of a scraper and a leaf-shaped arrowhead, blades and a blade core in the eastern portion of the grid reflects some degree of manufacture, the clustered recovery of a tranchet axe fragment, a truncation and blades (two serrated) in the west rather suggests the 'importation' of a mobile tool kit onto the site (*i.e.* without contemporary working debris). The former, eastern cluster corresponds to the location of two small pits from which sherds of Neolithic pottery were recovered. However, only four pieces of worked flint of Early Neolithic attribution were retrieved from this portion of the grid and the majority of this cluster would seem to consist of later material (23 later Neolithic/Early Bronze Age pieces and nine of later Bronze Age date). (**10**) Although the evidence of the flint working may otherwise suggest more prolonged 'stays', generally the site's low density of burnt to worked flint when compared to Wardy Hill – 1/2.8 *vs.* 2.5/1 (excavated assemblage; *i.e.* excluding the evidence of the pot-boiler mound) – does itself attest to only low intensity usage (see Edmonds *et al.* 1999).

Amongst the components of the nearby Trinity Lands excavations – on-going at the time of writing – aside from the recovery of a fine polished axe (from a Roman ditch; Fig. 9.3) and a Neolithic bowl in the upper profile of a tree-throw, has been a large pond-like hollow within a colluvium-sealed palaeochannel. Much burnt flint was recovered from within it and spread throughout the vicinity, where characteristic 'burnt flint' pits were also found. While obviously associated with water processing activities, a fragment of human skull was recovered from its deposits; these are thus far dated by later Bronze Age flintwork and pottery (with radiocarbon determinations still forthcoming, an Early Iron Age component also seems to be present; Fig. 9.5). (**11**)

Palynological study has yet to elucidate the island's Neolithic and Bronze Age cover. However, the sequence now achieved from the West Fen Road investigations, not unexpectedly, shows the greatest abundance of shrubs and trees during the later Iron Age (primarily oak and ash); subsequent reduction in these within the respective profile suggests progressive woodland clearance during that period (Scaife in Regan 2001). Given the recognition that settlement mobility was a distinct component of the Neolithic and, at least the earlier, Bronze Ages – the 'archaeology of paths and clearances' as it were (*e.g.* Tilley 1994; Bruck 1999; Pollard 1998 & 1999) – it is surprising that the distribution of lithics on clay-based sites is not further interrogated. Whilst rarely amounting to 'sites' as normally understood, they provide insight into early patterns of what probably would then have been life in, or at least seasonal usage of, woods (Evans *et al.* 1999). Involving only localised lithic incidents and very minor, low-density clusters, they have little if any distinct ploughsoil 'signature'. Accordingly, there is an accidental quality to their recovery and, aside from the Trinity Lands hollow, none of the Ely sites has been excavated solely for the purposes of its lithic phases (*i.e.* their recovery has been secondary to the investigation of later phases of usage). (**12**) Nevertheless, it is for these very reasons that the documentation of such small scale event-like depositions addresses imbalances inherent in much fieldwalking-generated data alone. Many survey scatter sites reflect multiple occupations – this being a main cause of their ready surface register – and, accordingly, the record is biased towards multi-period usage and, thereby, locational continuities.

Aside from that of the Bronze Age occupation at Wardy Hill, unequivocal evidence has yet to be found of pre-Iron Age settlement on Ely's clays. Whilst the determination of what constitutes settlement *per se* is by no means straightforward prior to the mid second millennium BC, the same is not generally true for the later Bronze Age and, for the purposes of this paper, West Row Fen can be considered a 'typical' configuration (Martin & Murphy 1988). Given the scale and density of the flint scatters that have been investigated what can be said, however, is that widespread traces of 'low level' activities have been identified throughout all phases of later prehistory from the later Mesolithic/ Early Neolithic to the later Bronze Age. Normally held to represent 'off-site' activities, such a

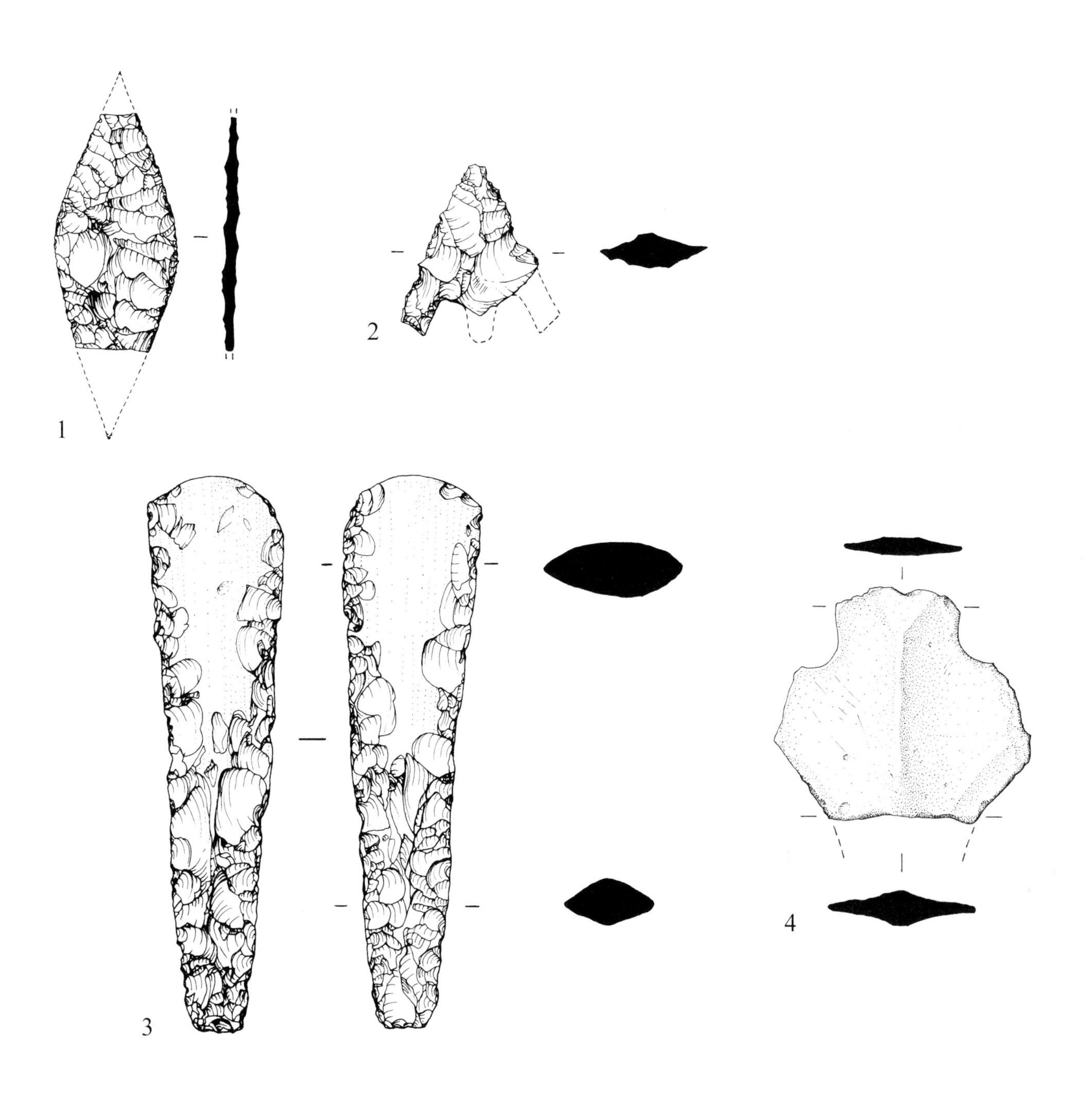

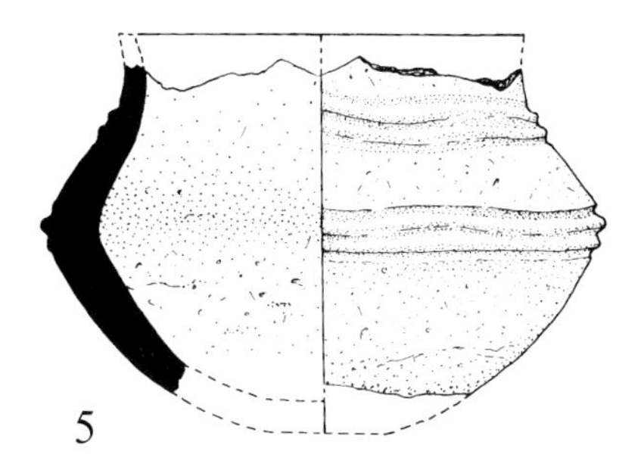

Figure 9 *Recent Ely clayland findings* – 1) Leaf-shaped arrowhead from Wardy Hill Ringwork (<2354>); 2) Barbed-and-tanged arrowhead, West Fen Road, Ely (<2564>); 3) Polished axe recovered from early Roman ditch, Trinity Lands, Ely excavations (<2142>); 4) The West Fen Road rapier fragment (<9114>); 5) Late Bronze Age/ Early Iron Age 'PDR' bowl from Trinity Lands 'hollow' (<11177>; 3 & 5 shown half-sized; remainder, 1:1)

determination is only really appropriate if the recognition of the 'on-site' (their would-be permanent parent settlements) is unproblematic.

To this extent the Ely investigations contribute to the study of 'taskscape' activities (Ingold 1986; Edmonds *et al.* 1999). They challenge us to find an appropriate language to study this spectrum of low density usage. For between lithic 'events' – primarily in this case, localised and immediate visits, typical, thus far, of later Mesolithic/Early Neolithic usage – and more permanent 'settlement' (*e.g.* Wardy Hill's later Bronze Age), there seems a medial level as represented by the later Neolithic/Bronze Age usage at West Fen Road (and Soham; Edmonds *et al.* 1999). In this regard 'stays' might be considered an apt term. Reflective of more extensive scatters, in reference to the earlier 'events' these seem to involve more extended occupation involving the working of flint (though 'events' can also encompass working). Alternatively, of course, what this could attest to is that the basic mobile-*cum*-residential unit was smaller in the later Mesolithic/Early Neolithic than in subsequent periods. This distinction should, however, not imply a strictly chronological division. The Trinity Lands hollow probably represents a 'stay' site of the later Bronze Age; permanent settlement would then itself have involved off-site 'tasking' and a mobile component has, moreover, been identified for Iron Age settlement in the region (Evans & Hodder, forthcoming).

Gatherings and Deposition

Progressing towards conclusion, return should here be made to the West Fen Road rapier fragment. With a dark green patina and a distinct mid-rib, the notched butt is broken at the blade (Fig. 9.4). Though damage to the hilt end makes it impossible to assign it to a distinct type, it probably relates to either Burgess and Gerloff's Groups III or IV (1981). (**13**) As it was recovered through metal-detecting of machined topsoil it is without direct feature attribution and can only be generally located to the western half of the site. While the area clearly saw later Bronze Age activity, this can, therefore, only be classed as a 'non-wet' 'off-site' find and is likely to have been deposited within a probable woodland setting (unless broken in conflict, accidental 'dropping' of such a piece seems implausible).

Spanning, in effect, (clay-)land-use between the later Mesolithic and later Bronze Age, the West Fen Road flint plots show no obvious indication of what is widely held to be the marked changes in the nature of settlement that occurred over the course of the second millennium BC (*i.e.* 'settling down'). Yet, the results from Ely do seem to reflect a different character of usage during the later Bronze Age, albeit essentially one of degree. Of course, this may be biased by the conditions of survival in the case of the Trinity Lands hollow – primarily its pitting and the quantity of pottery present. Nevertheless, the results there suggest the repetition of quasi-specialised activities whose focus on the pond/hollow indicates a need of guaranteed water sources. Beyond this, the combined recovery of the human skeletal remains at the Trinity Lands site and, arguably, the rapier from West Fen Road could also attest to an element of ritual activity. While the deposition of skulls – like the provision of year-round water sources (*i.e.* wells) – are also attributes of permanent settlement of the period (*e.g.* Edmonds *et al.* 1999; Bruck 1995), they are equally held to be a distinct component of watery depositional rites (Healy & Housley 1991; Healy 1996). Relevant here are the hints that a range of ritual deposition widely associated with the fen marshes proper, may also have had expression in its neighbouring clay uplands (see Needham 2001 concerning hoard, contexts and variability).

The recent Ely fieldwork, therefore, raises issues concerning the context of wetland metalwork deposition with the later Bronze Age. Was it something tied to individual settlements and immediate family units, or did it occur within a broader framework of *en masse* gathering? Based on the evidence of Flag Fen (Pryor 1991 & forthcoming), the latter would seem the more appropriate model (though this may only apply to a range of higher level items, for example shields and swords, and, in the case of Flag Fen, its helmet). Given the evidence of the island's land-use patterns at this time, two possible factors may have been alternatively influential (or complementary). First, by the marshland context of this material, deposition may have occurred in connection with cross-fen causeways. Their routes – unfortunately not reconstructable by the general provenancing of the Coveney finds – would themselves have facilitated communication and interaction between dispersed communities (smaller items may, of course, have been individually offered to assure passage across these rickety structures). The second is that gatherings could well have been held on Ely's clay uplands; presumably in the autumn to spring when seasonal, off-island fen-edge pastures may have been otherwise flooded, and there must have been 'peak times' in the annual round when its woodlands were sought out for collection (and hunting). (**14**) While further later Bronze Age settlement may well be found on the island's heavy soils (and, potentially, even field/land boundary divisions), balancing the evidence to date it would appear that Ely's clays would then have only largely seen seasonal usage, probably drawing the communities of its skirtland terraces – and potentially even further afield – to its upland resources. Social *gatherings* and their attendant rituals may well have been the display venue for much metalwork deposition; either extra-residential groups brought together through seasonal festivals coinciding with collection activities and/or causeway maintenance and construction.

However provisional, the results from the island highlight the need to further 'problematise' the region's later prehistoric land-use. Attempting to advance beyond simple geographically deterministic and positivist discovery-led narratives, we must begin to scrutinise the 'background noise' and apparent distributional 'blanks' – just how empty are these? Equally, if wishing these materials and our sites to speak beyond the level of subsistence economics and other baseline categories, it is imperative that earlier stray find data is integrated with recent survey and environmental studies. The Fenland Survey (and later FMP fieldwork) certainly provides a basis to facilitate further research. The challenge now is to address just what constitutes and lies *beneath* its record.

Acknowledgements

Aside from the pleasure of acknowledging now long-term collaboration with David Hall, advice and information provided by R. Bradley, N. Brown, P. Clay, S. Needham and F. Pryor must be cited. The results presented should, moreover, be understood as reflecting the efforts of many colleagues at, and associates of, the CAU, particularly C. Conneller, A. Dickens, M. Edmonds, K. Gdaniec, D. Gibson, JD. Hill, M. Knight, G. Lucas, P. Masser, J. Pollard and M. White. In this capacity R. Mortimer and R. Regan, the Directors of C.A.U.'s West Fen Road excavations, are to be singled out and I am grateful to be able to draw upon their results. Finally, Tom Lane has proven a most sympathetic editor, whose patience has been much tried in the production of this paper.

With individual graphics by A. Hall (Fig. 9) and M. Berger (Fig. 8) – the latter also providing computer support for the West Fen Road analyses – otherwise the illustrations within this paper are the work of C. Begg; their collective talents are here acknowledged.

End-notes

1) Fox attributed the paucity of Bronze Age metalwork in the Ouse valley when compared to the Cam and its neighbouring 'open' chalk downland to the fact that it was bordered by 'cold claylands' (1923, 62) – his caricature providing the title for this paper. (Noting the paucity of hoards on clay soils, Fox attributed 'forest associated' hoards elsewhere in the region to the supply of charcoal fuel, *ibid.*) Whilst markedly fewer bronzes are known from the lower Ouse, in recent years a socketed spearhead has been recovered from Meadow Lane, St Ives (Pollard 1996; Needham *et al.* 1997, No. 26, illus. 17.3) and mid-rib casting moulds – either from spear or sword production – have been found in association with a later Bronze Age settlement at Barleycroft Farm (Evans & Knight 2000a).

2) This must now include both the Wilburton and Ewart Park swords from the Fengate Power Station site (there is also a Ewart Park-related short sword), from where dirks and a rapier were also recovered (Coombs 1992; Pryor 1991 & forthcoming; see also Pryor 1978 concerning recent Whittlesey finds).

3) High ground would surely not have been the only places named and here the pocketed nature of Ely's marshland embayments may also have relevance *viz.* metalwork deposition within distinctly 'bounded' wetlands. On Ely these would include Grunty Fen in the southeast and *The Cove* in the north (Coveney denoting 'the island in the Cove'); see Needham's 1998 cultural geography of the Bronze Age Atlantic Zone.

4) The context of the region's renowned scrap hoards – primarily Wilburton and Isleham – may well have differed and could relate to production (see Prigg 1888; Fox 1923: 59-60 concerning the apparent sword foundry excavated at Chippenham).

5) Extending over 12 sq km, the Setchel Fen skirtland terraces flanking the southern side of the Isle of Ely would also have been lost to marsh over the course of the second millennium BC.

6) Coinciding with the line of the Aldreth causeway, based on analogy with the Stuntney/Little Thetford crossing and that its route is commanded by an Iron Age ringwork, Belsar's Hill – and that a later Bronze Age sword has been dredged from the Old West river at this point (Fox 1923, pl. IX.1) – in all probability this 'way' is also of later Bronze Age attribution (see below for discussion of other causeway routes).

7) The Coveney Site 2 scatter lies on a low sandy skirtland rise just north of the main island; Littleport 17 and 18 are on glacial sand and gravels which cap the clays (Hall 1996).

8) Hurst Lane, however, is the only of the three recent eastern Cove sites that has produced evidence of 'earlier' Iron Age occupation, the others all being of later Iron Age attribution.

9) While no pre-Iron Age sites as such were identified in the 1991 Bray's Lane/Waitrose site within Ely itself (TL551804; Hunter 1992) (the only substantial exposure to date on the Greensand) 146 worked flints were recovered. Although not a substantial number in itself, this was a limited trench-based excavation and its lithic densities are substantially greater than from the Hurst Lane site.

10) Of course, there is a possibility that some of the later Bronze Age-ascribed flintwork in this and the other Ely assemblages is actually of earlier Iron Age manufacture. That no mobile, lithic-only associated component of Iron Age settlement systems has yet to be identified does not itself preclude their existence, only make a later Bronze Age date more likely.

11) See Gdaniec, *et al.* 1997 for the comparable Bronze Age utilisation of a large pond-like hollow on chalkland at Hall Farm west of Isleham (TL635741).

12) A lithic-retrieval experiment was, however, undertaken in the course of developer-funded fieldwork on the clays at Prickwillow Road, just north of Ely itself, in 1997 (TL551812). Aside from a general low density 'scattering' of later Neolithic/ Bronze Age flintwork, during the evaluation trenching a small pit/hollow, cut by a Roman field boundary, produced Early Neolithic flints – a blade core and seven blades. ('Crumbs' of Early Neolithic pottery were recovered from the adjacent excavation of the Roman feature; it also produced blades re-fitted with the original core, thus demonstrating that later displacement is not a major factor in these conditions.) To further the study of Early Neolithic site maintenance (*i.e.* 'tidying up'; see Evans *et al.* 1999), during subsequent fieldwork the area of this feature was targeted for further study (Dickens 1997). A 15 x 15m square was opened centred upon it and, following initial topsoiling to a depth of 0.25m, two-bucket samples were taken across the area on a 5m grid; this procedure was repeated again following further stripping to a depth of 0.5m. This produced a further ten worked flints (and four burnt pieces). All probably of Bronze Age date, this would indeed indicate that the Early Neolithic 'spread' was largely localised to the area of the original feature, which, in effect, held a knapping incident.

13) Given the size of the piece – and the presence of the mid-rib – this could even be from a dirk rather than a rapier.

14) Effectively amounting to a system of transhumance, see Evans 1987 for a critique of the over-use of such models in fenland studies.

Bibliography

Bradley, R., 1990, *The Passage of Arms: An archaeological analysis of prehistoric hoards and votive deposits* (Cambridge University Press)

Brooks, H., 1993, 'Fieldwalking and excavation at Stansted Airport', *Flatlands and wetlands: Current themes in East Anglian Archaeology*, East Anglian Archaeology 50, 40-57

Brown, A., 1996, 'Use and Non-Use: aspects of the prehistoric exploitation of the fen-edge at Isleham' in Hall, D., *The Fenland Project, Number 10: Cambridgeshire Survey, Isle of Ely and Wisbech*, East Anglian Archaeology 79, 202-12

Bruck, J., 1995, 'A place for the dead: The role of human remains in Late Bronze Age Britain', *Proc. Prehist. Soc.* 61, 245-77

Bruck, J., 1999, 'What's in a settlement? Domestic practice and residential mobility in Early Bronze Age southern England', in Bruck, J and Goodman, M. (eds), *Making Places in the Prehistoric World: Themes in settlement archaeology* (London, U.C.L. Press)

Burgess, C.B. and Gerloff, S.,1981, *The Dirks and Rapiers of Great Britain and Ireland,*

Prähistorische Bronzefunde, Abteilung IV, Band 7

Burgess, C.B. and Colquhoun, I., 1988, *The Swords of Britain*, Prähistorische Bronzefunde, Abteilung IV, Band 5

Coles, J.M., 1962, 'European Bronze Age Shields', *Proc. Prehist. Soc.* 28, 156-90

Coombs, D., 1992, 'Flag Fen platform and Fengate Power Station post alignment – the metalwork', *Antiquity* 66, 504-17

Cooper, L., 1994, 'Kirby Muxloe, A46 Leicester Western by-pass', *Transactions of the Leicestershire Archaeological and Historical Society* 68, 162-5

Dickens, A., 1997, *Further Archaeological Investigations at land off Prickwillow Road, Ely, Cambridgeshire*, Cambridge Archaeological Unit Report 214

Edmonds, M., Evans, C. and Gibson, D., 1999, 'Assembly and Collection – Lithic complexes in the Cambridgeshire Fenlands', *Proc. Prehist. Soc.* 65, 47-87

Evans, C., 1987, 'Nomads in 'Waterland'? – Prehistoric transhumance and Fenland archaeology', *Proceedings of the Cambridge Antiquarian Society* 76, 27-39

Evans, C., 1992, 'Commanding gestures in lowland: The investigation of two Iron Age ringworks', *Fenland Research* 7, 16-26

Evans, C., 1993, 'Lithic 'noise' – low density scatters – missing settlements? The Langwood Farm Environs', *Fenland Research* 8, 14-6

Evans, C., 1997a, 'Hydraulic communities: Iron Age enclosure in the East Anglian Fenlands' in Gwilt, A. and Haselgrove, C. (eds), *Re-constructing the Iron Age*, 216-27 (Oxford, Oxbow Monograph 71)

Evans, C., 1997b, 'Sentimental Prehistories: The construction of the Fenland Past', *Journal of European Archaeology* 5, 105-36

Evans, C., 2000a, 'Testing the ground – Sampling Strategies' in Crowson, A., Lane, T. and Reeve, J. (eds), *The Fenland Management Project Excavations 1991-1995*, Lincolnshire Archaeology and Heritage Reports Series 3, 15-21

Evans, C., 2000b, 'Wardy Hill, Coveney' in Crowson, A., Lane, T. and Reeve, J. (eds), *The Fenland Management Project Excavations 1991-1995*, Lincolnshire Archaeology and Heritage Reports Series 3, 44-51

Evans, C., 2000c, 'Langwood Farm West and Environs', in Crowson, A., Lane, T. and Reeve, J. (eds), *The Fenland Management Project Excavations 1991-1995*, Lincolnshire Archaeology and Heritage Reports Series 3, 25-36

Evans, C., 2000d, 'Archaeological Distributions: The Problem with Dots (#3)', in Kirby, T. and Oosthuizen, S. (eds), *An Atlas of Cambridgeshire and Huntingdonshire History* (Centre for Regional Studies, Anglia Polytechnic University)

Evans, C., forthcoming a, *Power and Island Communities: Excavations of the Wardy Hill Ringwork, Coveney, Ely* (East Anglian Archaeology)

Evans, C., forthcoming b, Britons and Romans at Chatteris: Investigations at Langwood Farm, Cambridgeshire

Evans, C., Pollard, J. and Knight, M., 1999, 'Life in Woods: Tree-throws, 'settlement' and forest cognition', *Oxford Journal of Archaeology* 18, 241-54

Evans, C. and Knight, M., 2000a, 'A Fenland Delta: Later Prehistoric land-use in the lower Ouse Reaches', in Dawson, M. (ed), *Prehistoric, Roman and Saxon landscape studies in the Great Ouse Valley*, Council for British Archaeology Research Report 119, 89-106

Evans, C. and Knight, M., 2000b, *Investigations at Hurst Lane, Ely, Cambridgeshire: Integrated Assessment and Updated Project Design*, English Heritage/Cambridge Archaeological Unit

Evans, C. and Hodder, I., forthcoming, *The Haddenham Project (II): Marshland Communities and Cultural Landscape*, Cambridge, McDonald Institute Research Series

Fox, C., 1923, *The Archaeology of the Cambridge Region* (Cambridge University Press)

Gallois, R.W.,1988, *Geology of the country around Ely*, British Geological Survey (London, Her Majesty's Stationary Office)

Gdaniec, K., Edmonds, M and Wiltshire, P, 1997, *Neolithic and Bronze Age Settlement and Environmental Reconstruction at Prickwillow Road and the Relict Snail river, Isleham, Cambridgeshire*, Cambridge Archaeological Unit Report 233

Gibson, D. and Knight, M, forthcoming, 'Settling Enclosure: Different histories of land enclosure and settlement in the Bronze Age'

Hall, D., 1992, *The Fenland Project, Number 6: The South-western Cambridgeshire Fenlands*, East Anglian Archaeology 56

Hall, D., 1996, *The Fenland Project, Number 10: Cambridgeshire Survey, The Isle of Ely and Wisbech*, East Anglian Archaeology 79

Hall, D. and Coles, J., 1994, *The Fenland Survey: An essay in landscape and persistence*, English Heritage Archaeological Report 1 (London)

Healy, F., 1996, *The Fenland Project, Number 11: The Wissey Embayment: Evidence for Pre-Iron Age Occupation accumulated prior to the Fenland Project*, East Anglian Archaeology 78

Healy, F. and Housley, R., 1991, 'Nancy was not alone: Human skeletons of the early Bronze Age from the Norfolk peat fen', *Antiquity* 66, 948-55

Hill, J.D., Evans, C. and Alexander, M., 1999, 'The Hinxton Rings – A Late Iron Age cemetery at Hinxton, Cambridgeshire, with a reconsideration of northern Aylesford-Swarling distributions', *Proc. Prehist. Soc.* 65, 243-74

Hunn, J., 1993, 'The Block Fen Fieldsystem: 1992 Investigations', *Fenland Research* 8, 10-11

Hunter, J., 1992, *Archaeological Investigations at Bray's Lane, Ely, 1991*, Cambridge Archaeological Unit Report 8

Ingold, T., 1986, *The Appropriation of Nature* (Manchester, University of Manchester Press)

Lethbridge, T.C., 1934, 'Investigation of the Ancient Causeway in the Fen between Fordey and Little Thetford', *Proceedings of the Cambridge Antiquarian Society* 35, 85-9

Lethbridge, T.C., 1936, 'Fen Causeways', *Proceedings of the Cambridge Antiquarian Society* 36, 161-2

Liddle, P., 1982, *Leicestershire Archaeology: The present state of knowledge to the end of the Roman period*, Leicester Museums, Art Galleries and Records Service Report No 4

Malim, T., 2000, 'Prehistoric Trackways (#11)', in Kirby T. and Oosthuizen S. (eds), *An Atlas of Cambridgeshire and Huntingdonshire History* (Centre for Regional Studies, Anglia Polytechnic University)

Martin, E. and Murphy P., 1988, 'West Row Fen, Suffolk: A Bronze Age fen-edge settlement site', *Antiquity* 62, 353-8

Mortimer, R., 2000, *The Cotmist Field, West Fen Road, Ely: Assessment Report*, Cambridge Archaeological Unit Report 362

Needham, S., 1998, 'Discussion Contribution', in Jorge, S.O. (ed), *Existe uma Idae do Bronze Atlantico?* 185-7, Trabalhos de Arqueologia 10 (Instituto Portugues de Arqueologia)

Needham, S., 2001, 'When expediency broashed ritual intention: The flow of metal between systemic and buried domains', *Journal of the Royal Anthropological Institute* (N.S.) 7, 275-98

Needham, S., Bronk Ramsey, C., Coombs, D., Cartwright, C and Pettitt, P., 1997, 'An independent chronology for British Bronze Age metalwork: The results of the Oxford Radiocarbon Accelerator Programme', *Archaeological Journal* 154, 55-107

Pollard, J, 1996, 'Iron Age Riverside Pit Alignments at St Ives, Cambridgeshire', *Proc. Prehist. Soc.* 62, 93-115

Pollard, J., 1998, 'Prehistoric settlement and non-settlement in two southern Cambridgeshire River Valleys: The lithic dimension and interpretative dilemmas', *Lithics* 19, 61-71

Pollard, J., 1999, 'These places have their moments: Thoughts on occupation practices in the British Neolithic', in Bruck, J. and Goodman, M. (eds), *Making Places in the Prehistoric World: Themes in settlement archaeology*, 76-93 (London, U.C.L. Press)

Prigg, H., 1888, 'On a recent discovery of a Bronze Age sword at Chippenham, Cambridgeshire',

Proceedings of the Suffolk Institute of Archaeology 6, 184

Pryor, F.M.M.,1978, 'Three new Bronze Age weapons', *Durobrivae* 6, 14-6

Pryor, F.M.M., 1982, Problems of Survival: Later prehistoric settlement in the Southern East Anglian Fenlands, *Analecta Praehistorica Leidensia* 15, 125-43

Pryor, F.M.M., 1991, *Flag Fen: prehistoric Fenland Centre* (London, Batsford)

Pryor, F.M.M., 1996, 'Sheep, stockyards and field systems: Bronze Age livestock populations in the Fenlands of eastern England', *Antiquity* 70, 313-24

Pryor, F.M.M.,1998, *Farmers in Prehistoric Britain* (Stroud, Tempus)

Pryor, F.M.M., forthcoming, *Archaeology and Environment of the Flag Fen Basin* (London, English Heritage Archaeological Report)

Regan, R., 2001, *West Fen Road, Ely, Cambridgeshire: Cornwell Field*, Cambridge Archaeological Unit Report 413

Rowlands, M., 1976, *The Production and Distribution of Metalwork in the Middle Bronze Age in Southern England*, Brit. Archaeol. Rep., British Series 31 (Oxford)

Tilley, C., 1994, *A Phenomenology of Landscape* (Oxford, Berg)

Trump, B.A.V., 1968, 'Fenland Rapiers', in Coles, J.M. and Simpson, D.D.A. (eds), *Studies in Ancient Europe*, 213-25 (Bristol, Leicester University Press)

Tura, E., 1982., 'A Late Bronze Age site at Glenfield: Interim Report', *Transactions of the Leicestershire Archaeological and Historical Society* 57, 81-2

Wait, G.A., 1985, *Ritual and Religion in Iron Age Britain*, Brit. Archaeol. Rep., British Series 149 (Oxford)

Waller, M., 1994, *The Fenland Project, Number 9: Flandrian Environmental Change in Fenland,* East Anglian Archaeology 70

5. INFIELD AND OUTFIELD: THE EARLY STAGES OF MARSHLAND COLONISATION AND THE EVOLUTION OF MEDIEVAL FIELD SYSTEMS

by Stephen Rippon

Introduction: Infields and Outfields

In recent decades we have come a long way in our understanding of medieval field systems, and in particular the origins and structure of the Midland open fields. The work of David Hall in Northamptonshire and elsewhere has been one of the most important contributions, most notably for the way in which documentary, cartographic and earthwork evidence are integrated. Though the structure of these field systems is now relatively well-understood, their origins are less clear. Large-scale fieldwalking has shown that the medieval pattern of nucleated villages and open fields replaced a landscape characterised by dispersed settlement, though little is known of the structure of their associated field systems. There has been speculation that open fields may have evolved from infield-outfield systems (*e.g.* Astill 1988, 63; Baker and Butlin 1973c, 655-6; Finberg 1969, 150; Fox 1981, 64, 89-90), and though Taylor (1981, 13) is quite right in suggesting that 'systems such as run-rig and infield-outfield ... are well documented as having existed in many places in this country', such arrangements have received relatively little attention in recent overviews of British field systems (Astill 1988; Rowley 1981; Taylor 1987, 68).

Infield-outfield agriculture is a system of cultivating land whereby certain core areas are regularly cropped and manured, with other areas only occasionally cultivated when and as required. It is best known in Scotland though the evidence is in fact relatively late (mainly from the fifteenth century and later [Dixon 1994, 30; Whittington 1973]), and in certain places at least may represent a relatively brief episode which replaced a more enclosed landscape (Dodgshon 1994). Infield-outfield systems are also known elsewhere in the western fringes of the British Isles (Buchanan 1973, 584-98; Jones 1973, 435), though it is less clear whether they were ever widespread in lowland Britain. Documentary and cartographic evidence testifies to the occasional cultivation of outfields during the medieval period from as far afield as Cumberland (Elliott 1973, 42, 54-6), Yorkshire (Harris 1959, 6-7; 1961, 24-5), Staffordshire (Baker and Butlin 1973a, 20), Nottinghamshire (Beresford and St Joseph 1979, 45-6), East Anglia (Bailey 1989; Postgate 1973, 300-3), Kent (Baker 1973, 417), Somerset (SRO DD/CCH bx7/6; Hallam 1978, 44), and Devon (Finberg 1969, 147-8; Hoskins 1954, 63) (and see Uhlig 1961). On the whole, what this documentary evidence describes is the simple practice of dividing land between that which was more or less permanently cultivated and manured – the infield – and areas that were only infrequently manured and cultivated on a temporary basis – the outfield. This is infield-outfield cultivation in principle, but when the location of the infield and outfield areas can be located, the permanently cultivated areas were not necessarily concentrated into a central core area close to the village (*e.g.* Postgate 1973, 301; Baker 1973, 417). This leads to the question of whether these infield/outfield systems are the last surviving remnants of an approach to landscape exploitation that was once more common, or a relatively late development that simply enabled at least some cultivation of the last remaining areas of poor ground within a township (*e.g.* Baker and Butlin 1973b, 20; Bailey 1989; Sheppard 1973, 154.

The obvious spatial configuration for an early infield-outfield system in the less crowded landscapes of the early medieval period is for a nucleus of manured arable land around or immediately adjacent to the settlement, with a less intensively used zone further out. Did such idealistic arrangements ever exist in practice? Detailed fieldwalking studies have suggested that such systems existed in the Roman period (*e.g.* Gaffney and Tingle 1989; Rippon 2000a), and the possibility of medieval infield –outfield cultivation has also been raised through detailed fieldwalking at Wharram Percy. Here heavily manured fields concentrated to the north and west of the village, with a few examples to the east, with areas beyond this core being less intensively manured. This may reflect simply convenience (distance from the village) or some form of infield/outfield cultivation (Hurst 1983, 99), and documentary evidence certainly testifies to the latter on the Yorkshire Wolds (Sheppard 1973, 154).

Field-names might also give clues to the presence of early core agricultural areas. Fox (1981, 89) has suggested that 'old field' and possibly 'longlands' field-names may indicate an 'original nucleus of arable land' associated with early settlements (and see Ford 1979, 158-61; Sheppard 1973, 179-80; Uhlig 1961, 293). Physical evidence for such arrangements is less common, though careful integration of documentary material with evidence contained within the historic landscape in a number of areas has revealed oval-shaped enclosures that are potential infields (*e.g.* Lancashire: Atkin 1985; Wheldrake in Yorkshire: Sheppard 1966; Cockfield in Co. Durham: Roberts 1981; around Exmoor: Green 2000; Gillard *et al.* 2000, 7; the Kentish Weald: English 1997). The rest of this paper relates to another area where potentially early core agricultural areas have been identified: the coastal wetlands of the Severn Estuary Levels.

The Early Medieval Colonisation of Coastal Marshes

At first sight, it might seem that coastal wetlands have little to contribute to the debate over the origins of field systems in dryland areas. However, it appears that the reclamation of these areas was going on at the same time as open fields were evolving at the end of the first millennium AD (Rippon 1997a; 2000b): might similar approaches to the cultivation of land have been going on in both areas? Marshland landscapes contain within their fabric a record of how they evolved (*e.g.* Fig. 1), which is probably more complete than in dryland areas, where features such as field-boundaries are more expendable: in a marshland landscape even very early boundaries will tend to survive since, once created, ditches would have become an invaluable part of the drainage system. Overall, these marshes provide a model for how early medieval landscapes evolved under relatively controlled circumstances: on a flat surface, with few pre-existing features to constrain subsequent events, and where the need to maintain drainage meant that boundaries, once created, tended to survive.

In recent decades, most of our extensive coastal wetlands have seen programmes of research into their landscape history. A common feature of these studies has been the interdisciplinary nature of that research, integrating geomorphological, palaeo-environmental, archaeological, documentary and cartographic sources. A number of studies have used the fabric of the present – or historic – landscape as a framework around which this other evidence can be woven, notably David Hall's (1996) work in the Cambridgeshire Fens, Hallam's (1965) seminal study of the Lincolnshire fens, Williams' (1970) *Draining of the Somerset Levels*, Silvester's (1988; 1993) work on the Norfolk Marshland, Eddison and her colleagues' research into Romney Marsh (Eddison 1995; Eddison and Green 1988; Eddison *et al.* 1998), and Rippon's (1996a; 1997a) studies of the Severn Estuary Levels. However, in all these cases it is the twelfth and thirteenth

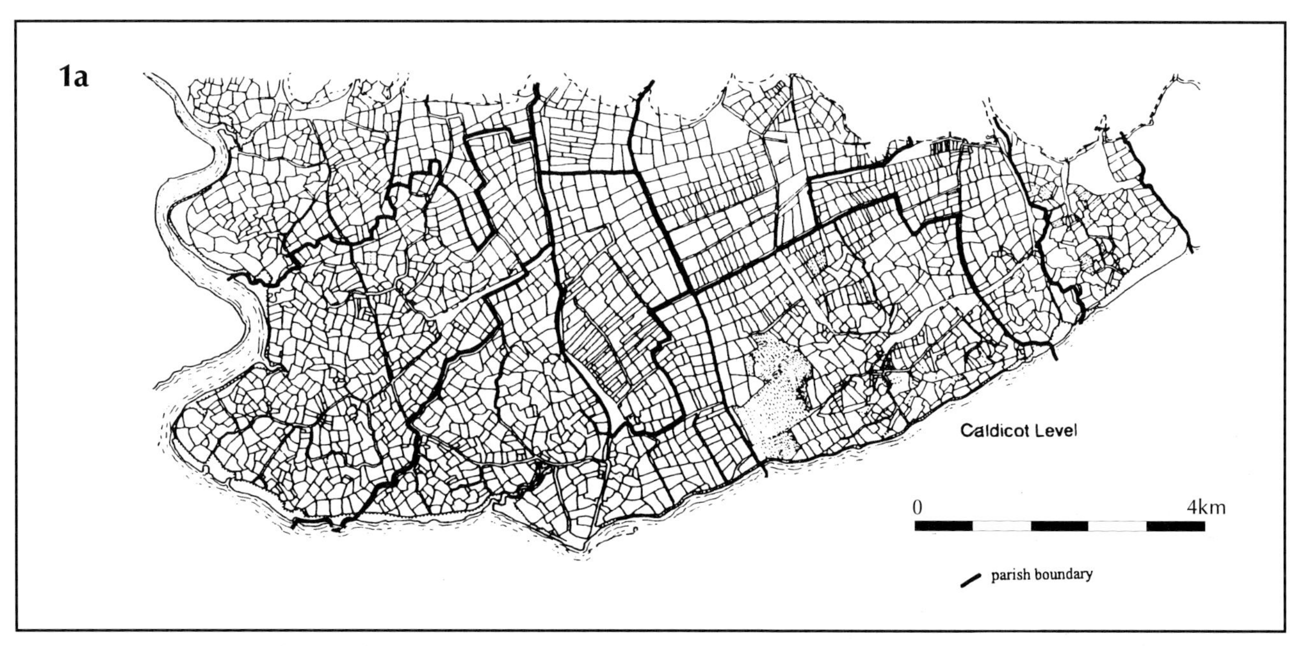

Figure 1a The Caldicot Level, Gwent, South East Wales. The historic landscape in 1831 (Commissioners of Sewers Map: Gwent Records Office D.1365/2), showing the pattern of fields and roads. Note the distribution of surviving open fields. Caldicot Moor (on the far right) survived as an intertidal marsh used as common pasture

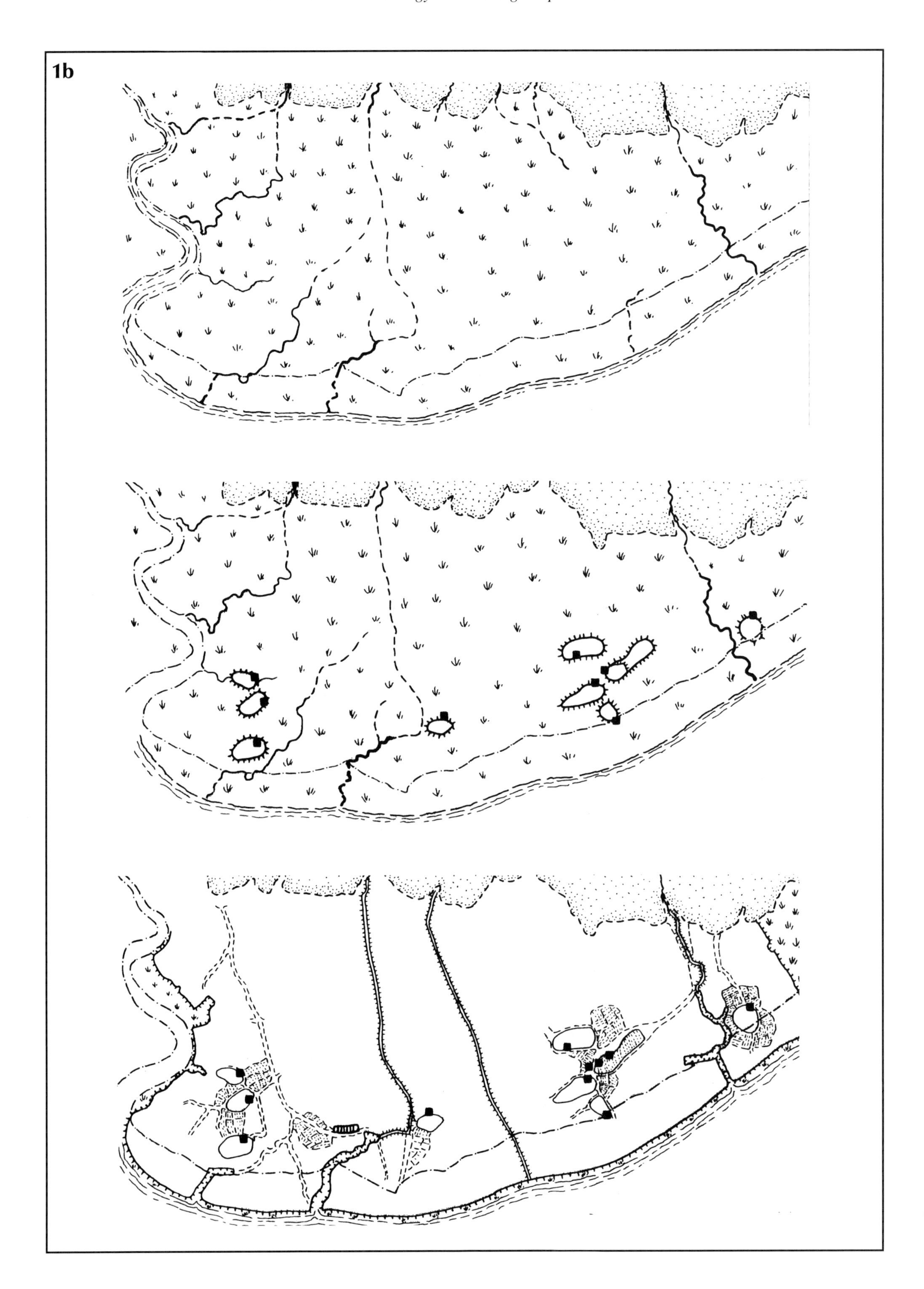
1b

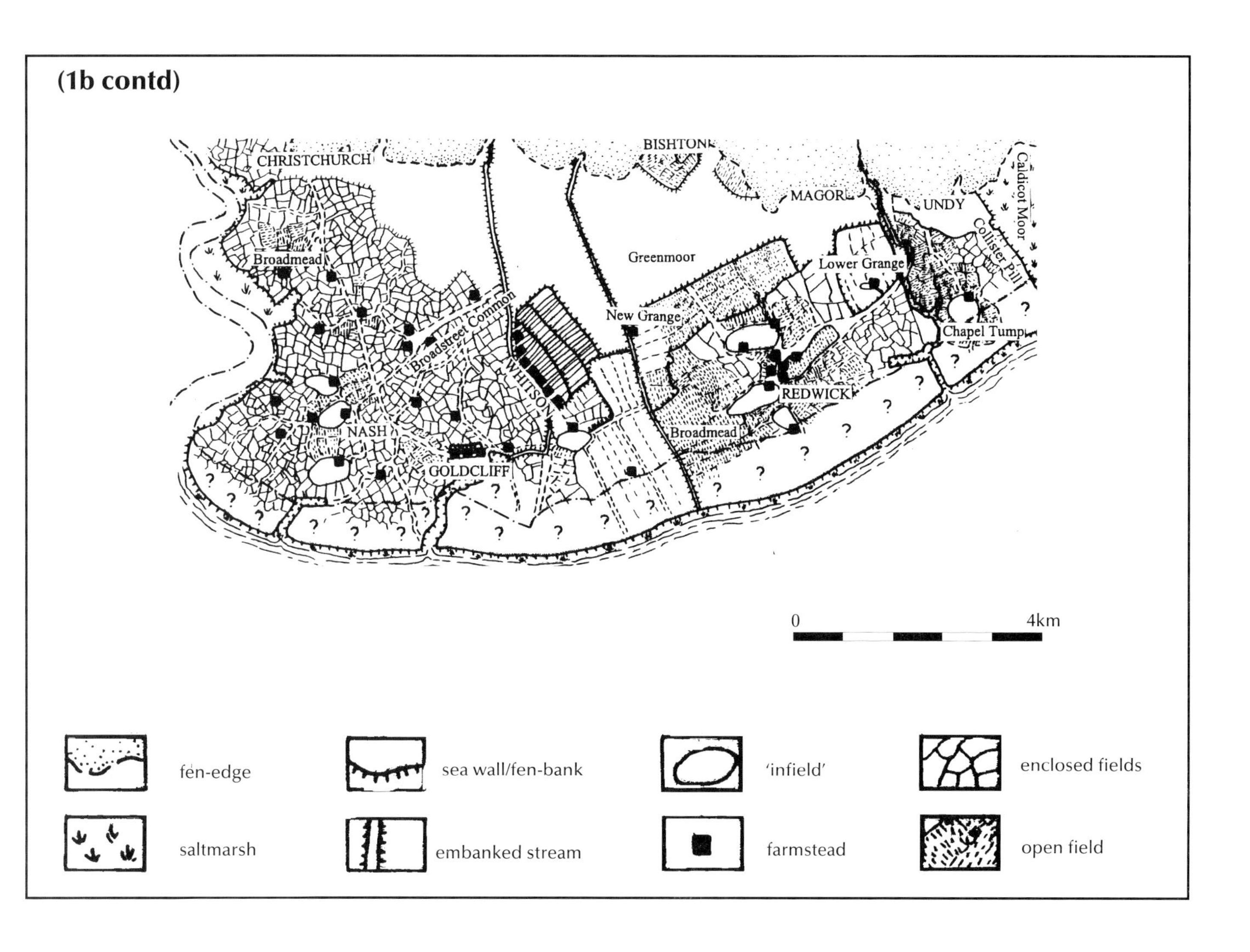

Figure 1b Suggested sequence for the earlier phases of landscape evolution. The higher, coastal parts of the intertidal saltmarsh were colonised through the construction of a series of small, oval-shaped ring dikes, which may initially have only afforded protection from flooding during the summer months. The course taken by a number of the streams that flowed off of the adjacent uplands is unclear.

A sea wall was subsequently constructed along the coast, and streams flowing off the adjacent uplands were canalised to avoid freshwater flooding of the areas now protected from tidal inundation. The early ring-dike enclosures became the focus for settlement, perhaps acting as infields.

As population increased, and the demand for land increased, further land was enclosed and drained, initially in a piecemeal fashion (hence the irregular landscapes of the higher coastal areas), and later in a more planned fashion (hence the more regular landscapes towards the lower-lying, backfen areas). Fen-banks protected these lower-lying areas from freshwater flooding. Different estate owners followed different strategies with regard to the development of their estates, reflected for example in the more nucleated settlement associated with common fields in Redwick, and the dispersed settlement pattern and predominantly enclosed fields in Nash

centuries onwards – well documented and with well-dated ceramic sequences – that have received most attention: the origins of these landscapes are more difficult to uncover, and have been rather neglected. The earliest phases of reclamation remain particularly obscure.

By the nineteenth century, local legend in a number of areas claimed that the first attempts at drainage were undertaken by 'the Romans' (*e.g.* the Caldicot Level, Gwent: Knight 1962; Fenland: Hall 1977; Romney Marsh: Eddison 2000), but the results of recent survey, excavation, and palaeo-environmental analysis has shown that very few coastal wetlands were in fact reclaimed in the Roman period (Rippon 2000b). That particular transformation of the landscape appears to have been restricted to the Severn Estuary, and though elements of these drainage schemes may survive in a handfull of places (Fulford *et al.* 1994), in most marshland areas of Britain the Roman-period landscape is buried under later alluvium, with the result that the historic landscapes of these coastal wetlands post-date this major episode of marine transgression (Rippon 2000a).

The extent of settlement, population, and ploughteams in Domesday suggests that most of the more extensive coastal wetlands were reclaimed by the later eleventh century, and the physical relationship between medieval settlement patterns (revealed through fieldwalking, documents, or standing buildings) to the extant networks of fields and roads suggests that the basic fabric of the historic landscape in these areas was also in place by that time. It would appear, therefore, that the origins of our marshland landscapes lie after the period of late/post-Roman flooding, and before the later eleventh century. There are three key issues: when were these marshlands colonised, what was the process whereby intertidal saltmarshes were transformed into freshwater, reclaimed landscapes, and who was responsible for this major undertaking? The issues of dating and who was responsible for initiating reclamation are dealt with elsewhere (Rippon 2000b, in press); what follows is a tentative contribution to the second issue, that of how the colonisation of coastal marshes began.

Reclamation and Construction of Sea Walls

Today, our coastal wetlands shelter behind massive embankments that hug the coast. It has been assumed that this was always the case, with the earliest sea wall built along the coast and major tidal rivers, with the area so protected from inundation being settled later, starting with the higher coastal areas (*e.g.* Rippon 1996a, fig 4; 1997a, fig 7). However, recent archaeological work has shown that this was not always the case, and that there was sometimes an initial phase of settlement, perhaps seasonal, on the open saltmarsh.

In Fenland, for example, the earliest phases of medieval colonisation have been researched through the Fenland Survey and subsequent Fenland Management Project (see Crowson *et al.* 2000; Hall and Coles 1994; and individual *Fenland Survey* volumes). In general, the sequence appears as follows (see Rippon 2000b). During the fifth and sixth centuries, when 'Early Saxon' pottery was in circulation, settlement concentrated around the margins of the coastal saltmarsh and inland, freshwater, backfen. Around the seventh century, as 'Middle Saxon' Ipswich ware type pottery came into use, settlement shifted onto slightly raised relict creek-banks in the higher coastal marshes, and though some attempt was made to improve drainage through the construction of ditches, these areas remained an essentially intertidal environment. It was only around the tenth century that a sudden environmental change occurred, with freshwater replacing intertidal conditions, indicating that the area was now protected from inundation by a sea wall. Settlement concentrated in a series of nucleated villages often located around small greens, at the head of long droveways that led down into the lower-lying backfens. The patterns of roads and fields around these early settlements, on the higher coastal areas, was irregular in layout resulting in part from the incorporation of naturally meandering saltmarsh creeks into the post-reclamation field boundary pattern, and otherwise suggesting a gradual and piecemeal approach towards enclosure and drainage. By contrast, as more land was required, and settlement expanded down the droveways towards the backfen, a more co-ordinated and systematic approach towards reclamation was adopted. As lower-lying ground in the backfens was enclosed the major source of flooding became freshwater runoff from the adjacent uplands, leading to a series of fen-banks constructed parallel to the fen-edge/coast (*e.g.* Fig. 1).

This initial phase of settlement on the unreclaimed marsh is paralleled on the continent during both the Roman and early medieval periods, and experiments on modern saltmarshes in Germany have shown that it is possible to raise a number of crops in such environments (see Rippon in 2000b for a fuller discussion). In Britain, the relatively few areas of extensive saltmarsh that were left unreclaimed by the post-medieval period appear to have been used mostly as common pasture, though there are references to their having been cropped for meadow (*e.g.* Rumney Wharf near Cardiff: Reeves 1977, 300). Analogy with mainland Europe also suggests that the initial attempts at embankment may not have been designed to provide year-round protection from inundation. An alternative sequence is for there to have been seasonal 'summer dikes' which protected small areas of marsh associated with individual settlements from summer floods, that were only later replaced by a continuous sea wall built along the coast (Fig. 1). A number of such low embankments that probably provided only seasonal protection have been recorded in the Netherlands dating to the Roman period, including Broekpolder in the west (Linda Therkorn *pers comm.*, August 2000), and sealed beneath *terpen* mounds at Donjum-Heringa, Peins-Oost and Wijnaldum-Tjitsum in the north (Bazelmans *et al.* 1999; Besteman *et al.* 1999). Summer, or 'ring', dikes were also constructed during the early medieval period on the coastal marshes of mainland North West Europe, before being replaced by a continuous embankment (Bazelmans *et al.* 1999; Behre 1990, 38-9; Mayhew 1973, 48; Schmid 1990). Such summer dikes still continued to function as late as the early nineteenth century on the island of Ameland, off the Netherlands, before their destruction through enclosure and reallotment schemes (Bazelmans *et al.* 1999). The Ameland enclosure was used as a common meadow, sub-divided between large numbers of tenants each of whom received a proportion of the strips each spring (a system that is very similar to that which prevailed in British common meadows, including those of the Somerset Levels: Brian 1999).

Around the Severn Estuary, the majority of saltmarshes were eventually reclaimed through constructing a sea wall along the coast. The one notable exception was Caldicot Moor, being that part of the Gwent Levels that fell within the lordship of Chepstow (Fig. 1; Rippon 1996a, 77-8; in press). This remained an area of common pasture, which was occasionally flooded by the sea, though an attempt was made to enclose one area of the higher ground known as 'Twimple' (PRO MPC 116; Bradney 1929, 110-23). Though very little is known about this enclosure, it does not appear to have been settled, or regularly ploughed (other areas of ancient enclosure being covered in well-developed ridge and furrow). There are eighteenth century accounts of rudimentary divisions being made of the intertidal marshes (*e.g.* Bradney 1929, 115), and it is tempting, based on its position, morphology, and similarity to the Ameland enclosure, to see it as a seasonal embankment designed simply to protect an area of meadow during the summer months.

Early enclosures on the Severn Estuary marshes

As with Fenland, in the coastal marshes of the Severn Estuary the earliest areas to be settled are characterised by highly irregular landscapes (*e.g.* Fig. 1). However, in this area, pottery does not appear to have circulated widely in the rural landscape until around the eleventh or twelfth century, and although tenth century material is now being recognised on a number of sites, the region is aceramic before that date. In common with other major coastal wetlands, the extent of settlement and ploughteams recorded in Domesday suggests that extensive areas had already been reclaimed by that date, but in the absence of datable material culture, and earlier documentary sources, we must interrogate the historic landscape itself in order to understand the earliest stage of wetland colonisation.

When the patterns of roads, fields and settlements of these historic landscapes are carefully dissected, a relative sequence of features can be identified. The earliest appear to have been distinctive oval-shaped enclosures around which the rest of the historic landscape formed (*e.g.* Figs. 2-4). Soon after their recognition these features were given the name 'infields' (Rippon 1994; 1996a; 1997a), though this interpretation is in need of more careful consideration. Taken collectively, these enclosures have a number of common characteristics:

- they are restricted to the higher, coastal areas of the Levels (that were the first to be settled, enclosed and drained) either in clusters (*e.g.* Redwick on the Caldicot Level: Fig. 1; Rippon 1996a, fig 27; and Withy in Huntspill: Fig. 2; Rippon 1994, fig 12.4) or individually (*e.g.* Puxton in North Somerset: Fig. 3; Rippon 1996b; 1997b; 1998; 1999; and Vole in Somerset: Fig. 4)

- roads and droveways run towards the enclosures (suggesting that they are stratigraphically early in the formation of the historic landscape), but then pass around them

- their shape is generally oval (also suggesting that they were created relatively early, in a landscape that was not too cluttered with other features: see below)

- occasionally there is evidence for a bank running around the enclosure's perimeter
- their size is typically *c*.5-19 ha (12-47 acres); average 13 ha (32 acres)
- extant farms are almost always located on the edge or just outside the enclosed area (suggesting that they represent areas of agricultural land, not an enclosed settlement, which has been confirmed by survey and excavation at Puxton: see below)
- a number are associated with churches or chapels (suggesting some pre-eminence in the settlement pattern, again possibly indicating their relatively early origins)

Accounting for the oval shape

One of the main character defining features of these enclosures is their oval shape which may potentially be accounted for in a number of ways, notably that they:

- are related to small bedrock islands
- are related to morphologically-similar early Christian sites
- have adopted the most economical shape for the first areas to be enclosed within a previously unsettled landscape.

Few of these sites have been surveyed in detail. Relatively crude surveys carried out in advance of the construction of the M5 motorway suggest that Withy Farm, Withy Bow Bridge and Withy Road Farm show no elevation difference compared to the surrounding areas (data was plotted to the nearest foot); Hackness may be slightly lower-lying that the surrounding areas. More accurate surveys at Middle Lane and Ham Farm in Kingston Seymour suggests those enclosures are *c*.0.10-0.15 m above the surrounding areas (Gilbert 1996, 56), though the significance of such differences, in a landscape that, due to long-term subsidence into deeply buried rock-cut features and more recent palaeochannels, is never completely flat, is unclear. Work at Puxton,

Figure 2 A cluster of 'infields' at East Huntspill, Somerset (Hackney, Cote, Withy Road Farm, Withy Bow Bridge and Withy Farm). Note the series of fields within the enclosure at Withy Bow Bridge (on the far left) with a reversed-S profile, and how farms all lie at the edges of the enclosures. Withy is relatively well documented, being a detached part of Glastonbury Abbey's manor of Shapwick

the only site to have seen detailed survey and excavation, showed that it was only a small number of platforms that were raised, and that this was accounted for by a build up of occupation debris, not the occurrence of a bedrock 'island'. Indeed, none of the Severn Estuary enclosures are shown on geological or soil survey maps as being bedrock islands, and excavations for a trout lake at Middle Lane in Kingston Seymour to a depth of 3 m, and archaeological investigations at Puxton to a depth of 2 m, failed to reach bedrock (Gilbert 1996, 56; Rippon 1996a). In contrast to a number of low bedrock islands in the Levels (*e.g.* Chedzoy and Sowy in the Parrett Valley, Somerset; Godney in the Brue Valley, Somerset; Hillsea in Yatton, North Somerset), none of the 'infield' enclosures have '-ey' (island') names (though there is a Hackney Farm at Hackness, in Huntspill: Fig. 2). Overall, there is no evidence that the shape of these enclosures results from their being located on bedrock.

A number of the 'infields' are associated with medieval churches or chapels (Table 1), though their scale is altogether different to the curvilinear churchyard enclosures that are characteristic of many parts of Wales and Cornwall, and which are typically just 0.2 – 0.4 ha (Brook 1992, 85; Preston-Jones 1992, 106; Silvester 1997, 114). A closer parallel

	area	**church or chapel**
Central Somerset		
Withy Farm (East Huntspill)	17.9 ha (44.2 acres)	
Withy Bow Bridge (East Huntspill)	16.5 ha (40.8 acres)	
Withy Road Farm (East Huntspill)	14.1 ha (34.8 acres)	
Hackness (East Huntspill)	11.8 ha (29.2 acres)	
Cote (East Huntspill)	16.5 ha (40.8 acres)	
Huntspill Court (West Huntspill)	15.3 ha (37.8 acres)	
Manor Farm (Lympsham)	7.9 ha (19.5 acres)	medieval church
Vole (East Brent)	9.4 ha (23.2 acres)	
Rooksbridge (East Brent)	17.6 ha (43.5 acres)	
Chapel Farm (East Brent)	12.6 ha (31.1 acres)	chapel place-name
East Bower (Bridgwater)	7.4 ha (18.3 acres)	
average	*13.4 ha (33.1 acres)*	
North Somerset		
Middle Lane (Kingston Seymour)	30.0 ha (74.1 acres)	
Poplar Farm (Kingston Seymour)	16.5 ha (40.8 acres)	
Ham Lane (Kingston Seymour)	7.9 ha (19.5 acres)	
St Georges (Banwell)	13.7 ha (33.9 acres)	medieval chapel
Chestnut Farm (Hewish)	13.0 ha (32.1 acres)	
Puxton	6.3 ha (15.6 acres)	medieval chapel
average	*14.6 ha (36.1 acres)*	
Caldicot Level		
Greenstreet (Redwick)	21.6 ha (53.4 acres)	medieval church
Longlands (Redwick)	17.7 ha (43.7 acres)	
South Row (Redwick)	15.7 ha (38.8 acres)	
Sea Street (Redwick)	8.2 ha (20.3 acres)	
Chapel Tump (Undy)	partly eroded	chapel place-name
Farmfield (Nash)	12.9 ha (31.9 acres)	
Nash	9.8 ha (24.2 acres)	medieval church
Burnt House Farm (Nash)	5.9 ha (14.6 acres)	
Whitson	2.9 ha (7.2 acres)	medieval church
average	*11.8 ha (29.2 acres)*	
Wentlooge Level		
St Brides	9.7 ha (24.0 acres)	medieval church
Overall Average	*13.0 ha (32.1 acres)*	

Table 1 'infield' enclosures of the Severn Estuary: areas of better preserved examples

might be the larger enclosures associated with a number of early Christian sites in these areas (*e.g.* James 1992; Kissock 1997, 132-5; Preston-Jones 1992, fig 11.11) and also elsewhere (*e.g.* Oxfordshire: Blair 1994, figs 44, 47 and 51; and see Faith 1997, 16-36). However, the character of these larger enclosures is unclear, and their function need not have been distinctively ecclesiastical: they may simply have been areas of early demesne land. There is also no evidence that any of the Severn Estuary enclosures were linked with minster churches, and indeed, some never progressed beyond chapel status: most lack any evidence for ecclesiastical sites (*e.g.* Vole: Fig. 4).

It would appear, therefore, that the Severn Estuary enclosures represent the earliest intakes of formerly waste or underused land, where there was a lack of pre-existing features to constrain the shape of the area enclosed. Indeed, the same phenomena can be seen in the early phases of colonisation in a number of other areas, notably zones of woodland (*e.g.* the Kentish Weald: English 1997; Wraxall in North West Kent: Rippon 1997a, fig 49) and moorland fringe (*e.g.* Hound Tor and Holne Moor on Dartmoor: Aston 1985, fig 79; Fleming and Ralph 1982). Medieval deer parks adopted an oval shape for the same reason: an oval gives the shortest length of boundary per area enclosed. In the case of deer parks this was important due to the cost of the park pale, while in the case of the Severn Estuary enclosures it would appear to have been because of the cost of constructing an embankment.

The only site to have seen any systematic archaeological investigation is Puxton, in North Somerset (Fig. 3), which was occupied from at least the tenth century (Somerset is aceramic in the centuries before then; Rippon 1996b, 1997b, 1998, 1999). The 6.3 ha (15.5 acres) oval-shaped enclosure was surrounded by a low embankment *c.*13 m wide, which, though damaged by modern ploughing, survives to a height of *c.*0.5 m. A key question is the function of such banks: were they to protect an area from tidal flooding (*i.e.* the very first sea wall?), or were they precursors to 'fen-banks' in protecting already-embanked areas from freshwater flooding due to run-off from the adjacent uplands? The geographical distribution of the enclosures rules out the latter: most of these sites lie on the higher coastal areas where freshwater flooding is unlikely to have been a problem (Fig. 1). The morphology of the bank at Puxton may also be significant: such a broad but low bank may at first seem rather odd, though in a tidal environment it would have suffered less from erosion than a steeper-sided structure. Had the Puxton bank acted as a sea wall for a sustained period of time then there should have been a build up of sediment on its outside, leading to an elevation difference when compared to inside. Allen (1991; 1999) has used this as a technique for locating early sea walls in a number of coastal

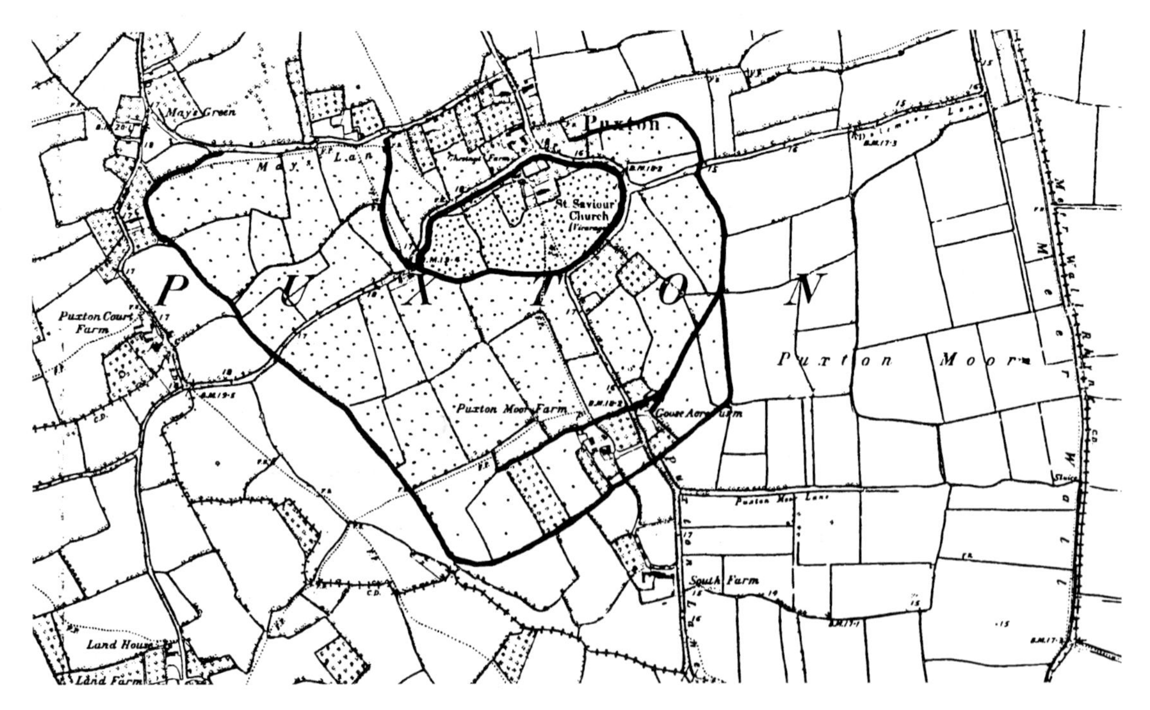

Figure 3 The sequence of enclosures at Puxton, North Somerset.
The primary enclosure, by the church, was occupied by the tenth century

wetlands, and though no such difference was disernable at Puxton, this might be due to a number of factors: that it lay a considerable distance inland, that it was above Mean High Water Spring Tide (MHWST) but below Highest Astronomical Tide (HAT), and/or that by the time the occasional tidal floods reached this area they had dumped most of their sediment. Alternatively, the Puxton embankment may only have functioned as a sea wall for a very brief time as very soon after its construction it was made redundant through the creation of a sea wall further towards the coast.

For the Severn Estuary enclosures to have functioned as sea walls, they must have lain below HAT (which in the Estuary is around 1.3-1.4 m above MHWST), though establishing what this was in the medieval period is difficult. High water level in the sally port at Bristol Castle lay between 11.8 and 12.4 m OD, some 4 m above the modern MHWST (6.95 m), but the value of this observation is questionable as sluice gates may have been used to retain tidal and river-waters within the ditch for defensive reasons (Ponsford 1981, 104). More accurate measures of medieval MHWST have been gained from the height of accreted marsh deposits at the waterfronts at Dundas Wharf (c.6.4 m OD) and Canynges House (c.6.6-6.7 m OD), that is some 0.5 m below that of today at this point on the river (Jones 1991, 19). It is difficult to scale this back to the open Estuary but the difference between medieval and modern MHWST is likely to have been more rather than less due to the attenuation/ weakening of tidal waves in the river Avon (J. Allen *pers comm.* 2000). In the Inner Severn Estuary, Allen (1991) has compared the elevations of still actively accreting saltmarshes with those that were reclaimed during the medieval period, and suggests that MHWST around AD 1300 was c.0.9 m lower than today (and see Allen and Rae 1988).

Most of the Severn Estuary 'infield' enclosures lie on the more extensive areas of marshland adjacent to the outer Estuary. They generally lie at around c.5.4 m OD in East Huntspill and Brent, c.5.5-5.8 m OD in North Somerset, and c.6.1 m OD on the Gwent Levels (the surface of these marshes reflecting the increase in MHWST up the Estuary: Hawkins 1992, fig 6). The MHWST for these stretches of coast are approximately 5.8 m OD, 6.1 m and 6.7 m OD respectively, with the Highest Astromical Tides (HAT) around 1.3 m higher. Assuming that the medieval figures were around 0.9 m lower, it would appear that the Severn Estuary infields were about 0.3-0.5 m above their contemporary MHWST, but nearly 1 m below the HAT (Table 2).

The possible function of the Severn Estuary enclosures as agricultural core areas

So what was the function of these early enclosures? There is no evidence that they were enclosed settlements. Earthwork, soil chemistry, and fieldwalking surveys at Puxton all indicate that occupation was restricted to a series of slightly raised platforms in the north eastern corner of the enclosure by the church, with the remaining area being occupied by lightly manured paddocks (Rippon 1997b, fig 11). The enclosure appears, therefore, to have been an area of agricultural land with the associated settlement tucked to one side (as is still the case with the farms that are associated with these enclosures all around the Estuary [e.g. Figs. 2-4]). At Withy Bow Bridge (Huntspill), the enclosure is filled with reversed-S profile fields indicating prolonged arable cultivation (Fig. 2; Rippon 1994, fig 12.4), with another possible example within the earlier of the two enclosures at Greenstreet, Redwick (GwRO D.1365/2).

The Severn Estuary 'infields' average around 13 ha (32 acres; Table 1), though most fall into one of two size groupings between 6-10 ha (15-25 acres; 35%) and 12-19 ha (30-47 acres; 54%). Both would have provided sufficient arable to support one family

	height of 'infield'	*current MHWST*	*medieval MHWST*	*current HAT*	*medieval HAT*
Huntspill/ Brent	c. 5.4 m	c. 5.8 m	c. 4.9 m	c. 7.1 m	c. 6.2 m
North Somerset	c. 5.6 m	c. 6.1 m	c. 5.2 m	c. 7.4 m	c. 6.5 m
Gwent Levels	c. 6.1 m	c. 6.7 m	c. 5.8 m	c. 8.1 m	c. 7.2 m

Table 2 Approximate measures of medieval tidal levels around the Severn Estuary

Plate 1 Vole, Somerset (TUD/UK 15119 part III print 5237 [13th Jan. 1946].
Crown Copyright 1946/MOD.)
(Reproduced with permission of the Controller of HMSO)

within a mixed-agricultural regime, as Taylor (1987, 62) suggests that around 30 acres (12 ha) of land *in total* would support one family, with similar estimates from local studies in Southwest Britain. On Glastonbury Abbey's marshland manor of East Brent, for example, the average size of a tenant holding in 1189 was 15.4 acres (6.2 ha; Harrison 1997, table 5.04a), while in Devon, Finberg (1951, 40) suggests that a peasant required 15 or 16 acres of arable (6.1-6.5 ha). Green (2000, 35-9) found that morphologically very similar enclosures in northern Devon/western Somerset were mostly 20-70 acres (8-28 ha). The Severn Estuary examples are broadly comparable, though lying towards the lower end of the Devon/Somerset range, which may be accounted for in terms of the greater soil fertility on the Levels, and the abundance of rich meadow and pasture.

Infields and Outfields?

It is argued here that these enclosures represent core agricultural areas – infields in one sense – that initially afforded some protection from tidal flooding, notably during the summer months, before the construction of a continuous sea wall along the coast. The use to which the surrounding marshes were put is unclear, though they would

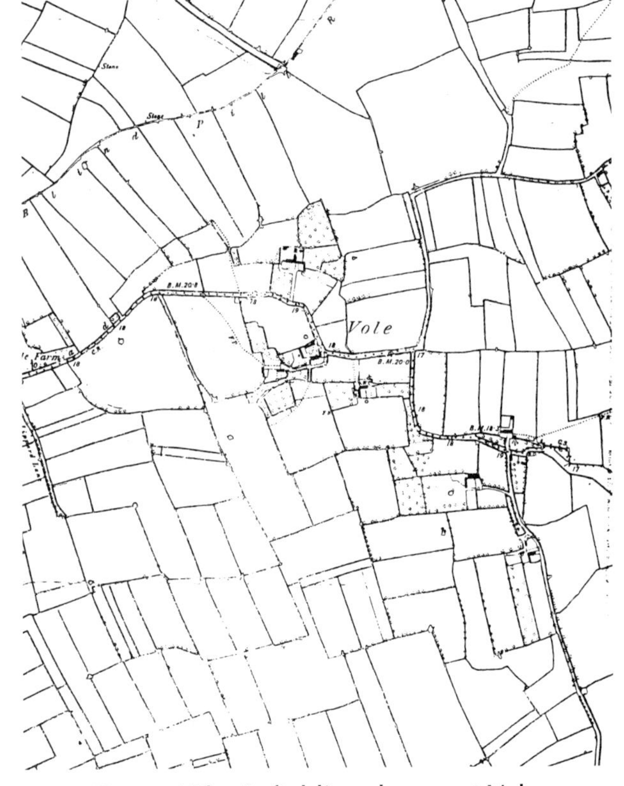

Figure 4 The 'infield' enclosure at Vole, East Brent, Somerset

have provided excellent grazing and would have been perfectly capable of supporting rich meadow, as was case into the post-medieval period on areas of saltmarsh that remained unreclaimed (Reeves 1977, 299).

Once that coastal embankment had been constructed, the old 'infields' became redundant although their location next to settlements, some of which had become manorial and/or parochial centres, ensured their continued use as core agricultural areas. At Puxton, a sequence of intakes is recognisable (Fig. 3), and though the intensity with which the different areas were exploited is unclear, the primary enclosure appears to have been the most heavily manured. There is little firm evidence for the occasional cultivation of 'outfield' areas on the Severn Estuary Levels as might be expected in an area of fertile soils and an abundance of pasture. Over a long time perspective, however, there were fluctuations in the extent of enclosure and drainage that is evidenced by relict landscapes on Huntspill (Rippon 1997a, 210-12) and Banwell Moors (Rippon 1997b, 44-6). A number of closely spaced drainage features excavated on Banwell Moor (Rippon 1997b, fig 6) were associated with small amounts of medieval pottery and may represent one or more attempts to drain or even cultivate part of this, one of the lowest-lying parts of the North Somerset Levels. The complex disposition of arable, pasture and meadow in the reclamations of Glastonbury Abbey's manors in the Brue and Parrett valleys may also indicate the occasional and unsystematic extension of arable cultivation of what were mainly areas of arable and pasture (Musgrove 1999). Reference in the thirteenth/fourteenth centuries to 'Stubbrech' meadow in Sowy, and 'la Breche' in the moors of Walton, may suggest occasional cultivation of the moors beside the river Parrett (Musgrove 1999, 309).

Parallels for the Severn Estuary 'infields'

It is difficult to find comparable features on other coastal marshes in Britain, although the turf dike that enclosed some 425 acres at Wheldrake, in the Vale of York, may represent an infield on a far larger scale (Sheppard 1966). In the Norfolk Marshland, an irregular landscape on the higher coastal marshes is not that dissimilar to the pattern seen around the Severn in suggesting a gradual and piecemeal colonisation. This landscape contains a number of possible 'infield' enclosures such as Walpole St Peter (15 ha) and West Walton (25 ha). In contrast, just across the Nene Estuary on the Cambridgeshire silt fens, a far more regularly arranged landscape suggests some degree of planning and co-ordination in its initial colonisation, and potential 'infields' are noticeably absent. On Romney Marsh another highly irregular landscape that clearly results from gradual and piecemeal enclosure and drainage, contains a small number of possible 'infields', notably at Snave. Further work is needed on the cartographic and air photographic sources, but it would appear that the Severn Estuary is not alone in seeing the creation of these early enclosures.

Discussion

It is argued here that the oval-shaped enclosures that are so characteristic of the higher coastal marshes of the Severn Estuary Levels represent the earliest elements of the historic landscape. It is suggested that they represent individual intakes in what remained an intertidal marsh, and that it is possible that they were initially only intended to protect a small area of agricultural land from summer floods (as was the case on the near continent). They acted as infields in the sense of being a core agricultural area, and although it is not known whether there was cultivation on the open marsh this area was certainly used less intensively. Probably not long after the construction of these ring dikes, the decision was taken to construct sea walls along the coast, making the earlier embankments redundant. Although the ring dike's banks may have been removed (as they would have hindered the post-reclamation drainage), their associated drainage ditches remained a valuable part of the drainage system and so have survived to this day.

It is not suggested that these early enclosures were infield/outfield systems in the classic sense, but it is possible that they reflect an approach current in the late first millennium AD towards the colonisation of land that was based upon a small core area that was surrounded by less intensively used ground. Even after the enclosure and drainage of the surrounding areas, the location of the early enclosures next to the settlements ensured that they remained core agricultural areas for some time. On dryland areas such early arrangements may have been swept away by later landscape evolution, but the premium placed upon drainage on coastal wetlands ensured that such early features have survived.

In recent decades there have been great advances in our understanding of landscapes characterised by open field systems, though less attention has been paid to more irregularly-arranged common fields and the wholly enclosed patterns of fields that occurred outside the Midlands. Although coastal marshes, like upland fringes and the poor sandy soils of Breckland, can all be regarded as physically challenging environments that would normally be cultivated only after areas that were more suited to settled agriculture had been colonised, the excellent preservation of their historic landscape allows this processes to be observed in great detail, and may provide a model for how contemporary landscapes were evolving elsewhere. Whilst one key feature of the Severn Estuary infields – their encircling bank – is a direct response to difficulties in the natural environment (the threat of tidal flooding), another feature – their oval shape – was not. This results from their being created in a relatively featureless landscape, with little to constrain their shape other than the desire to create as short a perimeter per area enclosed as possible. As such, the creation of a small, roughly oval-shaped, enclosed infield, with less intensive exploitation of an outfield beyond, is the logical way that any previously unsettled landscape will have been created. It is not surprising, therefore, to find similar features in a variety of woodland and upland-fringe environments.

Overall, there may not be anything special about the Severn Estuary 'infields' other than the fact that they have survived where others have been lost, either in the transformation of landscapes through the creation of open fields, or more gradual and piecemeal evolution in more ancient landscapes. 'Infield-outfield' systems are a logical way of exploiting an uncrowded landscape particularly in newly settled areas, and as such may provide a model for other, dryland, landscapes.

Acknowledgements

I would like to thank Jos Bazelmans, Danny Gerrets and Linda Therkorn for discussing the results of their recent excavations in the Netherlands, and Terry Green and Martin Gillard for access to their on-going research into the landscape of the Greater Exmoor region, and John Allen, Bob Jones and Toby Parker for discussing medieval sea levels in the Severn Estuary.

Bibliography

GwRO (Gwent Records Office) D.1365/2: Commissioners of Sewers Map, Redwick

PRO (Public Records Office) MPC 116: Map of the Manor of Caldicot

SRO (Somerset Records Office) DD/CCH bx 7/6: Manorial Court Rolls of Wootton Courtney 1538-53

Allen, J.R.L., 1991, 'Salt-marsh accretion and sea-level movement in the inner Severn Estuary: the archaeological and historical contribution', *Journal of the Geological Society of London* 148, 485-94

Allen, J.R.L., 1999, 'The 'Rumensea' Wall and the early settled landscape of Romney Marsh' (Kent), *Landscape History* 21, 5-19

Allen, J.R.L. and Rae, J.E., 1988, 'Vertical saltmarsh accretion since the Roman period in the Severn Estuary, southwest Britain', *Marine Geology* 83, 225-235

Astill, G., 1988, 'Fields', in Astill, G. and Grant, A. (eds), *The Countryside of Medieval England* (Oxford, Blackwell), 62-85

Aston, M., 1985, *Interpreting the Landscape* (London, Batsford)

Atkin, M.A., 1985, 'Some settlement patterns in Lancashire', in Hooke, D. (ed), *Medieval Villages* (Oxford, Oxford University Committee for Archaeology), 171-85

Bailey, M., 1989, *A Marginal Economy: East Anglian Breckland in the Later Middle Ages* (Cambridge University Press)

Baker, A.R.H., 1973, 'Field systems of Southeast England', in Baker, A.R.H. and Butlin, R.A. (eds), *Studies of Field Systems in the British Isles* (Cambridge University Press), 377-429

Baker, A.R.H. and Butlin, R.A., 1973a, *Studies of Field Systems in the British Isles* (Cambridge University Press)

Baker, A.R.H. and Butlin, R.A., 1973b, ' Introduction: materials and methods', in Baker, A.R.H. and Butlin, R.A. (eds), *Studies of Field Systems in the British Isles* (Cambridge University Press), 1-40

Baker, A.R.H. and Butlin, R.A., 1973c, 'Conclusions: problems and perspectives' in Baker, A.R.H. and Butlin, R.A. (eds), *Studies of Field Systems in the British Isles* (Cambridge University Press), 619-56

Bazelmans, J., Gerrets, D., de Koning, J. and Vos, P., 1999,'Zoden aan de dijk: Kleinschalige dijkbouw in de late prehistorie en protohistorie van noordelijk Westergo', *De Vrije Fries* 17, 7-74

Behre, K-E, 1990, 'History of landscape and habitation in the coastal region of Niedersachsen', in Behre, K-E (ed), *Environment and Settlement History in the North German Coastal Region* (Wilhelmshaven), 5-66

Beresford, M.W. and St Joseph, J.K.S., 1979, *Medieval England: an aerial survey* (Cambridge University Press)

Besteman, J.C., Bos, J.M., Gerretts, D.A., Heidinga, H.A. and de Koning, J., 1999, *The excavations at Wijnaldum. Reports on Frisia in Roman and Medieval times I.* (Rotterdam)

Blair, J., 1994, *Anglo-Saxon Oxfordshire* (Stroud, Alan Sutton)

Bradney, J., 1929, *History of Monmouthshire, volume 4, part 1: The Hundred of Caldicot, Part 1* (London, Mitchell, Hughes and Clarke)

Brian, A., 1999, 'The Allocation of Strips in Lammas Meadows by the Casting of Lots', *Landscape History* 21, 43-58

Brook, D., 1992, 'The Early Christian Church East and West of Offa's Dyke', in Edwards, N. and Lane, A. (eds), *The Early Christian Church in Wales and the West* (Oxford, Oxbow Monograph 16), 77-89

Buchanan, R.H., 1973, 'Field systems of Ireland', in Baker, A.R.H. and Butlin, R.A. (eds), *Studies of Field Systems in the British Isles* (Cambridge University Press), 580-618

Crowson, A., Lane, T. and Reeve, J. (eds), 2000, *Fenland Management Project Excavations 1991-1995*, Lincolnshire Archaeology and Heritage Reports Series No. 3

Dixon, P. 1994,' Field-systems, rig and other cultivation remains in Scotland: the field evidence', in Foster, S. and Smout, T.C. (eds), *The History of Soils and Field Systems* (Aberdeen, Scottish Cultural Press), 26-52

Dodgshon, R. A., 1994, 'Rethinking Highland Field Systems', in Foster, S. and Smout, T.C. (eds), *The History of Soils and Field Systems* (Aberdeen, Scottish Cultural Press), 53-65

Dodgshon, R.A., 1998, 'The evolution of Highland townships during the medieval and early modern periods', *Landscape History* 20, 51-63

Eddison, J. (ed), 1995, *Romney Marsh: the debatable ground* (Oxford)

Eddison, J., 2000, *Romney Marsh: survival on a frontier* (Stroud, Tempus)

Eddison, J. and Green, C. (eds), 1988, *Romney Marsh: evolution, occupation, reclamation* (Oxford, Oxford University Committee for Archaeology)

Eddison, J., Gardiner, M. and Long, A. (eds), 1998, *Romney Marsh: Environmental Change and Human Occupation in a Coastal Lowland* (Oxford, Oxford University Committee for Archaeology)

Elliott. G., 1973, 'Field systems of North West England', in Baker, A.R.H. and Butlin, R.A. (eds), *Studies of Field Systems in the British Isles* (Cambridge University Press), 41-92

English, J., 1997, 'A possible early Wealden settlement type', *Medieval Settlement Research Group Annual Report* 12, 5-6

Faith, R., 1997, *The English Peasantry and the Growth of Lordship* (London, Leicester University Press)

Finberg, H.P.R., 1951, *Tavistock Abbey: a study in the social and economic history of Devon* (Cambridge)

Finberg, H.P.R., 1969, *West country historical studies* (Newton Abbott, David and Charles)

Fleming, A. 1994, 'Medieval and post-medieval cultivation on Dartmoor: a landscape archaeologist's view', *Devon Archaeol. Soc. Proc.* 52, 101-18

Fleming, A. and Ralph, N., 1982, 'Medieval settlement and landuse on Holne Moor, Dartmoor: the landscape evidence', *Medieval Archaeology* 26, 101-37

Ford, W.J., 1979, 'Some settlement patterns in the central region of the Warwickshire Avon', in Sawyer, P.H. (ed), *English Medieval Settlement* (London, Edward Arnold) 143-63

Foster, S. and Smout, T.C. (eds), 1994, *The History of Soils and Field Systems* (Aberdeen, Scottish Cultural Press)

Fox, H.S.A., 1981, 'Approaches to the adoption of the Midland System', in Rowley, T. (ed), *The Origins of Open-Field Agriculture* (London, Croom Helm), 64-103

Fulford, M.G., Allen, J.R.L. and Rippon, S.J., 1994, 'The Settlement and Drainage of the Wentlooge Level, Gwent: Survey and Excavation at Rumney Great Wharf, 1992', *Britannia* 25, 175-211

Gaffney, V. and Tingle, M., 1989, *The Maddle Farm Project: an integrated survey of prehistoric and Roman landscapes on the Berkshire Downs* (Oxford)

Gilbert, P., 1996, 'The pre-Conquest Landscape at Kingston Seymour on the North Somerset Levels: Report on Survey 1996', *Archaeology in the Severn Estuary* 7, 53-7

Gillard, M., Higham, R.A. and Rippon, S.J., 2000, 'Greater Exmoor: potential for medieval settlement studies and work in progress', *Society for Landscape Studies Newsletter*, spring/summer 2000, 4-7

Green, T., 2000, *Early enclosures in a landscape of dispersed settlement: an examination of patterns detected in the field-boundaries of North Devon and West Somerset*, Unpublished MA Dissertation, Department of Archaeology, University of Exeter

Hall, D., 1977, 'The sea bank in Cambridgeshire', *Proc. Camb. Ant. Soc.* 67, 67-9

Hall, D., 1996, *The Fenland Survey, Number 10: Cambridgeshire Survey, The Isle of Ely and Wisbech*, East Anglian Archaeology 79

Hall, D. and Coles, J., 1994, *Fenland Survey: An Essay in Landscape and Persistence*, English Archaeology Report 1 (London)

Hallam, H.E., 1965, *Settlement and Society: a study of the early agrarian history of south Lincolnshire* (Cambridge University Press)

Hallam, O., 1978, 'Vegetation and Land Use on Exmoor', *Somerset Archaeology and Natural History* 122, 37-51

Harris, A., 1959, *The Open Fields of East Yorkshire*, East Yorkshire Local History Series 9

Harris, A. 1961, *The Rural Landscape of the East Riding of Yorkshire* (Oxford University Press)

Harrison, J., 1997, *The Composite Manor of Brent: a study of a large wetland-edge estate up to 1350*, Unpublished PhD thesis, University of Leicester

Hawkins, A.B., 1990, 'Geology of the Avon Coast', *Proceedings of the Bristol Naturalists Society* 50, 3-27

Hoskins, W.G., 1954, *Devon* (London, Collins)

Hurst, J.D., 1983, 'The Wharram Pesearch Project: Results to 1983', *Medieval Archaeology* 28, 77-111

James, H., 1992, 'Early medieval cemeteries in Wales', in Edwards, N. and Lane, A. (eds), *The Early Christian Church in Wales and the West* (Oxford, Oxbow Monograph 16), 90-103

Jones, G.R.J., 1973, 'Field systems of North Wales', in Baker, A.R.H. and Butlin, R.A. (eds), *Studies of Field Systems in the British Isles* (Cambridge University Press), 430-79

Jones, R.H., 1991, 'Industry and environment in medieval Bristol', in Good, G.L., Jones, R.H. and Ponsford M.W. (eds), *Waterfront Archaeology*, Council for British Archaeology Research Report 74, 19-26

Kissock, J., 1997, '"God Made Nature and Men Made Towns": Post-Conquest and pre-Conquest Villages in Pembrokeshire', in Edwards, N. (ed), *Landscape and Settlement in Medieval Wales* (Oxford, Oxbow), 123-38

Knight, J., 1962, 'The Goldcliff Stone: a reconsideration' *Monmouthshire Antiquarian* I(ii), 34-6

Lane, T., 1995, *The Archaeology and Developing Landscape of Ropsley and Humby*, Lincolnshire Archaeology and Heritage Reports Series 2

Mayhew, A., 1973, *Rural Settlement and Farming in Germany* (London, Batsford)

Musgrove, D.J., 1999, *The Medieval Exploitation of the Peat Moors of the Somerset Levels*, Unpublished PhD thesis, University of Exeter

Ponsford, M.W., 1981, 'Bristol' in Milne, G. and Hobley B. (eds), *Waterfront Archaeology in Britain and Northern Europe*, Council for British Archaeology Research Report 41, 103-4

Postgate, M.R., 1973, 'Field systems of East Anglia' in Baker, A.R.H. and Butlin, R.A. (eds), *Studies of Field Systems in the British Isles* (Cambridge University Press), 281-324

Preston-Jones, A., 1992, 'Decoding Cornish Churchyards' in Edwards, N. and Lane, A. (eds), *The Early Christian Church in Wales and the West* (Oxford, Oxbow Monograph 16), 105-24

Reeves, A.C., 1977, 'The Custumal of Rumney Manor', *Bulletin of the Board of Celtic Studies* XXVII(ii), 298-302

Rippon, S., 1994, 'Medieval Wetland Reclamation in Somerset', in Aston, M. and Lewis, C. (eds.), *The Medieval Landscape of Wessex* (Oxford, Oxbow) 239-53

Rippon, S., 1996a, *Gwent Levels: The Evolution of a Wetland Landscape*, Council for British Archaeology Research Report 105

Rippon, S., 1996b, 'Roman and medieval settlement on the North Somerset Levels: survey and excavation at Banwell and Puxton, 1996', in *Archaeology in the Severn Estuary 1996* (volume 7), 39-52

Rippon, S., 1997a, *The Severn Estuary: Landscape Evolution and Wetland Reclamation* (London, Leicester University Press)

Rippon, S., 1997b, 'Roman and medieval settlement on the North Somerset Levels: second season of survey and excavation at Banwell and Puxton, 1997', *Archaeology in the Severn Estuary 1996* (volume 8), 41-54

Rippon, S., 1998, 'Roman and medieval settlement on the North Somerset Levels: the third season of survey and excavation at Puxton, 1998', *Archaeology in the Severn Estuary 1998* (volume 9), 69-78

Rippon, S., 1999, 'Roman and medieval settlement on the North Somerset Levels: the fourth season of survey and excavation at Puxton, 1999', *Archaeology in the Severn Estuary 1999* (volume 10), 65-73

Rippon, S., 2000a, 'The Romano-British exploitation of coastal wetlands: survey and excavation on the North Somerset Levels, 1993-7', *Britannia* 31, 69-200.

Rippon, S., 2000b, The *Transformation of Coastal Wetlands: exploitation and management of marshland landscapes in North West Europe during the Roman and Medieval periods* (London, British Academy)

Rippon, in press, 'Reclamation and regional economies of medieval Britain', in Raftery, B. (ed), *Recent developments in wetland research* (Dublin)

Roberts, B., 1981, 'Townfield Origins: the case of Cockfield, County Durham', in Rowley, T. (ed), *The Origins of Open-Field Agriculture* (London, Croom Helm), 145-61

Rowley, T., 1981, *The Origins of Open-Field Agriculture* (London, Croom Helm)

Schmid, P., 1990, 'Habitation and Diking in Land Wursten', in Behre, K-E (ed), *Environment and Settlement History in the North German Coastal Region* (Wilhelmshaven), 95-6

Sheppard, J.A., 1966, 'Pre-enclosure field and settlement patterns in an English township: Wheldrake, near York', *Geografiska Annaler* 48B, 59-77

Sheppard, J.A., 1973, 'Field systems of Yorkshire', in Baker, A.R.H. and Butlin, R.A. (eds), *Studies of Field Systems in the British Isles* (Cambridge University Press), 145-87

Silvester, R.J., 1988, *The Fenland Survey, Number 3: Norfolk Survey, Marshland and the Nar Valley*, East Anglian Archaeology 45

Silvester, R.J., 1993, "The addition of more or less undifferentiated dots to a distribution map'?: the Fenland Project in Retrospect', in Gardiner, J. (ed), *Flatlands and Wetlands*, East Anglian Archaeology 50, 24-39

Silvester, R.J., 1997, 'Historic Settlement Surveys in Clwyd and Powys', in Edwards, N. (ed), *Landscape and Settlement in Medieval Wales* (Oxford, Oxbow), 113-21

Taylor, C.C., 1981, 'Archaeology and the origins of open-field agriculture', in Rowley, T. (ed), *The Origins of Open-Field Agriculture* (London, Croom Helm), 13-21

Taylor, C.C., 1987, *Fields in the English Landscape*, 2nd edition (Gloucester, Alan Sutton)

Uhlig, H., 1961, 'Old hamlets with infield and outfield systems in western and Central Europe', *Geografiska Annaler* 43, 285-312

Whittington, G., 1973, 'Field systems of Scotland', in Baker, A.R.H. and Butlin, R.A. (eds), *Studies of Field Systems in the British Isles* (Cambridge University Press), 530-79

Williams, M., 1970, *The Draining of the Somerset Levels* (Cambridge University Press)

6. A REVIEW OF 25 YEARS OF FIELDWALKING WITH DAVID HALL

by Paul Martin

Introduction

I first met David Hall in the Summer of 1972. David was conducting an excavation on behalf of the Brixworth Archaeological Research Committee. Prior to this I had carried out surveying work over several years, concentrating on settlement distribution within the confines of the parish of Brixworth. David and I quickly established a rapport when it was understood that similar work performed by him around the Wollaston area (David's home village) closely matched that of the work I had undetaken at Brixworth. Following that meeting in 1972, survey work undertaken by us throughout the winter months began to establish settlement patterns dating from the Mesolithic through to the Middle Saxon period.

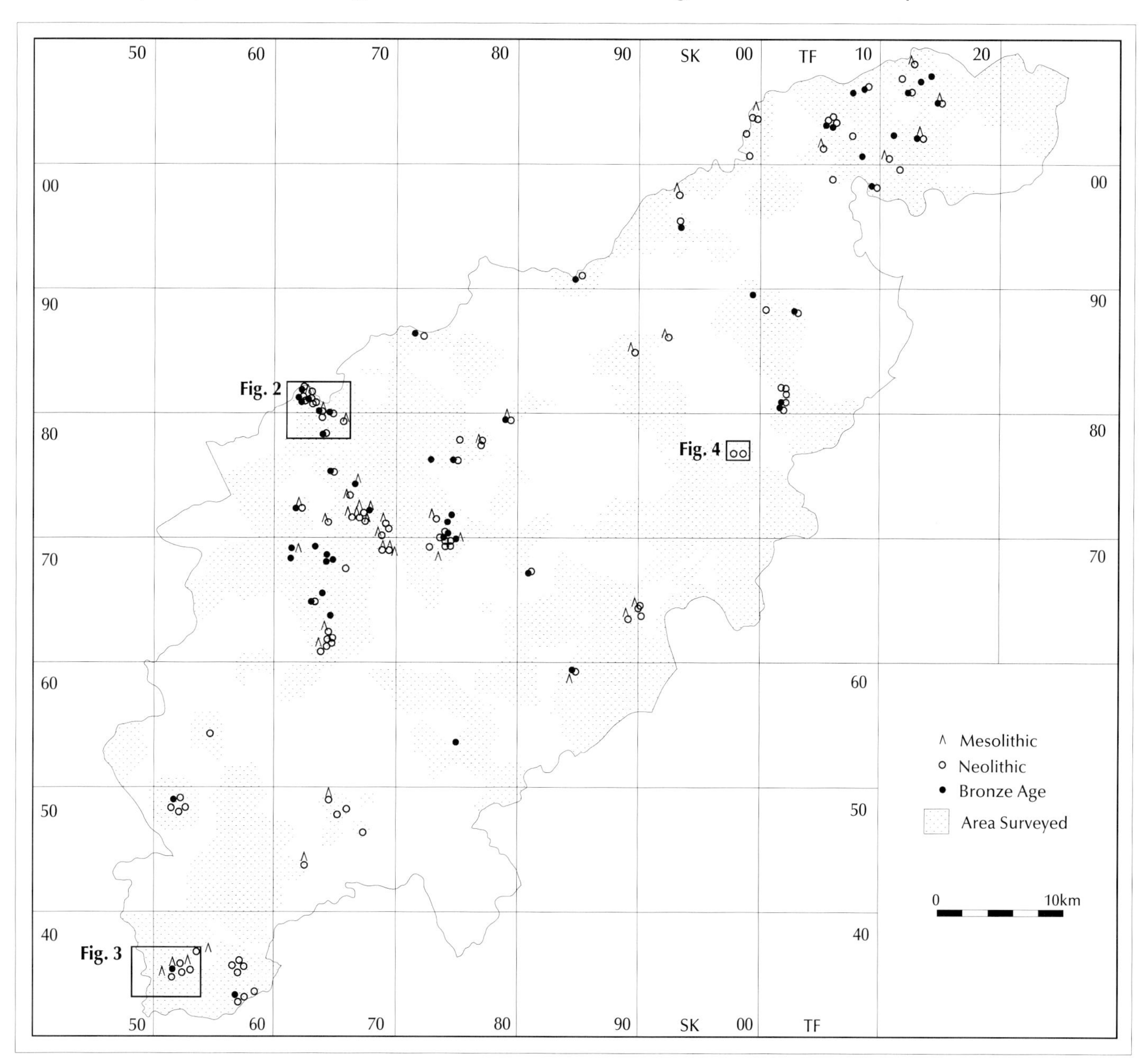

Figure 1 Distribution of Northamptonshire lithic sites. Mesolithic, Neolithic and Early Bronze Age settlements located by Paul Martin and David Hall, 1972-1997

To enable us to understand these complex patterns in context, we knew that surveying on a much larger scale would be required. This afforded opportunities for David to demonstrate his broad range of the 'non technical' skills that are essential to success in the world of archaeology. David's organisational abilities were soon put to good use. His experience told him that careful planning and a systematic approach were crucial, as one single field missed could result in the overlooking of the key to a number of factors ranging from furlong boundaries to prehistoric flint scatters, indicating settlement. Moreover, his persuasive skills came to the front when faced with contrary farmers. Diplomacy and a wide knowledge of farming practices were needed to maintain a constant flow of available land to study. As we were both brought up in the countryside we were well aware that taking sides concerning politics, fox hunting *etc.* had to be carefully balanced with each individual farmer. We had to be *Socialists* one day and *Tories* the next, or pro-fox hunting and anti-fox hunting depending on whichever farmer we were communicating with. David's eccentric ways and dress sense (he was once described by a friend of mine as a walking scarecrow), almost certainly encouraged the more contrary farmers to grant us permission to survey their land.

Our earlier years together included rescue excavations (Plate 1) combined with fieldwalking. It should be remembered that the major excavations at Raunds and the Irthlingborough barrow were both first brought to fruition because of David's knowledge of important sites within the wider region. I would also like to acknowledge, as I am sure David would, the help and encouragement that other people gave to our County survey, notably the Northamptonshire Field Group consisting at the time of Dennis Jackson, Robert Moore, Bill Bellamy, Glenn Foard, Richard Harper, Pat Foster and Brian Giggins, along with two other well loved individuals, Arthur Goldsworthy and Peter Hardy, both of whom sadly passed away several years ago.

The importance of the role which amateur archaeologists can play in establishing new archaeological practices may be illustrated as follows: the Northamptonshire Field Group (including David and myself) helped to establish a network system in which members were allocated an area and were then held responsible for checking every development site in their assigned plot for archaeological remains. The importance of some of our finds soon established the fact that

Plate 1 1972 excavations to try and locate one of the Saxon cemeteries at Sandpits Field, Brixworth. David Hall in the background, and Arthur Goldsworthy in the foreground

Northamptonshire contained many important archaeological sites.

Indeed, for many years the Midland counties had been classed as being almost barren of earlier prehistoric settlement. Known barrow sites such as Woodford and the Grendon complex were examples of the limit of the knowledge of earlier prehistory in Northamptonshire. David and I both sought to understand the settlement patterns of early prehistory in Northamptonshire, which would then inform those of later periods throughout the County. Remnants of settlement pertaining to the Mesolithic, Neolithic and Early Bronze Age seemed to follow a familiar pattern. Settlement of particular periods tended to occur on specific soil types.

Most of the work David and I carried out in the 1970s and the early 1980s occurred in areas where acidic soils dominated. Alas, these soils appeared to be where most settlements had occurred. Observations showed that, due to the acidity, surviving faunal and pottery remains were limited,

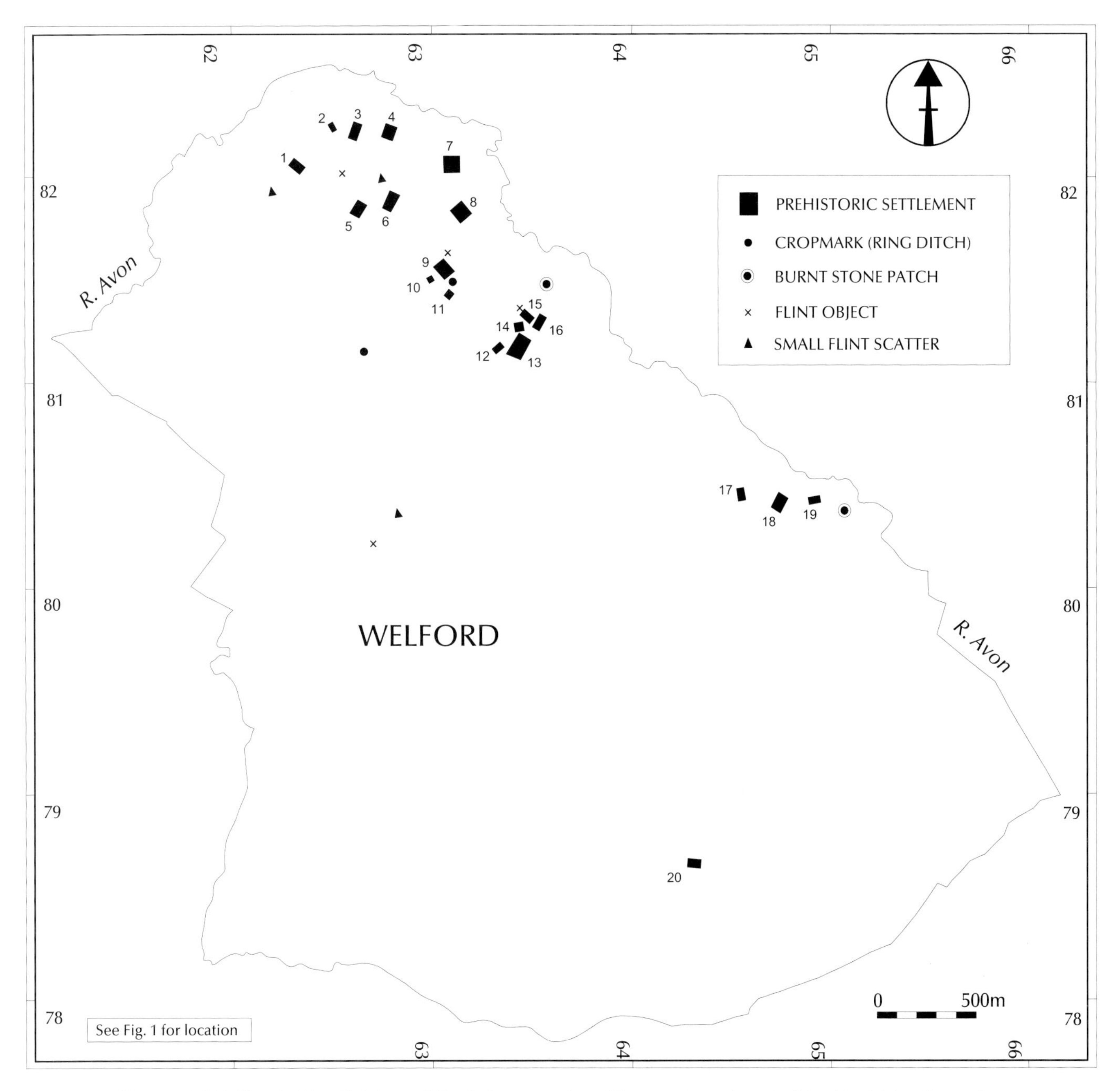

Figure 2 Welford. Neolithic and Early Bronze Age flint scatters located by Paul Martin and David Hall in December 1979. Scatters located on gravels South of the river Avon. Note no major flint scatters found on the heavier boulder clays of the central and southern areas of the parish, except for site 20 which was located on a patch of glacial gravel

with the only clue to past activity being the lithic remains. As our work expanded we confronted different geology notably the limestones to the northeast and the southwest of the County. These gave us new insight into our ever-expanding settlement patterns. Unlike the acidic soils in the central areas of the county, these alkaline rich soils provided us with faunal and ceramic remains to accompany the lithics.

Important to settlement was the availability of water. From our earlier days working together we both independently recognised that lighter soils and closeness to running water were a cocktail for earlier prehistoric settlement (Martin and Hall 1980, 13). As can be seen from our distribution map of Mesolithic, Neolithic and Bronze Age lithic sites (see Fig. 1), the clustering alongside main watercourses is irrefutable. In one case study the Welford parish survey bore out our theory that, in the main, settlement was confined to lighter soils

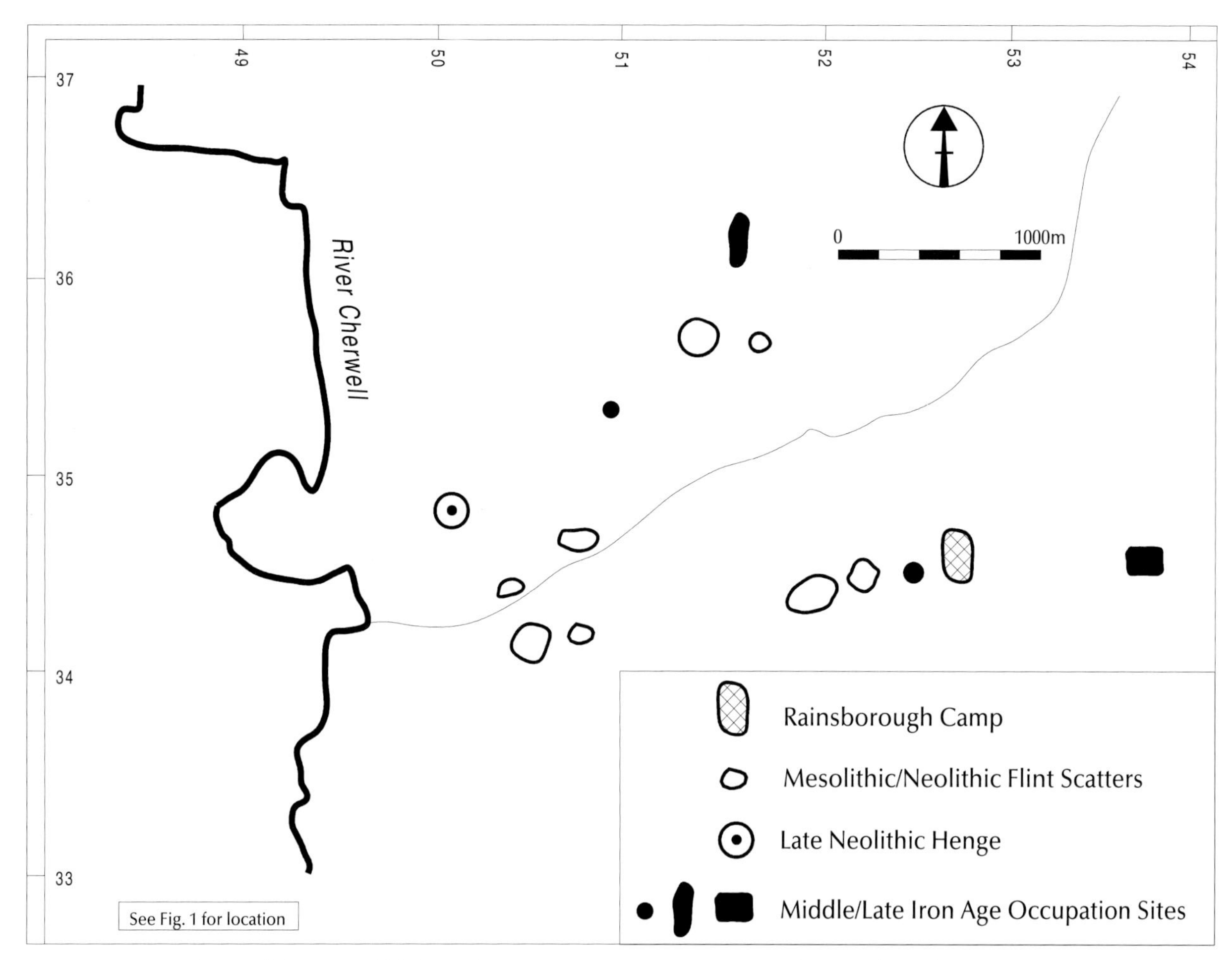

Figure 3 Mesolithic/Neolithic and Iron Age occupation sites located in close proximity to Rainsborough Camp. Sites found in the winters of 1994 and 1995 by David and myself on Limestone and Northampton Sand. The Late Neolithic henge was located by Glenn Foard from an aerial photograph

and not to the heavier clays. From the distribution map of Welford (see Fig. 2) it can be clearly seen that lithic scatters were located on the gravels alongside the river Avon and not on the clays in the central areas of the parish (Martin 1982, 56-59).

Combining our fieldwork with Glenn Foard's aerial reconnaissance, David and I appeared to have stumbled upon previously unknown settlement areas dating to the Neolithic. One of these areas was of special significance. Rainsborough Camp the Iron Age hill fort situated between Aynho and Kings Sutton was always classed as an anomaly due to its location. In fact its tactical position was classed as weak (Avery *et al.* 1967, 291). Indeed, surveying around Rainsborough yielded some fascinating results. It seems that the area around this hillfort had been settled since the Mesolithic (see Fig. 3). Could Rainsborough be like other Iron Age hillforts throughout the country in having Neolithic beginnings? Fieldwork could be one of the key factors in answering this question by understanding the wider settlement framework rather than concentrating on the nucleus itself.

Further investigations, using modern technology, would I feel give Rainsborough a much earlier date than has been previously shown. Evidence such as that from the triangular area between Banbury, Brackley and Aynho highlights the increasing numbers of flint scatters (settlement) in these regions and their significance in the understanding of Mesolithic, Neolithic and Early Bronze Age settlement patterns. Evidence to date suggests that the upper reaches of the main river systems flowing through or bordering Northamptonshire are providing us with a network of later Neolithic crop marks (hengi-forms) similar to those in southern England.

Moreover, the importance of field survey was again shown when investigating Hinton-in-the-Hedges parish, where an upstanding mound was discovered. This mound, which the RCHM classed as undated (RCHM 1982, 92), seems in all probability to be a long barrow measuring 60m x 25m. Flint scatters found in the surrounding area on Great Oolite Limestone certainly provides evidence to support a Neolithic date for the long barrow.

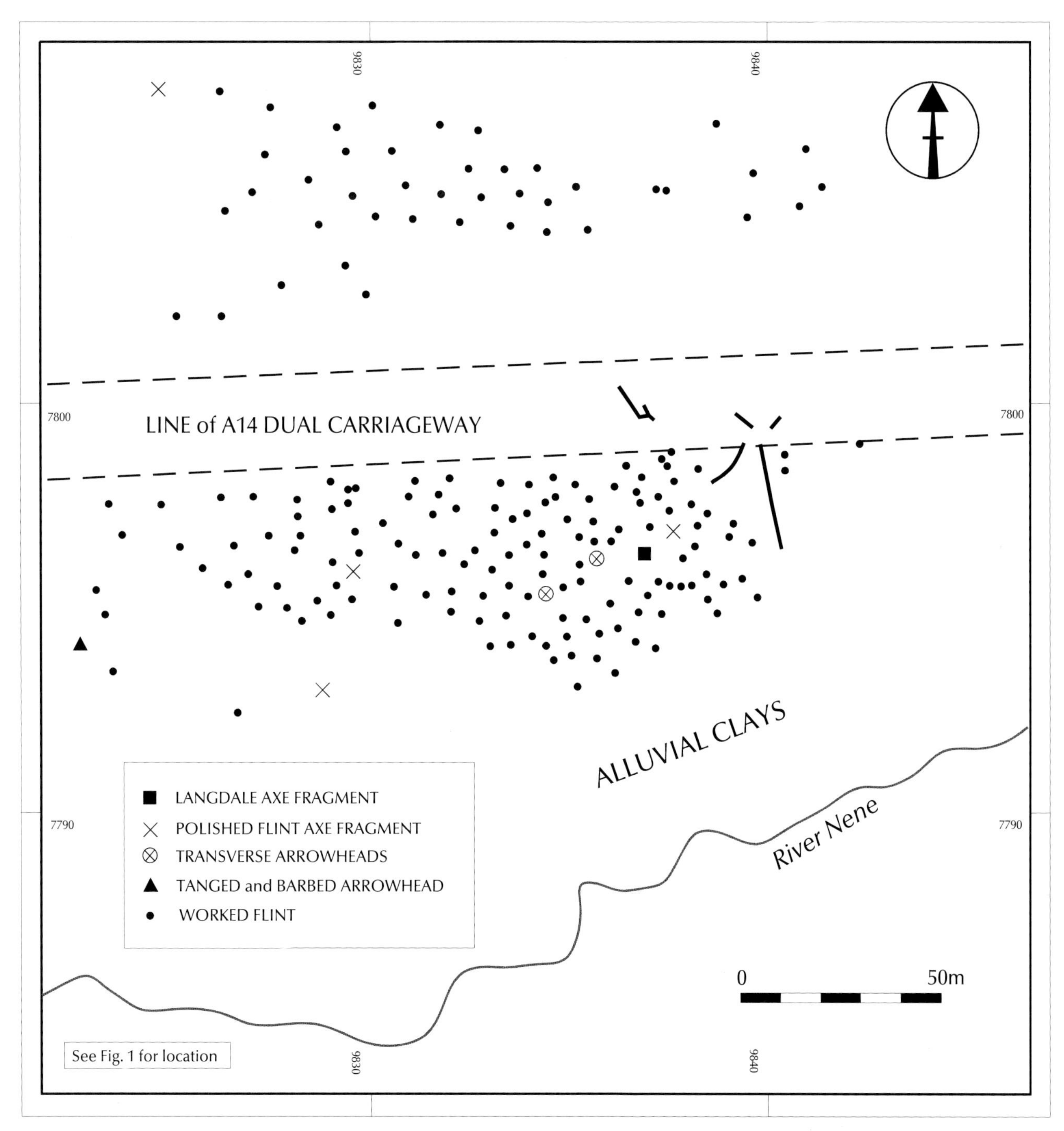

Figure 4 Islip. Secondary Neolithic/Early Bronze Age flint scatter located by Paul Martin and David Hall next to one of the river Nene tributaries, February 1989. Excavations by the Northamptonshire Archaeological Unit prior to the A14 dual carriageway located sherds of Secondary Neolithic and Early Bronze Age pottery in the features to the east of the scatter

Surveying along the fringes of the river Welland and river Avon also revealed similar Neolithic and Early Bronze Age flint scatters. Furthermore, the parishes of Collyweston, and Duddington also proved to be of particular interest to David and myself, as aerial photographs in this region showed a complex of cropmarks resembling hengi-form types. Finds from within and around these crop marks clearly point towards the Later Neolithic period.

The brief, fast methods of surveying carried out by David and me, are I feel, just the beginning. They invite more detailed research in the future which will hopefully expand on our pioneering work in these areas.

Post-Roman Settlement Patterns

One important area of research carried out during our twenty-five years together was the establishment of an Early/Middle Saxon settlement pattern. Again the early work was initiated whilst undertaking the Brixworth parish survey. Early Saxon cemeteries found within the parish of Brixworth were investigated by myself, David and Arthur Goldsworthy (Plate 1), to try and establish the connection with the numerous areas of occupation found through field walking within the parish (Hall and Martin 1979). The work carried out in Brixworth coincided with Glenn Foard's work at Earls Barton (Foard 1978). Satellite settlements such as those at Brixworth and Earls Barton paved the way for a better understanding of the transition of post-Roman settlement to the nucleation of the modern day village. What transpired from this earlier research work in the 1970s was a pattern not too dissimilar from the Brixworth survey found throughout the Northamptonshire county. Excavations on one such settlement during the construction of the Brixworth bypass revealed a rectangular pattern of post holes comprising two, possibly three, structures in association with classic hand-made Early/Middle Saxon pottery (Shaw 1990; Jackson 1991, 112).

The Significance of Surface Scatters

The importance of surface scatters of artefacts in denoting settlement was established in the early days of our surveying. Several of the surface scatters which we located have since been excavated and have indeed provided evidence of settlement. We designate the term 'settlement' on Neolithic and Bronze Age sites in cases where 20% or more of the total flint assemblage is composed of tools. One such site was a Late Neolithic/Early Bronze Age flint scatter found at Islip to the west of the county in February 1989 (Fig. 4). This site, located on Northampton Sand and excavated by the Northamptonshire Archaeology Unit prior to construction of the A14 dual carriageway, revealed pits and shallow ditches which contained pottery from at least three vessels dating to these periods (Dix and Holmes 1990, 38) below where the flint scatter was found. The Islip and other similar flint scatters are of great importance in our understanding of Neolithic and Bronze Age settlement in that they are protected in part by alluvial clays (see Fig. 4). Similarly, a late Neolithic/ Early Bronze Age pit was located under a flint scatter during an evaluation for the Brixworth bypass (Jackson 1991, 112). In the light of these excavations it is possible to interpret the large number of flint scatters which David and myself found throughout the county over a number of years as being settlement.

Bureaucracy always took back stage with David and myself, with most communications taking place verbally or on the backs of beer mats. Alongside archaeology, our love of real ale saw us frequent many public houses across Northamptonshire, especially in our dinnertime breaks. One could muse as to the percentage of sites found pre-pub or post-pub, for after all, we were independent, surveying the county for the love of the work and not the money. Pubs were also a safe refuge from the rain. On one such occasion whilst surveying the deserted village of Glassthorpe in Flore parish we were caught in torrential rain far from our vehicles. We could have chosen to return home, but we didn't. Instead, we drank several pints of real ale in front of a log fire, at *The Saracens Head* in Little Brington. Why we chose to stay was that we had just located evidence for an early Saxon settlement at Glassthorpe, so no rain was going to deter us from investigating this further.

The variations in geology and archaeology within our parameters from the Soke of Peterborough in the northwest of the county – we did still class the Soke as falling within our boundaries – to Aynho on the Oxfordshire border were considerable. One day we could be picking up Roman Castor ware from a kiln site near Peterborough and the next Roman Oxford wares from a ploughed out site in the Banbury area, such is the length and diversity of the county.

To conclude, I feel it has been a privilege to work with David and hope to repeat this experience in our Autumn Years. David's contribution to Northamptonshire archaeology and history is second to none. I feel his work compares favourably with that of Bridges and Baker, both well known eighteenth and nineteenth century historians, and trust that his work will be recorded in the annals of history.

Bibliography

Avery, A., Sutton, J.E. and Banks, J. W., 1967, 'Rainsborough, Northants, England : Excavations 1961-5', *Proc. Prehist. Soc.* 33, 207-307

Dix, B. and Holmes, M., 1990, 'M1-A1 Link Road', *South Midlands Archaeology*, 20, 38

Foard, G., 1978, 'Systematic fieldwalking and the investigation of Saxon settlement in Northamptonshire', *World Archaeology* 9, 357-74

Hall, D.N. and Martin, P.W., 1979, 'Brixworth, Northamptonshire – an intensive archaeological survey', *Journal of the British Archaeological Association* 122, 1-6

Jackson, D.A., 1991, 'Migration and Early Medieval', *Northamptonshire Archaeology* 23, 112

Martin, P.W. and Hall, D.N., 1980, 'Brixworth, Northamptonshire : new evidence for early prehistoric settlement and agriculture', *Bedfordshire Archaeological Journal* 14, 5-14

Martin, P.W., 1982, 'Welford, Northamptonshire : Neolithic and Bronze Age settlement patterns', *CBA Group 9. A review of Archaeology in Bedfordshire, Buckinghamshire, Northamptonshire and Oxfordshire. Newsletter* 12, 56-59

RCHM, 1982, *An Inventory of Archaeological Sites in South-West Northamptonshire* Vol 4, (London, Her Majesty's Stationery Office)

Shaw, M., 1990, *Archaeology and the Brixworth bypass : A Saxon site and other finds made during the construction of the Brixworth bypass,* Northamptonshire Archaeology Unit (Contracts Section)

7. WOODS, FENS AND ROADS: WHERE ARE THE FENS?

by Brian K. Roberts

This paper uses a reconstruction of the distribution of early woodland in England to frame the question "Where are the Fens?" This is, of course, easily answered with reference to an atlas. However, if it were not possible to consult a map, if one were travelling and yet not in possession of that well-known image of England with the distinctive rectangular enclave of the Wash and the rounded swell of East Anglia, then the question would be sharper, significant, even urgent. River crossings, fens and fen edges would raise important issues, while distances and direction, hours of light or darkness, fine weather or storm, road or causeway and mud or stone surface would loom large. Using a map of early woodland and maps of the seventeenth century, fourteenth century and Roman road systems, the consequences and repercussions of the location of the great ice-scooped hollow of the Fenland can be explored. Maps, of course, are important in codifying our experiences of the world. Generalisations of real world space, brought to the scale of the page, they allow the identification of structural settings – contexts – both physical and cultural, within which events, past, present or future, take place. This should be emphasised, for it includes all of the things we study, at all times and at all scales, local, regional and national, All events possess a location. Maps give us a glimpse of the articulation and discontinuities in the changing real worlds of the past amid the seamless robes of time and space.

Perversely, this discussion will begin with the medieval Gough map (Fig. 1) rather than that of Roman conditions or a modem rescension of Ogilby's road book. This discussion builds around the Ordnance Survey Facsimile of the Bodleian Library's medieval map, prepared in 1870, published in 1935 and reprinted in 1959, but now out of print. Catherine Delano-Smith and Roger Kain in their recent book describe the Gough map as 'extraordinarily well-constructed' and 'based not only on widely gathered information but also on mathematically calculated co-ordinates for a handful of towns' (Delano-Smith and Kain 1999, 47-48). They accept a date of approximately 1360. Building their arguments on the evidence of surviving maps from the thirteenth century, they argue that itineraries were fundamentally important for establishing lists of places and the distances between them. Figure 1 has been constructed not by using a cartogram within the distorted coastline of the original map, but by relating the places depicted along the 'roads' on the Gough map to a 1930 Ordnance Survey reconstruction based on Ogilvy's road book of 1675. Approximately three fifths of the fourteenth century network is the same as that recorded in 1675. The radial pattern from London linked by major cross routes was already firmly established. Given the peripatetic nature of medieval great households, the widely scattered estates of the great religious houses and the need for the delivery of royal writs and other documents it is not hard to see that route itineraries were necessary if ephemeral documents in the medieval period. For those with the appropriate contacts, these would provide important sources for adding detail within an established general framework (Harvey 1991, frontispiece and 71-78).

The dislocations in the route system within the Gough map are well known, thus no links are shown between the southeast coast and London. Nevertheless the places joined by straight lines, normally bearing a figure indicating the distance between each pair, evidently depict a set of major routes. The placing of the other named and unnamed settlements, although not always accurate, provides a real sense of the spaces between these designated routes. They are sufficient in number to establish a framework for additional local route finding. River crossings are enigmatic, for while many rivers and streams appear, neither bridges nor ferries are noted. Many must have been present. Their location must have been subject to on-ground common sense. In this matter, the naming of places, is, for any stranger, essential. While it appears to be incomplete, the fact that the person who prepared the facsimile attached partial names to many places suggests a faded or partially illegible original. For the modern reader, common sense, supported by a road atlas, quickly suggests the names of places merely shown by a symbol in 1360.

One example is illuminating. The traveller from Richmond in Yorkshire to Kirby Lonsdale in Westmorland, one of the routes interlined, must cross from Swaledale to Yoredale ('the dale of the Ure'), to *Bolton*, *i.e.* Castle Bolton, then proceed up-valley, passing the unlocated *Moorhouse* to an

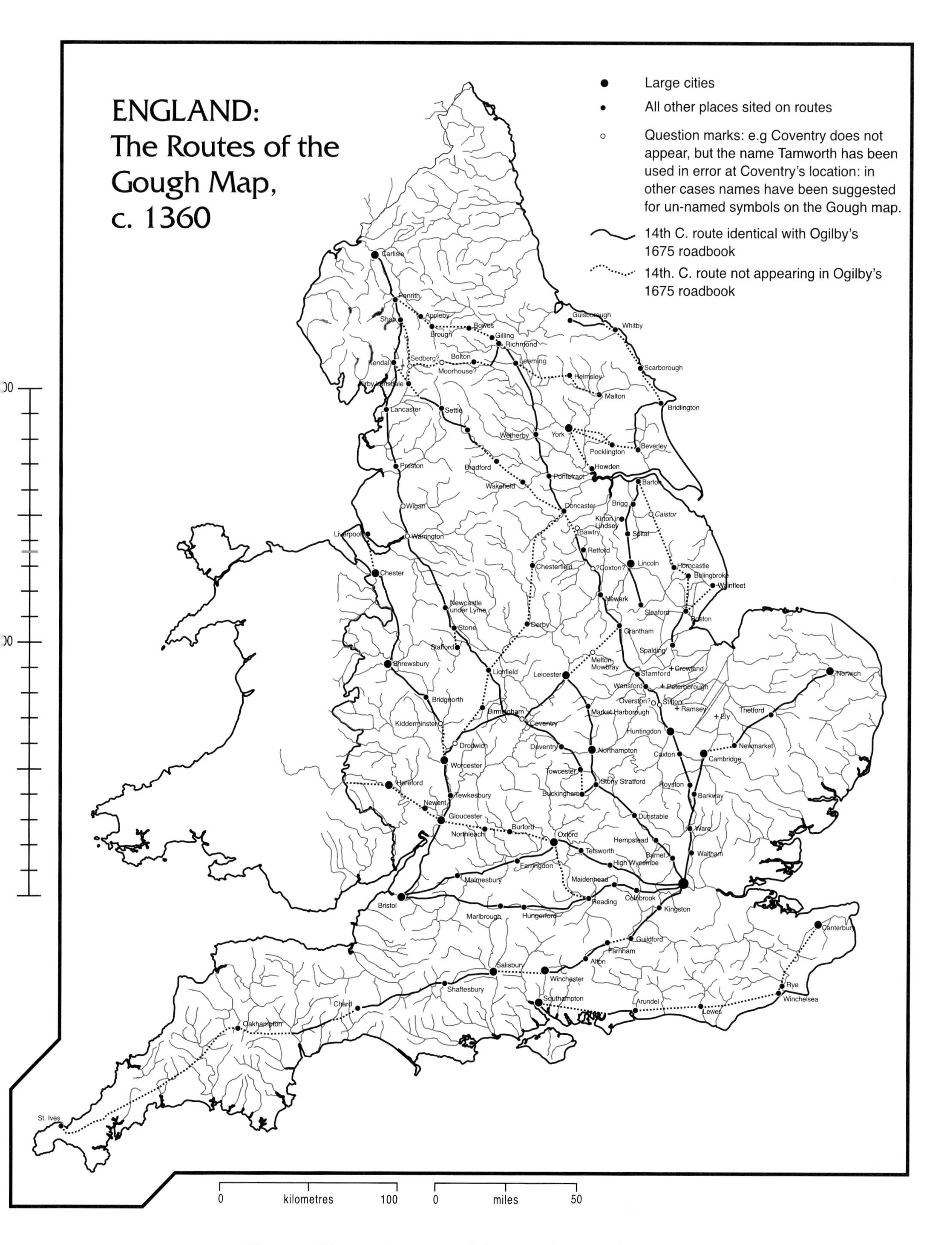

Figure 1 The road pattern of the Gough map of c. 1360

unnamed settlement, perhaps Sedbergh, and thence to Kirby Lonsdale. On this route severe weather would have provided the unwary traveller with a rude shock. Nevertheless, the instruction implicit in the map, namely *'from Bolton pass along the northern side of the Ure, to its head, and then straight on, largely westwards, to Kirby, a journey of 30* 'units' *beyond Bolton'* is sound enough, and the route is still followed by the A684. The distance is of the order of 40-45 miles, so that in this case at least, 30 *leagues*, each of a mile and a half, would be a very reasonable estimate of the distance involved. This detail, from a remote part of the remote north, is impressive, and begs a closer study of the map than is possible here. The Fenland is treated distinctively: the great monastic sites, Ely, Peterborough, Ramsey, Crowland are shown, with the island site of Ely being emphasised by a ring-like river surrounding it, a convention also used for the Isle of Axholme. In fact, this reflected medieval reality, for the island had to be approached by causeways (Darby 1940, 106-114). Thinking in terms of the location of the Fens, the main road northwards from London bifurcates somewhat north of Ware, the junction near Puckeridge of the present A10 and B1368. The route northwards, following the modern A10, heads towards Royston and thence via the A1198 to Huntingdon, with a note of Caxton to keep the traveller on course. The road then proceeds to Stamford via the modern A1. On the Gough map Stilton is shown slightly off the road, to the east, not on the main route as it now is, but the line passes through a place rendered *Ogerston* in the facsimile transcription. This cannot be certainly identified but the abbreviated Latin may be tentatively identified with the deserted village of Overston (TL 123895) whose location lies near or on the medieval route. Whatever the details, and local on-gound investigation is undoubtedly needed, this important north to south routeway essentially follows the line of the Ermine Street northwards, avoiding the fen edge to the east. A eastwards bifurcation begins at Puckeridge, passes via the village of Barkway – marked in 1360 – to head for Cambridge, and thence turns sharply eastwards to Newmarket, Thetford and eventually Norwich (Fig. 1). This dryland route kept well clear of the Fens.

Routes penetrating the Fens are generally not recorded, although from the north the Fenland is approached by one route from Lincoln to Sleaford, and another via Horncastle, Boston and Spalding along the silt ridge. Pinchbeck and Bourne, located but lacking link lines, do appear as places set east of the Sleaford-Grantham road, with Fosdyke set out near the ancient Sea Bank. While the Gough map is most certainly not a road map, it emerges as a remarkably sound basis for providing a series of reference locations from which itineraries could be defined or to which existing itineraries could be related. Thus the crossing of the Mimram (or Lea on some maps) at Ware, the Ouse at Huntingdon, and the Welland at Stamford are represented cartographically. Furthermore, the fact that Barkway lies near a northern tributary of the Lea – the river Rib – was discovered on the Gough map, before it was cross-checked on a modern map! The glimpse it affords of the Fens is one of impenetrability, with the great abbeys appearing as beacons amid the miasmas. Arising from these observations are fascinating questions about wayfinding and the use of local guides.

In 1936 R.A. Pelham noted that some of the routes appearing on the Gough map owe a debt to Roman antecedents, but commented that 'upon analysis these are seen to be by no means wholly Roman' (in Darby 1936, 260-15 fig 43). Figure 2 shows the Roman network in England, and in this case we are indeed dealing with a deliberately established system, even if it is now seen in a fragmentary form because of subsequent decay. The principle legs are considered to have been laid down for military purposes, with the Ermine Street being associated with the advance of the Ninth Legion from Colchester, round the Fens, and northwards to the Trent and the Humber (Frere 1998, 55, 291). Sheppard Frere also notes that the remarkable line of the Fosse Way, from Exeter to Lincoln, 'never deviating more than six miles from the direct alignment' (Frere 1998, 59), was both 'unitary and military'. This pattern is well known, and undoubtedly contributed to the network of Gough routes, of which perhaps one third are of Roman origin. However, as Figure 2 shows the significance of the Roman routes can be explored by placing the network over a national distribution map of woodland. This map incorporates all of the entries referring to woodland from Sir Clifford Darby's great analysis of Domesday Book, and adds to this data those pre-Conquest place-names indicative of the presence of wood. Its construction and limitations have been discussed in another context (Roberts and Wrathmell 2000) and it is used here merely to create a grey background to the over-printed roads. This correlation, which has far-reaching implications, suggests that the Fosse Way linked together great tracts of wold and clayland which had already been substantively cleared by the Roman period. It was a cross-country route of paramount military and economic importance.

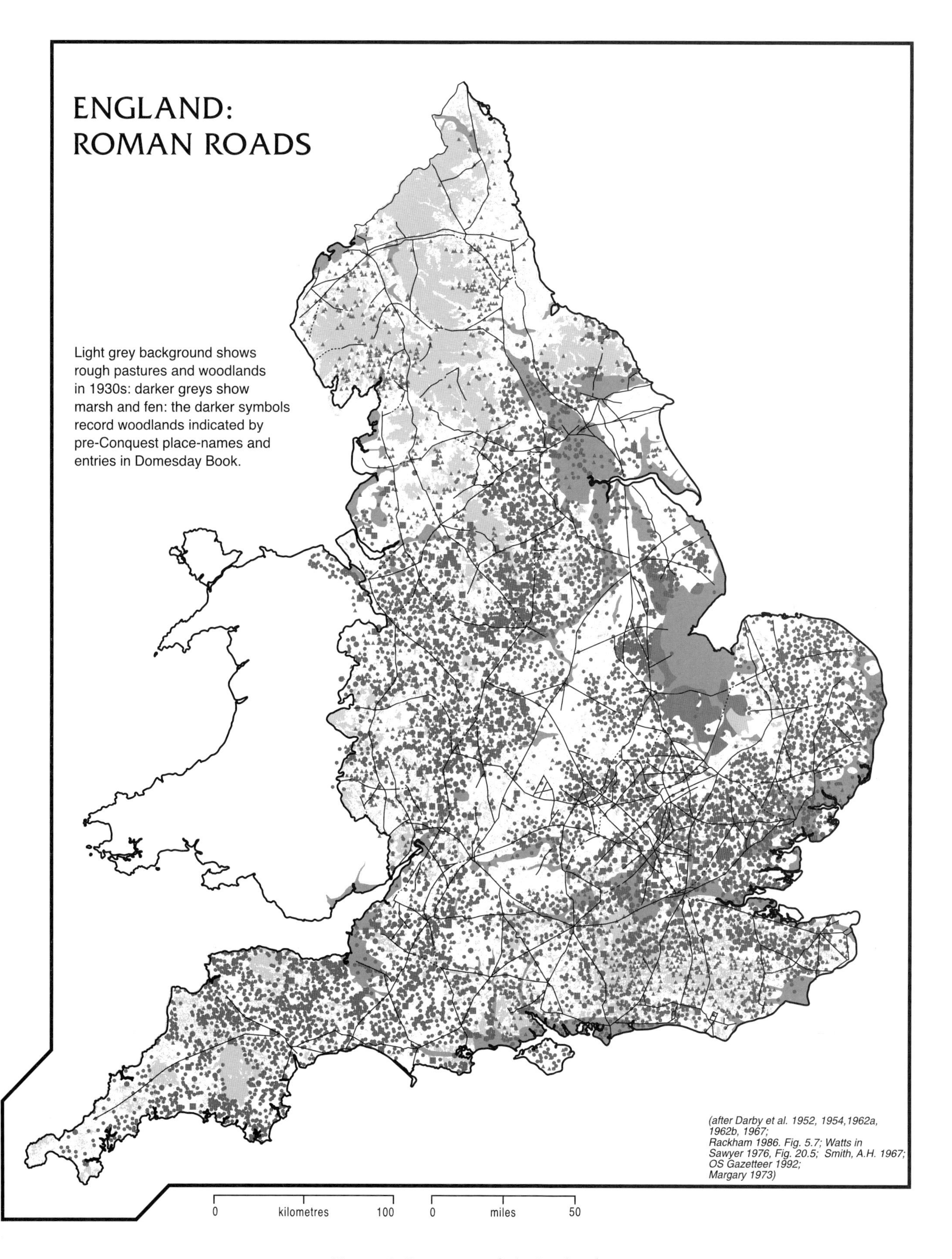

Figure 2 Roman roads in England

Returning to the Fens, the outstanding achievements of the Roman engineers and surveyors in laying out the lines of the Ermine Street is evident from Figure 2. The route was driven northwards from London, parallel to the Lea Valley with its woodlands, across the Chalk ridge and bleak clay Royston plateau beyond, to Godmanchester (*Durovigutum*), the Roman antecedent of Huntindon. It then skirted the Fens to Water Newton (*Durobrivae*). The bifurcation north of this point, with the roads meeting again at Ancaster (*Cavsennae*) is interesting. According to Ivan Margary (1973, 232) this diversion was also constructed at an early date. It is possible to argue that the western route avoids the lower, fen-edge, crossings of the Glen and the Welland, while the eastern route – the King Street – provides a possible link to the Car Dyke near Bourne. However, when the Roman road pattern is superimposed over the map of woodland, the two south to north roads essentially pass each side of a wooded area recorded in 1086. This is in Kesteven, a district recorded on the Gough map, whose first element incorporates the British *ceto*, Welsh *coed*, 'wood', with the second element being the Old Scandinavian *stefna*, 'a meeting place' (Ekwall 1960, 273). At one level this patch of woodland can be interpreted as bolted coppices that once used to supply charcoal for the kilns of *Durobrivae*. But other levels are implied by the survival of the British name element and 'the existence of a district with a common meeting place', subtle indicators of the survival of elements from very ancient woodland. The Roman engineers, isolating this block of territory may have had more in mind than river crossings and their drive northwards. The Roman name of Willoughby, *Vernemeton*, on the Fosse Way, some miles further west (SK 6425) and set firmly amid the great cleared tract, means 'very sacred grove' or ' great sacred grove', a reminder that there was more to woods than timber and charcoal (Rivet and Smith 1979, 495). Further, the name *Durobrivae*, meaning 'bridge(s) fort' iterates the importance of the Nene crossing and a native settlement there in pre-Roman times.

It has to be admitted that the Water Newton to Ancaster bifurcation is by no means an isolated case: the King Street thrusts northwards from Bourne to Sleaford, and then swings gently westwards to join the Ermine Street just south of Lincoln, demarcating another diamond shaped territory. While the southern portion of this, between Bourne and Sleaford, does indeed contain outliers of the Kesteven woodland, the northern portion, crossing the eastern flank of the Wolds, does not. This is not the place to pursue the arguments any further. One is quickly drawn into the details of local studies, involving elements as diverse as the distribution of *-ham* and *-by* names, the absence of names in *-leah* from the 'wooded' tract of Kesteven lying between the Witham, the West Glen and the East Glen (Fellows Jensen 1978, 236, 240 and 251) and a political context in which the territory of what Cyril Hart has termed 'outer Mercia' gives way to an intricate network of small tribal groupings (in Dornier 1977, fig 2) and where varied mixes of Scandinavian settlers colonised lands already well settled by the Anglo-Saxons (Stafford 1985, 115-121). Nevertheless, in any local and detailed presentation, the concentration of evidence for the presences of substantive woodland recorded in 1086 and a putative residual from antecedent prehistoric and Roman landscapes, cannot be ignored.

From the Ermine Street there was a road branching off at Wimpole Lodge, north of Royston, to continue north-east of Cambridge as Akeman Street crossing the southern Fenland in a direct line to Denver, near Downham Market (Margary 1973, 208-9). However, it was from *Durobrivae* that a Roman road crossed the Fens from west to east. Links from the Ermine Street lead to the Fen Road and Fen Causeway, as Margary says 'crossing the Fens from Peterborough through Whittlesey, March, and Nordelph to Denver' as Route 25, and thence onwards as Route 38 to higher land and northern East Anglia (Margary 1973, 230-2). A canal for sections of the route paralleled this, indeed in some sections the road was converted from the silted line of an earlier canal (Hall and Coles 1994, 107-8). In Roman times, in general, the water table was generally lower than in the prehistoric period, so that settlement extended on the fen edges and islands. As Hall and Coles have noted 'the Roman fen edge, islands and siltlands were more densely settled than at any time previously' (1994, 120). It was evidently the drier conditions that permitted this enhanced level of penetration and exploitation and it was not until the late Saxon period that rising water levels led to the construction of the Sea Bank (Hall and Coles 1994, 127). The distinctive qualities of Roman roads, their straightness, their engineered construction, their documentation in the Peutinger Table, the Antonine Itinerary, the Ravenna Cosmography and the *Notitia Dignitatum* (Rivet and Smith 1979, 148- 225) have encouraged scholarly exploration. If not completely understood most aspects have been commented upon. However, it has already been noted that two thirds of the routes recorded on the Gough map were *not* of direct Roman origin. There are few more striking latent patterns than the road net to

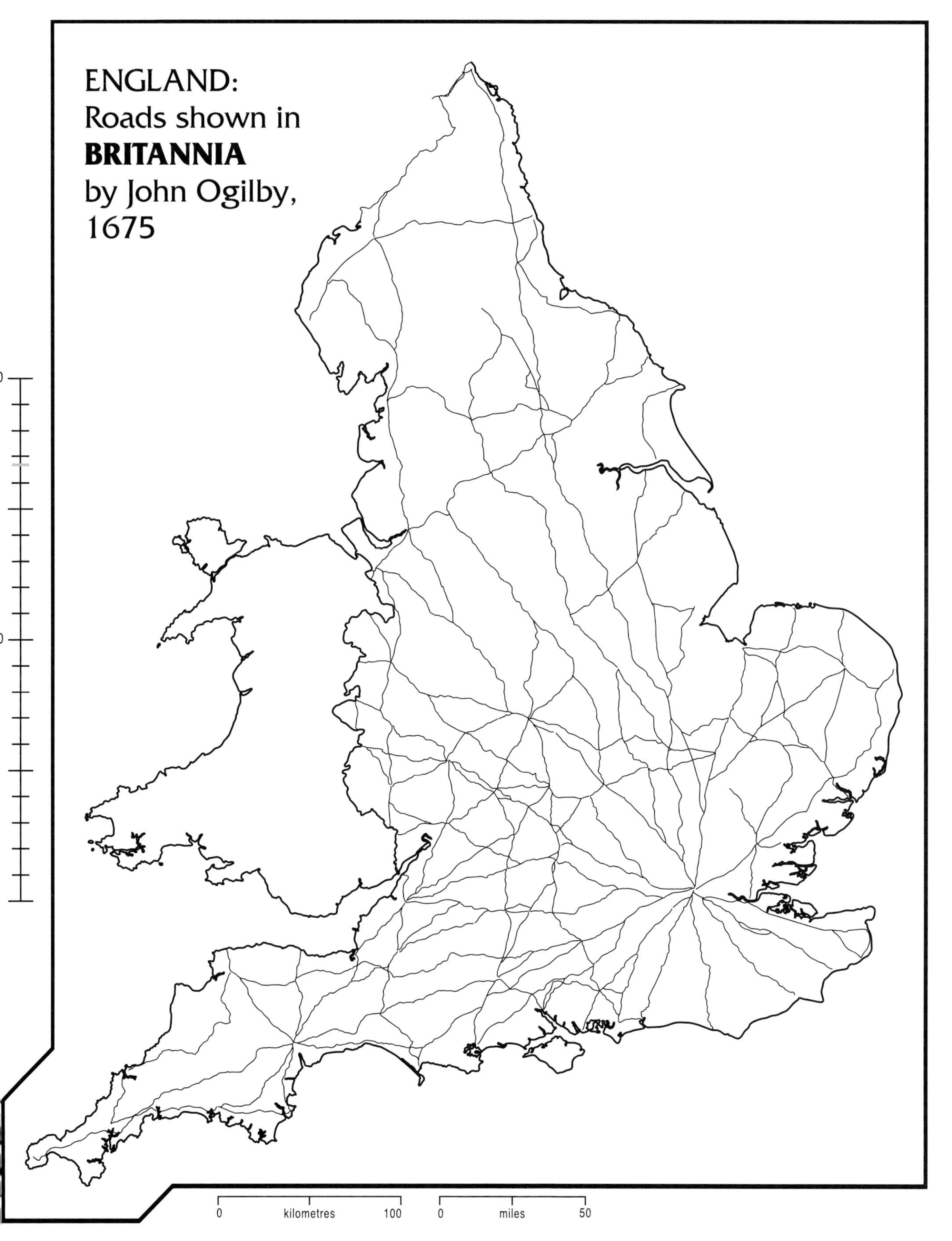

Figure 3 The road pattern recorded in John Ogilby's road book of 1675

be found amid the detail of the modern quarter inch to the mile maps, characteristically experienced as road atlases. To this network must be added the footpaths and bridleways, derived from large-scale maps, to create an aggregate network. If this can be assembled on a sufficiently large scale, and computers now allow this, then visible regional variations allow some deductions about the origins of the varied networks and their places within local regional cultures.

Ogilby's routes of 1675 are more complete and more rational, being drawn *'by Registring and Illustrating Your Majesty's High-Ways, Directly and Transversely, as from Shore to Shore, so to the Prescrib'd Limits of the Circumabient Ocean, from this Great Emporiam and Prime Centre of the Kingdom, Your Royal Metropolis'* (Fig. 3). The London-Puckeridge-Royston-Huntingon-Stamford-Grantham route is described, but by this date the traveller is told whether it is enclosed or unenclosed, and the bridges are – at least faintly – indicated, or 'imply'd where the Rivers or Brooks are not drawn through the Road' (Ogilby route 5). This time, however, routes only hinted at in 1360 are fully described. Thus, from Stilton an unenclosed road runs via Yaxley to Peterborough (Ogilby routes 41/36), past the gallows, windmills and a grove of willows to Paston, *Widrington* (Werrington) and Glinton, and thence to Peakirk, then along the Welland to Crowland and Cowbit, to cross the 'Witham' (*sic*) at Spalding. From there, now largely enclosed, the route passes through Pinchbeck, Surfleet with its wooden bridge, to Gosberton and Sutterton, again with a wooden bridge, to *Strugshil* (Struggs Hill) and Kirton, both with brick bridges, to reach Boston with its gibbet and stone bridge. The route is lined with windmills, while church spires and towers, both upon and adjacent to the route, with named isolated dwellings (*Dunber* and *Clout House*) provide guidance. Between Peakirk and Spalding the embankment bordering the river must have given a welcome sense of direction along this unenclosed stretch. A further route northwards from Peterborough (Ogilby route 41) takes the traveller via Peakirk, through Market Deeping to Bourne and Sleaford, and thence to Lincoln, mostly through unenclosed arable cornfields, but ending with a dozen miles of unenclosed heath.

Ely has, by 1675, emerged as a local node for the southern fenlands. A road from Puckeridge (Ogilby route 43) strikes boldly somewhat east of north, via Barkway and Cambridge, to Downham Market and King's Lynn. From Cambridge the way heads for Milton, by-passing Waterbeach with its windmills, to find the course of Akeman Street – 'Enter a lane & Enclosure on each side' to pass Denny Abbey, shown on the left but actually on the right hand side. The lane ends, but the road goes on, though 'fenny ground', 'pasture' and 'fenny grounds on each side', via the ferry across the Ouse or Old West river to Stretham, with its windmills, arable cornfields and some scattered woodlands to Ely. Fens now open ahead. From Chetisham the road winds to Littleport though 'fenny ground' with wood and meadows, to find that 'High bank or causey' running parallel to the Great River Ouse to Southery across the 'great Level of ye Fens'. Southery must be approached via a ferry across the Little Ouse, while a ferry may also be taken to Downham Market from this point. North of Southery an enclosed road, described as an 'open way' leads to Hilgay, with a bridge of wood across the river Wissey. To this is added the enigmatic note 'Helgaye River, 20 foot Riuv. Cut (*sic*)', but here the engraver was tired, or his exemplar was unclear, for Forham has become *Hardham*, while 'bridge' has become *bride*. A common, with a gate, finally brings the traveller to Denver and Downham Market itself.

A second route (Ogilby route 73) begins at Huntingdon, proceeds via the Hemingfords to the stone bridge over the Ouse at St Ives, thence via largely unenclosed roads to Erith. Beyond Erith the 'River Running to Lyn' is crossed, two watercourses associated with new drainage works, and *Critch Causeway* is followed to Sutton across the 'fenny ground' of South Fen. The unenclosed route to Ely through Wentworth and Witchford passes 'open arable or corn laines'. Leaving Ely, and crossing the Ouse by a drawbridge, the route zigzags though Stuntney by means of an enclosed lane, and then strikes across the open fen to Soham. The traveller learns that if at first there is 'fenny ground on both sides and the way bad and dirty' the entry to Soham comprises 'a very dirty way'! Nevertheless, Fordham Bridge on the county boundary sits amid countrysides of 'Great Corn Laines or open Arrable'. Throughout, windmills and church towers provide welcome reference points away from the road. Eventually rising land gives 'sheep downs for many miles'.

This is, of course, a different Fenland to that of the medieval period. During the seventeenth century the Duke of Bedford's capital was allied to the practical skills of Dutch engineers, and straight cuts to increase outfall were linked to a network of subsidiary drainage ditches and new large rectangular fields. However, although initially successful, the ventures were swamped by problems between 1650 and 1700 as the peat shrank and wasted and the dangers of flooding of the reclaimed lands increased. Windmills became increasingly common, and during the late seventeenth and eighteenth centuries gave increasing character to the fen landscapes. By the eighteenth century however, windmills were proving increasingly ineffective, and it was not until the advent of the steam engine that efficient, if destructive, drainage was ensured.

This discussion is necessarily incomplete. The mixture of generalisation and detail it contains has the objective of drawing attention to three things: first the extent to which the existence of the fenlands has affected the communication patterns of eastern England, causing bifurcations north of London and inhibiting cross-routes. It needs little knowledge of the visions of Saint Guthlac (Darby 1940, 8-9) or the medieval isolation of Ely beyond its causeways (Darby 1940, 106-114) to see from the three maps that the route patterns of the later seventeenth century represent a significant breakdown of isolation following the initiation of large-scale drainage ventures. Second, the national map of early woodland created by the author for English Heritage allows the distinctive terrains of the Fens to be placed in a broader context. The lands around their rim were far from homogeneous. Third, the question of the emergence of both national and local communication networks is one demanding further attention. While the contribution of the Roman engineers was undoubtedly important, establishing a skeleton, post-Roman contributions were of enormous importance in redefining, amplifying and extending antecedent patterns.

Bibliography

Bodleian Map of Great Britain (The Gough Map): Ordnance Survey Facsimile of the Bodleian Library's medieval map, prepared in 1870, published in 1935 and reprinted in 1959: now out of print

Darby, H.C., 1936, reprinted 1951, *An Historical geography of England before A.D. 1800* (Cambridge University Press)

Darby, H.C., 1940, reprint 1974, *The Medieval Fenland* (Newton Abbot, David and Charles)

Darby, H.C. *et al.* (ed), 1952, The Domesday Geography of England (7 volumes, Cambridge University Press 1952-77): Eastern England (1952); Midland England (1954); South-East England (1962); Northern England (1962); South-West England (1967); Gazetteer (1975); Domesday England (1977)

Delano-Smith, C. and Kain, R., 1999, *English Maps: a History* (London, The British Library)

Dornier, A. (ed), 1977, *Mercian Studies* (Leicester University Press)

Ekwall, E., 1960, reprinted 1970, *The Concise Oxford Dictionary of English Place-Names* (Oxford, The Clarendon Press)

Fellows Jensen, G., 1978, *Scandinavian Settlement Names in the East Midlands* (Copenhagen, Akademisk Forlag)

Frere, S., 1998, *Britannia* (London, Pimlico)

Hall, D. and Coles, J., 1994, *Fenland Survey: an Essay in Landscape and Persistence*, English Heritage Archaeological Report 1 (London)

Harvey, P.D.A., 1991, *Medieval Maps* (London, The British Library).

Margary, I.D.,1973, *Roman Roads in Britain* (London, John Baker)

Ogilby, J., 1675, reprint 1939, *Britannia, Volume the First.. or an Illustration of the Kingdom of ENGLAND and Dominion of Wales* (reprinted by A.Duckham and Co. Ltd. London)

Ordnance Survey, 1930, *A Map of XVII Century England* (Southampton, Ordnance Survey Office)

Ordnance Survey, 1992, *The Ordnance Survey Gazetteer of Great Britain* (London, The Macmillan Press Ltd)

Rackham, O., 1986, *The History of the Countryside* (London, J.M. Dent and Sons Ltd)

Rivet, A.L.F. and Smith, C., 1979, *The Place-Names of Roman Britain* (London, B.T. Batsford Ltd)

Roberts, B.K. and Wrathmell, S., 2000, *An Atlas of English Rural Settlement* (London, English Heritage)

Sawyer, P., 1976, *Medieval Settlement: Continuity and Change* (London, Edward Arnold)

Smith, A.H., 1956, *English Place-Name Elements,* English Place-Name Society vols. xxv, xxvi (Cambridge University Press)

Stafford, P., 1985, *The East Midlands in the Early Middle Ages* (Leicester University Press)

8. FLAT, FLATTER, FLATTEST – THE ENGLISH HERITAGE WETLAND SURVEYS IN RETROSPECT

by Robert Van de Noort

Abstract

Since 1973, English Heritage has supported four major regional surveys of England's wetlands – in the Somerset Levels, the Fens of Eastern England, the wetlands of the northwest of England and the Humber wetlands. Each of these projects developed a range of methods and techniques particular to the landscape that was studied and the results from the surveys reflect this diversity of approach. This paper compares and contrast these approaches, and evaluates their effect on the overall results of each of these surveys.

Introduction

> The story has been told by John Coles on many an occasion how David Hall introduced students from Cambridge to the Fenlands. From a distance, David pointed at the 'hills', sometimes not more than a few inches high, where archaeological finds were likely to be found. And on arrival, the 'hill' produced Mesolithic flint or Roman pottery, to the amazement and awe of the students.

The little anecdote of David Hall and the 'hills' of the Fenland serves to illustrate two important aspects of archaeological surveys of wetlands in general.

First, that the waterlain sediments that characterise wetlands are flat and that any undulations, or 'hills', represent either a landscape that predates the wetlands but protrudes through the waterlain sediments, or exists as a consequence of human action and may be a prehistoric barrow, a Roman period mound of briquetage or the result of more recent drainage work. Wetland surveys are limited by the burial of landscapes by younger peat, riverine or marine sedimentation. Many archaeological sites remain, therefore, undiscovered, until peat extraction, erosion or excavation removes this natural overburden.

Second, that the array of methods and techniques available to identify archaeological sites and finds is limited and that the extent to which any technique is successful depends on the thickness of the overburden. David Hall fieldwalked whole landscapes and discovered many sites (Hall 1992), many of these on the 'hills' within the wetlands. Aerial photography has proved highly successful in areas where little or no overburden was present (Hall and Coles 1994). However, the applicability of fieldwalking and aerial photography in wetlands varies with the thickness of the overburden and other survey techniques, including geophysical surveys (David 1995), have limited application only.

The title of this paper, 'flat, flatter, flattest', is the imaginative boasting of one wetland archaeologist to another. The flatter the wetland landscape, the more difficult the discovery of archaeological sites becomes, and the archaeologist working in the flattest landscape is faced with the greatest challenge. A 'hill' within wetlands or on the wetland margin, regardless of height, is more likely to produce archaeological remains than the flat land surrounding it – a paradox recognised by all wetlanders. In the same spirit, Francis Pryor has repeated (again on many an occasion) the tale told to Harry Godwin by a Fenlander that 'any fool can appreciate a hill', but that it takes a more sophisticated mind to appreciate flatness.

This paper is not intended to decide which of the large wetlands in England is the flattest. Rather, it will explore the methods and techniques used during the four wetland surveys commissioned by English Heritage – in the Somerset Levels, the Fenland of eastern England, the peatlands in the northwest of England and the Humber wetlands (Fig. 1). The aim of this paper is to compare and contrast the different methods and techniques of these surveys, and to assess how the overall results of each of the surveys were affected by the chosen approaches.

The Wetland Surveys

English Heritage and its predecessor within the Department of the Environment have been closely involved with wetland archaeology since 1973. Its support for the archaeological research in the Somerset Levels was followed by the survey of the

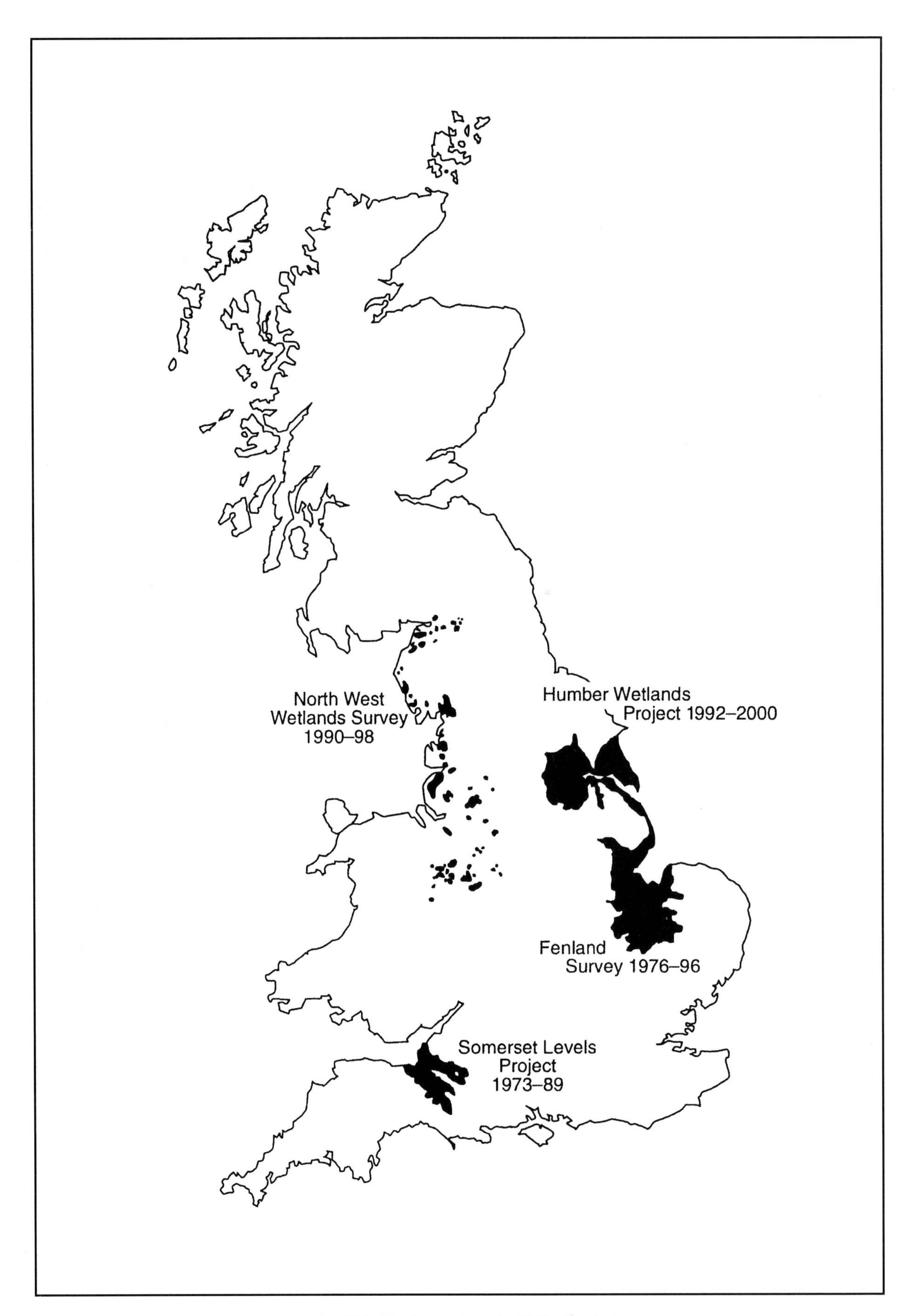

Figure 1 English Heritage-funded Wetlands Projects

Fenland in eastern England, the wetlands of the northwest of England and most recently by the survey of the wetlands in the Humber lowlands in northeast England. Together, these surveys constitute a programme of research that in terms of scale has few parallels in Europe. They also constitute a national strategy towards wetlands, matched by few archaeological research programmes in England or beyond.

The surveys have a number of common features. All four surveys were commissioned by Geoffrey Wainwright, formerly English Heritage's Chief Archaeologist, and Professor John Coles was closely involved in the running or management of the surveys. The wetland surveys also have a common rationale. This is based on the high preservation potential of waterlogged sites in wetlands combined with extensive threats to the wetlands and the archaeological remains contained within them – peat extraction, drainage and desiccation, the intensification of agriculture and urban and industrial development being the most prominent (Coles 1995). The publication record of the surveys is also remarkable, with the overwhelming majority of discoveries published – as articles in twelve volumes of the Somerset Levels Papers, in eleven monographs from the Fenland Project, six (to date) county-based monographs of the North West Wetlands Survey and seven monographs of the Humber Wetlands Project.

Nevertheless, each of the wetland surveys was distinctive in terms of organisation, management and the methods and techniques used to find sites, and the extend of exploration of the sites identified.

The Somerset Levels Project (1973-1988) was the first of the four wetlands surveys. It developed from strong concern about the physical destruction of archaeological sites through peat extraction. Peat extraction on the Somerset Levels was centred on the river Brue valley to the north of the Polden Hills, and in the decades of the Somerset Levels Project, it was mainly concentrated in the area to the south of the 'islands' of Westhay, Meare and Burtle. The most famous sites from the Somerset Levels – the Sweet Track, the Abbot's Way, Walton Heath Track, the Meare Heath track – are all from this area. The 'lake settlements' of Meare (East and West) and Glastonbury lie outside this area of peat extraction, but these sites had been discovered by Arthur Bulleid at the end of the nineteenth century (*e.g.* Coles and Coles 1986).

The Somerset Levels Project was essentially concerned with rescue archaeology. The peat extraction produced many more sites and opportunities for research than the project could handle. Therefore, all the sites identified and investigated were 'proper' wetland sites, that is sites that had been preserved within the anoxic, waterlogged matrix that also preserved the palaeoenvironmental context of the archaeological remains. The Project is recognised for its pioneering role of integrating archaeological objectives with palaeoenvironmental techniques to a level rarely seen at that point, especially the archaeological use of entomological and dendrochronological methods (*e.g.* Girling 1976, Morgan 1976).

Apart from the close integration of archaeological and palaeoenvironmental techniques, the methodology employed by the Somerset Levels Project was based around the peat extraction. Repeated walking of areas of surface peat milling and repeated survey of the cut faces of the peat formed the main method. The repetition formed an essential aspect of the methodology, as the continuous peat growth in prehistory could completely bury archaeological sites, leaving no clues on the modern surface until the removal of peat made identification possible (Coles 1975). In addition, the peat extractors themselves were increasingly used as sources of information; their number and everyday presence on the level greatly increased the chance of (early) discovery of sites. The rescue nature of the Project made excavation of the sites necessary, before their otherwise inevitable destruction. Few other methods and techniques were applicable for the research on the Levels and fieldwalking of arable or pasture fields, aerial photography, geophysical survey and the analysis of historical data were not developed.

The seasonal nature of much of the work resulted in the employment of large numbers of people on the Project. This is not only true for the field officers who walked the ditches and fields, as can be noted from the changing lists of field officers in each of the *Somerset Levels Papers*, but also for the excavators, who would join the project for several weeks at a time. As a consequence, the Somerset Levels Project is known by many in the archaeological profession.

To return to the title of this paper, the Somerset Levels was the flattest landscape among the English wetlands. The intrusive and destructive peat cutting provided the opportunities to develop methods for the identification of archaeological sites beneath and within the peat. Nearly all prehistoric sites were identified as a consequence

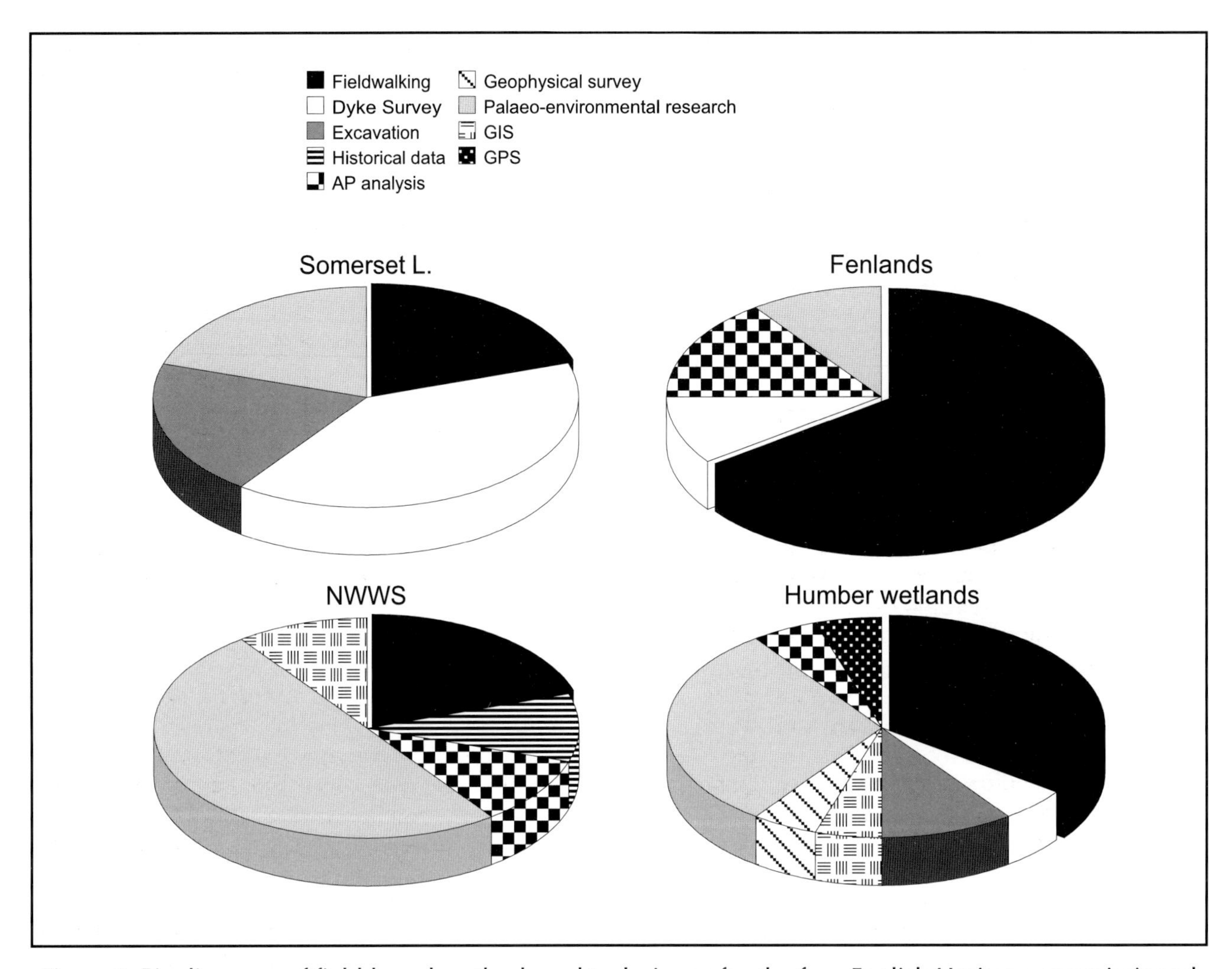

Figure 2 Pie diagrams of field-based methods and techniques for the four English Heritage commissioned wetland surveys – estimates, rounded to the nearest 5%

of peat cutting, either by the Project or the peat cutters themselves. The main exceptions to this are the 'lake settlements' of Meare and Glastonbury. The latter was discovered by Arthur Bulleid in the late nineteenth century, who noted the (not so flat) undulations in a field (Bulleid 1894, Coles and Minnitt 1995). These undulations existed as a consequence of differential desiccation of the organic and minerogenic sediments, the latter representing the clay brought in from outside the levels to form the house platforms. The Meare lake villages were discovered when a ditch was dug through one of the villages, and the finds were brought into Glastonbury Museum where they were recognised as dating to the Iron Age. The effects of continuing drainage have enhanced the effects of differential desiccation, and many of the unexcavated platforms can now be recognised in the micro-topography (Chapman and Van de Noort 2001).

The Fenland Project (1982-1988) was the second wetland survey in England, and it continued the work of the Fenland Research Committee (1932-1940). At the time of the appointment of David Hall as the Fenland Field Officer in 1976, little systematic archaeological research had been undertaken since 1940. Unlike the Somerset Levels, the main threat to the archaeological resource was not (or no longer) peat extraction, but the rapid desiccation of peat, erosion and the conversion of pasture land to arable land, bringing many archaeological sites within reach of ploughing activity (Hall and Coles 1994). These threats affected the whole of the Fens, and in particular the Fenland edge in Norfolk, Suffolk, Cambridgeshire and Lincolnshire.

The aims of the Fenland Survey, that ran from 1982 to 1988, were to be most ambitious and in line with the threats identified – to survey 420,000 ha through fieldwalking. At the close of the project, nearly 240,000 ha (or 60%) had been fieldwalked, with impressive results – over 2500 sites had been discovered by the Field Officers, who included Bob Silvester, Tom Lane and Peter Hayes in addition to David Hall. The sites range in date from the Mesolithic to the Medieval period (Hall and Coles 1994, 10). The survey was based on parishes, and fields were walked systematically according to their nature and condition, first set out by David Hall (1992) and shown in the 'Fieldwalking Intensity maps'.

The majority of sites identified were not waterlogged sites, although some included waterlogged components (Coles and Hall 1997). Past people's presence in the Fenland, essentially a lowland basin that had become gradually wetland as a result of sea-level change (*cf.* Shennan 1982), had through time been focused on the Fenland edge and on the 'islands' within the basin. From here, both the wetlands and the drylands could be exploited, a practice that has been described in greatest detail for the Fengate landscape (*e.g.* Pryor 1991). Additional human activity was encountered on the 'roddons', the minerogenic sediments making up the levees of tidal rivers and creeks. The majority of archaeological sites, therefore, were dry sites, that were covered and protected by peat growth or marine silts. The many small-scale excavations in the Wissey embankment undertaken prior to the survey illustrate this point most clearly – most finds came from within the peat, but rested directly on top of the pre-Holocene surface (Healy 1996).

Apart from fieldwalking, the Fenland Project developed several other methods. Most notably dyke survey; that is the examination of recently cleaned ditch faces that offered a third dimension to the survey and resulted in the discovery of the Flag Fen site and many other sites (Pryor 1991; French and Pryor 1993). The contribution of aerial photography cannot be understated. The large collection of the Cambridge University Committee for Aerial Photography, enhanced by targeted work by Rog Palmer and Chris Cox, not only allowed for the old rivers and creek systems to be recorded on maps, but also contributed significantly to the identification of archaeological sites and landscapes. The contribution of aerial photography to the project was determined environmentally by the advanced drainage and intensive agriculture of the Fens, allowing for soil marks to be readily noted from the air. The Fenland Project did not include excavations as a technique of recording – this was to be reserved for the Fenland Management Project.

Palaeoenvironmental research was undertaken by a fifth Field Officer, Martyn Waller, whose remit was to investigate the Holocene natural history on a Fenland-wide basis (Waller 1994). His task was enormous, despite the earlier work of the Fenland Research Committee, and the integration of archaeological with palaeoenvironmental research on the ground could not be achieved.

In terms of flatness then, the Fenlands are often perceived as a 'flat unpromising wilderness' (Hall and Coles 1994, 1). However, it was not the flatlands where the majority of archaeological remains were found, but the low 'hills' seen from a distance by David Hall, on the Fen edge or on the roddons.

The North West Wetlands Survey (1988-1997) was the third of the large-scale wetland surveys. The North West Wetlands Survey (NWWS) focused on the 37,000 ha of lowland peat in the counties of Cumbria, Lancashire, Greater Manchester, Merseyside, Cheshire, Staffordshire and Shropshire (Middleton and Wells 1990). The threats to the wetlands of northwest England included peat extraction, drainage and desiccation and the conversion of pasture land into arable (*e.g.* Leah *et al.* 1998). Nevertheless, throughout the area much pasture remains. In the areas of Greater Manchester and Merseyside, waste disposal, urbanisation and industrial development must also be recognised as significant threats to the wetlands. The Field Officer for Greater Manchester, David Hall, must have experienced this as a culture shock (Hall *et al.* 1995). The project was largely based at the Lancaster University Archaeology Unit with additional support, and unlike the Fenland projects, the NWWS integrated archaeologists and palaeoecologists in a single team. The NWWS was also the first wetland survey that worked within English Heritage (1991) management framework 'MAP2', although this was produced during, rather than prior to, the survey (LUAU 1993).

Fieldwalking was the main method employed for the identification of archaeological sites. In view of the relatively small acreage of wetland to be covered (*i.e.* less than 10% of the acreage of the Fens), and of the anticipated low artefact densities in northwest England, the peatland fringes were systematically fieldwalked at 10 m interval. This was at a higher density than employed in the Fenland, where systematic fieldwalking was conducted at a 30 m interval. Only areas of deep peat in the northwest and west midlands were walked at this resolution. Although a final synthesis has yet to be produced, it seems fair to suggest that the number of sites, and the quantity of finds, does not

	Somerset Levels Project	Fenland Project	NWWS	Humber Wetlands Project
Fieldwalking	20	65	20	35
Dyke survey	40	10	0	5
Excavation	20	0	0	10
Historical data	0	0	10	0
AP analysis	0	15	10	5
Geophysical survey	0	0	0	5
Palaeoenvironmental research	20	10	50	30
GIS	0	0	10	5
GPS	0	0	0	5

Table 1 Percentage of field-based methods and techniques for the four English Heritage commissioned wetland surveys – estimates, rounded to the nearest 5%.

match those from the Somerset Levels or the Fenland. I hasten to add that this is primarily a reflection of the distribution of past activity, rather than methodology.

Few other methods for the identification of archaeological sites were employed by the survey. Dyke survey was not a feasible systematic method of research, as large scale dyke-cleaning was not undertaken in the northwest. No excavations were undertaken as part of the survey. Aerial photography and remote sensing work was commissioned for the identification of peatlands, rather than for the identification of archaeological sites. Similarly, the often extensive documentary studies that accompanied the county-based surveys produced most valuable information on the location and extent of former and present wetlands, but less so on archaeology. As in any generalised statement, important exceptions exist (e.g. Stebbing Shaw's late eighteenth century discovery of Roman remains at Pipehill in Staffordshire [Leah *et al.* 1998, 115-7]).

The role of palaeoecology within the NWWS deserves additional attention. Palaeoecology, and in particular palynology and plant macrofossil analysis combined with high-resolution radiocarbon dating was used extensively during the project. Its role has been portrayed as an 'archaeological survey tool in its own right'. The (palaeo-)environmental archives contained within the peatlands were considered as 'sites' and their state of preservation and any light they might shed on past people's activity, either within or outside the wetlands, were assessed as part of the survey.

The NWWS was the first major survey in England to develop a Geographic Information System (GIS) as an integrated part of its work (Middleton and Wells 1990). The GIS functioned as a basis for the project's archive and as a tool that enabled data manipulation and rapid publication of the results. The use of a GIS is also indicative of the increasing role of archaeology in the planning process, following the publication of Planning Policy Guidance 16 (PPG16), Archaeology and Planning (Department of the Environment 1990). Within the planning system, it is crucial that data on sites and finds can be rapidly transferred to Sites and Monuments Record offices, where they will form the basis for future planning decisions.

How about the flatness of the northwest wetlands then? Overall, the retrieval of archaeological sites and finds from the wetland edge or the land surrounding the mires was good, but few finds were made from the peatlands themselves, and no new waterlogged sites such as trackways were discovered during the survey. The peatlands may be flat, but the archaeological survey relied on the surrounding hills and undulating land for the identification of archaeological remains.

The Humber Wetlands Project (1992-2001) was the final regional wetland survey commissioned by English Heritage. The Humber wetlands, a lowland basin in the Humber catchment in Yorkshire, Lincolnshire and Nottinghamshire, comprise some 330,000 ha. These represent, overwhelmingly, a landscape that became paludified and was silted up as a consequence of Holocene sea-level change, similar to the development of the Fens. Following a desktop assessment that established the need for such a survey (Van de Noort and Davies 1993),

English Heritage commissioned the survey in 1994. The survey was undertaken by a team of archaeologists and palaeoenvironmentalists, based at the University of Hull.

The aim of the Humber Wetlands Project was the systematic but selective survey of the area in six years. Each year was dedicated to the survey, analysis and publication of one physiographic region within the Humber wetlands. The surveys were undertaken within 'mapviews', areas measuring 5 x 4 km that were centred on wetlands, and within these mapviews, the different techniques employed by the Project were as closely integrated as possible (*e.g.* Van de Noort and Etté 1995).

The methods and techniques employed by the Humber Wetlands Project were by design multifaceted, and included on the archaeological side fieldwalking along the system developed in the survey of the Fenland, dyke survey whenever possible, systematic analysis of aerial photographs in archives, the selective deployment of English Heritage's geophysical survey team and small-scale excavations. The methods and techniques addressing the palaeoenvironmental aspect of the work included extensive coring programmes for lithostratigraphic analysis, and pollen analysis linked to selective but high-resolution radiocarbon dating programmes. Obviously, such a multifaceted approach reduced the actual acreage researched considerably.

The role of excavation of selected sites was recognised as an important tool, not only to enhance our understanding of the state of preservation of waterlogged archaeological sites and to raise the profile of the project, but specifically to link the finds from the surface found during fieldwalking to actual sites. Several excavations showed that the surface finds were all that was left of the archaeological resource, but on other occasions, important sites were discovered, for example two Roman roads with the foundations of their bridges across the river Idle at Scaftworth, on the Nottinghamshire-South Yorkshire border (Van de Noort *et al.* 1997).

The use of geophysical survey, both magnetometry and resistivity, was successful on the sandy 'islands' within the wetlands, but more notably on Roman period sites sealed within the alluvium as well. The mapping of the very extensive riverside-settlement at Trent Falls, at the confluence of the rivers Trent, Don and Ouse, showed the potential of this survey technique for wetlands (Fenwick *et al.* 1998). However, the identification of features was dependent on the presence of 'industrial' waste, dumped in the ditches. The application of this technique on prehistoric sites was, in general, less successful.

The Humber Wetlands Project followed the NWWS in the early adoption of GIS. Its application was extended into the field, with palmtop computers available for data input. The Humber Wetlands project was the first survey to apply differential Geographic Positioning Systems (dGPS), which provides a new method to analyse the micro-topography that may reflect wetland sites through the process of differential desiccation (Chapman and Van de Noort 2001).

The dGPS was also used extensively in the Humber estuary and the coast. The part-erosive nature of the tides offered unparalleled opportunities for the discovery and excavation of many archaeological sites, many of these being waterlogged in nature (Fletcher *et al.* 1999).

In all the Humber Wetlands Project identified over 400 archaeological sites, including 40 waterlogged sites, and many more finds and 'find scatters'. The majority of these were found on the hills and islands within the wetlands, but a significant proportion was found on the flat wetlands through the stubborn application of a system by the project's Field Officers.

Discussion

In the presentation of the methodological frameworks of the four large-scale wetland surveys commissioned by English Heritage, I have attempted to show the main characteristics of each of these projects. Without intensive analysis of costs, timetables and work sheets, it is not practicable to determine which strategy was the most effective and efficient. Such an assessment would have to include many other parameters, such as the natural history of each of the areas, the landuse, infrastructure and many other in a broader socio-economic context, ranging from rates of pay and changes in employment law to health and safety considerations.

Without the resources or time available to undertake such an exhaustive analysis, I have, therefore, estimated the percentage of time expended on the different activities by the four survey projects. The results are presented in Table 1. All percentages are rounded to the nearest (estimated) 5%, and some of the techniques used only occasionally have, therefore, not been recorded. The same information is presented in Figure 2 which gives four 'pie diagrams' showing the methodological components of the four wetland surveys. Several points of interest can be observed.

First of all, the methodology of the four wetland surveys varied greatly, and while these surveys may form a national strategy of wetland research, the characteristics of each of the wetlands, including their natural history and landuse, demanded pragmatic solutions. Peat cutting in the Somerset Levels, and cleaned dykes in the Fenland provided the essential third dimension to the survey required for the discovery of buried sites. These opportunities did not exist in the northwest and only to a small extent in the Humber wetlands.

Second, we notice an increase in the number of techniques employed by the surveys over time. The Somerset Levels Project and the Fenland Project employed four basic methods of research, the NWWS five and the Humber Wetlands Project eight methods. This reflects developments in the archaeological world in general, with a demand for an ever increasing number of specialists and specialist techniques and more multidisciplinary research. It also reflects, I believe, an increasingly critical approach to the inherent biases and difficulties in wetland surveys, with a greater emphasis on the integrity of the data rather than on the area of land covered.

Third, the wetland surveys have a number of common methodological characteristics. Most important is the integration of archaeological with palaeoenvironmental specialists within the projects, although the degree of integration varied between the different surveys. Another, but rather obvious commonality is the need for a third dimension to be added to the fieldwork in wetlands, either in the form of visiting peat cuttings, examining cleaned dykes, coring or excavation.

Finally, the first and last surveys, in the Somerset Levels and the Humber wetlands, included excavation within the survey methodology. Apart from its significant contribution to the survey itself, the function of excavation in increasing public appreciation of a particular wetland survey or wetland archaeology in general must be emphasised.

Conclusions

The four large-scale wetland surveys commissioned by English Heritage constitute a body of research that in terms of scale has few parallels in Europe. However, in order to appreciate fully the value of each of the constituents of this body of research, the methodologies must be appreciated. In this paper, I have argued that the methods and techniques applied by each of the surveys varied from its immediate predecessor. This should be seen as progress against a background of changes in landuse, archaeological practices and the development of more sophisticated techniques (such as geophysics, GIS and dGPS). The role David Hall played in this process is indisputable.

Bibliography

Bulleid, A., 1894, 'British village at Glastonbury', *Proceedings of the Somerset Archaeological and Natural History Society* 40, 141-51

Chapman, H.P. and Van de Noort, R., 2001, 'High resolution wetland prospection, using GPS and GIS: landscape studies at Sutton Common (South Yorkshire) and Meare Village East (Somerset)', *Journal of Archaeological Science* 28, 365-375

Coles, B., 1995, *Wetland heritage. A survey for English Heritage* (London, English Heritage and Exeter, WARP)

Coles, B.and Coles, J., 1986, *Sweet track to Glastonbury* (London, Thames and Hudson)

Coles, J.,1975, 'Archaeology in the Somerset Levels', *Somerset Levels Papers* 1, 5-8

Coles, J. and Hall, D., 1997, 'The Fenland Project: from survey to management and beyond', *Antiquity* 71, 831-44

Coles, J. and Minnitt, S., 1995, *'Industrious and fairly civilized'. The Glastonbury Lake Village* (Exeter, Somerset Levels Project)

David, A., 1995, *Geophysical survey in archaeological field evaluation* (London, English Heritage)

Department of the Environment, 1990, *Planning Policy Guidance No 16, Archaeology and Planning* (London, Department of the Environment)

English Heritage, 1991, *Management of Archaeological Projects (2nd edition)* (London, English Heritage)

Fenwick, H., Chapman, C., Hiad, R. and Lillie, L., 1999, 'The Archaeological Survey of the Lower Trent Valley and the Winterton Beck', in Van de Noort, R. and Ellis, S. (ed), *Wetland Heritage of the Ancholme and Lower Trent Valleys* (Hull, Humber Wetland Project, University of Hull), 195-97

Fletcher, W., Chapman, H., Head, R., Fenwick, H., Van de Noort, R., and Lillie, M., 1999, 'The archaeological survey of the Humber estuary' in Van de Noort R. and Ellis, S. (ed), *Wetland Heritage of the Vale of York; an archaeological survey* (Hull, Humber Wetlands Project, University of Hull), 205-41

French, C.A.I. and Pryor, F., 1993, *The South-West Fen Dyke Survey Project 1982-6*, East Anglian Archaeology 59

Girling, M.A., 1976, 'Fossil Coleoptera from the Somerset Levels: The Abbot's Way', *Somerset Levels Papers* 2, 28-33

Hall, D., 1992, *The Fenland Project, Number 6: The South-Western Cambridgeshire Fenlands,* East Anglian Archaeology 56

Hall, D. and Coles J., 1994, *Fenland Survey. An essay in landscape and persistence*, English Heritage Archaeological Report 1 (London)

Hall, D., Wells C. and Huckerby, E., 1995, *The wetlands of Greater Manchester,* North West Wetlands Survey 2 (Lancaster)

Healy, F., 1996, *The Fenland Project, Number 11: The Wissey Embayment: Evidence for pre-Iron Age occupation accumulated prior to the Fenland Project*, East Anglian Archaeology 78

Leah, M.D., Wells, C.E., Stamper, P., Huckerby, E. and Welch, C., 1998, *The wetlands of Shropshire and Staffordshire*, North West Wetlands Survey 5 (Lancaster)

LUAU 1993, *North West Wetlands Survey, project design* (unpublished)

Middleton, R. and Wells C., 1990, 'Research design for an archaeological survey of the wetlands of north-west England', in: *NWWS Annual Report 1990* 1-6

Morgan, R.A., 1976, 'Dendrochronological analysis of the Abbot's Way timbers', *Somerset Levels Papers* 2, 21-4

Pryor, F., 1991, *Flag Fen: prehistoric Fenland centre* (London, Batsford)

Shennan, I., 1982, 'Interpretation of Flandrian sea-level data from the Fenland, England', *Proceedings of the Geological Association* 83, 53-63

Van de Noort, R. and Etté J., 1995, 'The Humber Wetlands Survey: background, objectives and methodology' in Van de Noort, R. and Ellis, S. (ed), *Wetland Heritage of Holderness; an archaeological survey*, 1-7 (Hull, Humber Wetlands Project, University of Hull)

Van de Noort, R. and Davies, P., 1993, *Wetland Heritage; an archaeological assessment of the Humber wetlands* (Hull, Humber Wetlands Project, University of Hull)

Van de Noort, R., Lillie, M., Taylor, D. and Kirby, J., 1997, 'The Roman period landscape at Scaftworth' in Van de Noort, R. and Ellis, S. (ed), *Wetland Heritage of the Humberhead levels; an archaeological survey*: 409-28 (Hull, Humber Wetlands Project, University of Hull)

Waller, M., 1994, *The Fenland Project, Number 9. Flandrian environmental change in Fenland*, East Anglian Archaeology 70

9. CONVERSATIONS AROUND ARCHAEOLOGY AND COLOUR SCIENCE

by John Hutchings

Thirty six years, where have they gone? For thirty-six years David and I have met on an aimed-for target of once per week. Not that we have actually realised the target – wives, growing families, work, the reader will have knowledge of the problems. We have mourned the passing of ridge and furrow and pubs – thirteen of the latter. Thirteen of our meeting places in North Bedfordshire and South Northamptonshire have passed away with at least three more on the brink of closure.

During this period, conversation has inevitably taken in the world, but two topics keep returning – archaeology and colour. Much of my professional work has occurred within the subject of colour – colour measurement science, colour in biological nature and colour in anthropology and folklore.

There is a substantial overlap of colour with archaeology in its broadest sense. A look at the list of papers presented at the day school jointly organised by the Institute of Archaeology and the Colour Group (GB) in 1993 illustrates this.

Steve Mithen -	colour and symbolism in prehistoric art.
Peter Mactaggart -	use of colour pigments in the past.
Evelyn Baker -	colour in medieval floor tiles from Warden Abbey.
Michael Heyworth -	colour in ancient glass.
Chris Cox -	colour perception in aerial photographic and satellite image interpretation.
Paul Craddock -	use of colour in copper alloys.
Jerry Sampson -	colour on the exterior of medieval churches.
and me -	application of colour measurement to archaeology.

This programme at least scratched the surface, but important topics were omitted. The purpose of this paper is threefold. First, to remind the archaeologist that since palaeolithic times colour has been part of our daily life as individuals; second, to show that colour science can assist in the understanding of archaeological science and is thus useful for uncovering the technology of the past; third, to suggest that investigation of the archaeologist's colour vision attributes, coupled with basic training in colour, will help in the performance and interpretation of many archaeological situations.

Colour in Everday Life

Colour and appearance are essential to the well being of living organisms, essential to the lowliest of insects, to plants, to animals and to mankind (Hutchings 1997a). The ability of the human species to see colour has probably been inherited from ancestors who needed to see and select food that was safe and wholesome to eat. In common with that of other animal species, our total appearance, that is our colour, colour patterning, design and behavioural display, has adapted to physical, geographical, climatological and sexual environments. However, we act not only as animal organisms. We are creative. Our capacity for belief and power to imagine, coupled with our understanding of materials, have enhanced our ability to create profound effects on our fellows and on the appearance of our environment. The inheritance of colour vision has been exploited and colour now forms a highly significant part of modern life. Cosmetics, clothing, household pets, food, decorations inside and outside the house, landscape and architecture are all deliberately coloured and patterned in attempts to satisfy personal tastes and apparent needs for colourful surroundings. Examples of this essential nature of colour and appearance are abundant in anthropology, folklore, and, of course, archaeology.

All major colours have parts to play, but those most commonly occurring are red, black and white (Turner 1967). The following examples of folklore are current, or at least are from within living memory. In many households today white flowers are 'funeral' flowers and therefore unlucky, the presence of red and white flowers in the same vase is also an ill omen. While Scottish customs involve dark-haired men at New Year, there are unflattering beliefs about redheads, and fair-haired women are unlucky. The sight of a white horse is believed by some to bring good luck, black cats bring either good or bad luck, depending where you were brought up, and milk from a red cow has healing properties.

As for cures, silver (white metal) water prepared using a silver ring or coin has healing properties for humans and animals. Fifteen years ago David told me of the old man in Wollaston who said that, while the workmen were at lunch, he had buried a silver sixpence in the wet cement at the bottom of a stone wall "because it was the thing to do". Then there were the silver coins found in wall plaster. David was relating Hutch's finding of a thus buried coin when the piece of Roman plaster, then being excavated, broke open to reveal a silver coin.

Not all that many years ago it was believed that epilepsy, warts and appendicitis could be alleviated, respectively, by the burial of a black cock under the bed, a soot and water mixture, and a black snail. A red coral necklace is worn to protect children from disease and red wool keeps rheumatism, smallpox or a sore throat at bay. Examples of the necklace can be found in many eighteenth and nineteenth century paintings.

There are many folklore references to salt, soot or coal, and the rowan tree, which has red berries. Perhaps these objects act as tangible symbols of their respective colours. For example, black food, such as the traditional Scottish black bun and black pudding, appear to reinforce the black or dark-haired-man tradition of Christmas and New Year. There it is good luck for the coming year that the first person entering the house on New Year's Eve should be a dark-haired man bearing something black such as a lump of coal. A rowan tree in the garden is said to keep witches away (Hutchings 1997b). More will be said about this colour triad of red, black and white later.

Colour in Anthropology and Folklore – and Archaeology

Colour has but two uses. It acts as a signal, informing and communicating, and it is used to make things look pretty. Signals used by humans are of two types. Some are dictated by statute, passed by our elected or self-imposed rulers; traffic light colours and flag designs are examples. Other signals, however, are dictated by the community or the family. Traditional colours of foods eaten at wedding celebrations or the colours of wedding dresses themselves, for example, are only traditional within the more limited environment of smaller groups, perhaps a tradition practised within a single family. If the tradition of the family and community is a fact of modern everyday life, then it must be a respectable subject for the archaeologist to observe and study. Merrifield (1987) has encouraged the archaeologist to consider that where functional utility and accident are not interpretations of a particular finding then it is possible that the explanation is one involving religious or magic ritual. To go one step further, the possibility of the humble social family custom may also be included.

We know that differences of practice have long existed within single communities. For example, in Mousterian sites 70,000 years BP ochre was used in some burials, in others it was not. This is evidence of differences in local, hierarchical or family custom. Another observation can be drawn from this example. The colour itself, although it forms an important part of our (and their) lives, it is the total appearance of the ritual that is important. This leads, at different periods, as well as ochre to the appearance of shells, animal bones, the occasional mirror, urn, weapon, or personal adornment.

We can assume nothing of the reasons behind the inclusion of grave goods, except that perhaps they were of sentimental value or attached in some way to the deceased, or to the performer of the ceremony. We can follow the anthropologist, who considers ochre to be symbolically related to blood and, therefore, needed to sustain life beyond the grave. This belief exists within numerous communities. For example, Wrenscher (1980) quotes the Maori legend of the woman who went to the nether world, found a bowl of ochre, ate the ochre, became strong, and was restored to life. In a similar way we can get an idea of the symbolic meanings of other artefacts such as shells.

Materials used in 'art' of the Upper Palaeolithic (10-30,000 BP), however, form part of the total appearance of the created scene. Attempting to put ourselves in the shoes of ancient man, when we see in the cave a painting of a bison, do we prostrate ourselves (because it is a holy image), or laugh (because we admire it as a cartoon sketch), or wonder at the dangers we face outside the cave (because it is used for training young people to survive in the real world); do we sit back and admire (because it is 'fine art'), or die of fright (because this is the sign of an enemy tribe). Such is the background to consider when thinking of how people respond to images.

Archaeology is about people, how they lived, what they believed. What do we know of the way people use colour today? Can knowledge of this help the archaeologist? Anthropologically, there are three colours that very commonly occur in traditional behaviour and belief. These are red, white and black, which occur as a triad throughout archaeology, anthropology and folklore. They are also important in language, in the sense that colour words are added to languages in a specific sequence. The first two words are black and white, the third, red (Berlin and Kay 1979). Examples from current, or near current, folklore are given above.

Colours and their 'Meanings'

Colours carry messages. They are used for identification, such as the delineation of ritual areas, and for symbolism. Colours used for making pictures and for decorating stone figures, bone carvings or live bodies may have to *mean* something, although this is not essential. However, colours used for symbolic purposes, such as for amulets and cures, do have to *mean* something. It seems reasonable that *meanings* must be important for us as human beings. It would hardly be worth the trouble otherwise.

To be effective colour applied as part of a painting, an artefact or to a human body must be visible. To be visible it must have a contrast colour against which it is easily observed. The larger the colour difference the more visible the signal. Such are the principles behind early heraldic and flag designs. The largest contrast available to us is that existing between black and white, between dark and light. Both colours are widely available, blackish colours from fire, whitish colours from clays. The choice of the third colour for purely aesthetic purposes rests on its suitability as an effective colour-contrasting component of the picture. That is, a colour that will contrast with other colours used and with the background. Colour choice lies not only in its availability, but also to the artist's preference and its necessity for the desired picture.

Like *black* and *white*, the word *red*, used to describe the third triad colour, is a nominal description. *Reds* are widely available from minerals, blood, burned earth, and vegetable sources. We might imagine a pillar-box red, but this is rarely found in an anthropological context. *Red* colours include paler and darker reds, browns, oranges and some yellows. This range occupies a large part of colour space, only greenish, bluish and purplish hues are excluded. Indeed, dark tones of these colours can appear black under certain circumstances.

Is the choice of *red* as the third triad colour linked to its wide availability or has it a special meaning? There is evidence that the choice is more than coincidental. Australian aborigines use red for body decoration. They travel hundreds of miles to fetch their red ochre from the bloodstained battlegrounds of their ancestors. Similarly, in the Upper Palaeolithic period in Poland, haematite has been found in hunting camps 400km from the mining site (Malinowski 1980). Great effort is involved in the supply of red pigment. Anthropologists have equated the *meanings* of the triad colours to be symbolic of human bodily fluids, *black* to excrement, *white* to milk and semen, and *red* to blood (Brain 1979).

This importance of colour to humans occurs throughout the world and throughout historical times. From ancient Babylon to modern Europe, there are very many examples in which colour forms an essential part of a protection or cure. For example, red forms an *essential* element of protection against the evil eye in Italy, while in Christian Greece the protection *must* be the Islamic blue. Similarly, there are many examples of monuments and buildings of different historical periods and civilisations in which the deliberate use of traditional colours and colour patterns are indicated.

Interpretation can be more complicated. Colours can have many *meanings* even within one culture, hence each colour must be studied within its context. For example, in the matrilineal cultures of Central Africa the colour red may symbolise many things. They include woman, man, in-laws, rainbow, morning, desire, birth, and so on, according to the situation and context in which they are used (Turner 1967). This is a learned process. It is the same learned process of which advertisers make good use when they train potential purchasers to associate a particular colour or emblem with their product – Heinz beans, Cadbury's milk chocolate, for example.

Colour in amulets and cures acts as visible and tangible declarations of belief and psychological reinforcements of purpose. Colour and appearance in custom and belief makes distinct an individual (as the bride at her wedding), or an occasion (as Christmas decorations), or a site (as a laying-out area). A change in the look of a person or space immediately identifies the leading player and site to participants in the ceremony or occasion. In some rites colour is seen to be vital and every effort must be made to comply with custom. This extends even to the bride from a very poor Scottish family who went to her wedding dressed in old lace curtains. However, in many customs colour is irrelevant, it is appearance that is important. For example, providing her workmates identify the bride-to-be by decorating her with ribbons and pieces of coloured paper, the colours themselves are not important. The identification of the chief figure becomes the excuse for and is the focus of the party (Monger 1991).

Colour is a powerful stimulus and motivator that can be used in different ways to control our actions, direct our lives, and make us happy or miserable. This appears to have been the case ever since early man learned to hold a piece of ochre.

Driving Forces for Colour Use

These beliefs do not just happen. There are driving forces for the use of colour in individual, family or tribal tradition. The wearing of achromatic (black or grey or white, depending on local custom) working clothes for a funeral is an example of the economic driving force. These are the colours of every day working clothes that can be cleaned for the occasion of paying respect. This embodies the principle of adaptation of physical resources, that is, using what is available.

The historical driving force includes the use of colour in the patriotic sense. Examples are the red, white and blue of the United Kingdom and its use as a national symbol. In Japan, the introduction of red rice as a dish to celebrate happy occasions coincided with the introduction of the red and white national flag in 1870, the start of the period of Japanese industrialism and imperialism.

There is a supernatural part to the historical driving force. Colour itself can be sacred. Splashes of turmeric made on the wall by a married couple in India are worshipped. Also, in India the mere application of a streak of vermilion on the bride's head can be sufficient to create a Hindu marriage. In Australia specific colours have specific religious connotations in aboriginal pictures. Specific colours are apotropaic, that is, they protect. From ancient Babylon to modern Europe, colours have formed an essential part of a protection or cure (Hutchings *et al.* 1996).

The social driving force, includes the use of colour in symbolism, healing, rites of passage, calendar customs and food. Green, as all major colours, has many symbolic meanings that, in different contexts, can be positive or negative in meaning. These apparent contradictions can be resolved using the principle of singularity. This states that at any one time, to any one person, a colour symbolises only one emotion or feeling regardless of what that colour may symbolise to another person or to the same person on another occasion. Ireland is an extreme example where green must be worn (as a statement of nationhood) but must not be worn (because it is unlucky)(Hutchings 1997c).

In healing, a major principle of folk medicine is curing like with like. This includes the curing of jaundice with gin or beer containing saffron. Wedding colours, form part of the social driving force for colour use. These include preparation of the couple, *e.g.* in Scotland the groom-to-be is blackened, bride and groom wear special clothing, which differs in colour in different areas of the world, the marking of the bride with gold and the post marriage red colour of the wedding bed.

It seems central to the nature of human beings that we require life to contain certain elements. Alongside statutory regulations for wider government we require more localised rules within our immediate community, within our family and within ourselves. These control our moral behaviour as well as local ceremonial behaviour. Involved are codes of behaviour linking members of social groups. These include the needs, for example, to celebrate gods, rites of passage and seasons of the year. All involve the use of colour and appearance in some way (Hutchings 1998).

In archaeological times, only some of this information is available for us to examine; in present day anthropology and folklore times we can attempt to examine them all. The principles discussed herein provide clues to the archaeologist regarding the interpretation of finds. We may never be able to reconstruct in detail day to day belief systems of ancient peoples, but at least we can determine what fits and does not fit in with modern behaviour. Observation of the nominal colour of the unearthed artefact might reveal some of this behaviour. For example, grave goods from Roman burials exhibited in Mediterranean museums, such as those in some of the more modern galleries in Sicily, could further study of the ubiquitous red, white and black triad and its application within Roman belief.

Putting this the other way around is it putting it too strongly to say that it would be very surprising if no artefacts from the dig had significance as part of colour folklore?

Colour Measurement in the Service of Archaeology

Colour is the psychological response to electromagnetic radiation of wavelength 380 to 710 nm. The basis for daylight colour vision is the presence in the retina of the eye of three sets of cones that have different light response characteristics with respect to intensity and wavelength. Rods are the low light sensitivity structures in the retina responsible for our night vision. The signals to the brain from the cones and rods appear to be in the form of three signals – intensity in the form bright to dim, and two colour signals, the first when positive is reddish, when negative greenish, the second when positive yellowish, when negative blueish.

There are two broad approaches to objective colour studies of archaeological artefacts: pigment analysis and colour specification. Pigment and dye type and concentration can be determined by chemical analysis. Such analyses have been applied to the study of, for example, textiles (Billmeyer 1982). However, factors other than the colorant and its concentration affect the perceived colour. For example, processing has an overriding effect on the colour of glass and textiles.

Perceived colour can be specified by visually matching the colour of the object to a particular chip in a colour atlas, such as the Munsell Colour Atlas and the Munsell Soil Colour Charts. These are used for the specification of soil colour in archaeology (*e.g.* Fernandez and Schulze 1986; Escadafal 1989).

It is not possible to construct a colour *measurement* instrument as colour exists in the brain, but it is possible to build one that *specifies* colour. This is constructed in semi-imitation of the normal viewing set up. A standard light is used to illuminate the surface, and the light reflected from it is analysed with respect to human cone characteristics. This yields a set of three numbers, quantifying lightness (L*), degree of redness (+a*) to degree of greenness (-a*), and degree of yellowness (+b*) to degree of blueness (-b*). These are colour coordinates which can be plotted at right angles to form a three dimensional diagram. Because colour changes with illumination, this must be documented. In the following examples the standard °illuminants A, (tungsten light), and C (north European daylight) were employed. Different illuminants were used because two different instruments, portable and laboratory, were employed in this work. Colour coordinate calculations are made with reference to the officially designated 2° standard observer functions. The geometry of the portable Eel colorimeter is illumination at 45° and viewing at 0° to the normal. The Pretema reflectance spectrophotometer illuminates the sample diffusely, viewing taking place at 0°.

There are two main applications of colour measurement to archaeology. The first is the investigation of the effect of time on colour, for example, in fine art (Wright 1981), textiles (Sinclair 1987) and cave paintings (Fernandez 1986). The second is the understanding of the processes and technology of production of manufactured and naturally weathered materials. For example, a technique has been proposed for the use of nondestructive, reflectance spectrophotometry to determine pigments and impurities used in works of art (Simonot *et al.* 2000). Sections follow on fired clay, ancient glass and flint.

Source	+a*	+b*	L*
Warden Abbey	0, 1	18, 23	58, 64
Newcastle	9	22	63
Warrington	10, 12, 12, 15	25, 25, 26, 28	60, 59.5, 61.5, 62
Norton Priory	14, 17, 19	30, 34, 35	57, 58, 61

Table 1 "Moderately" fired medieval tiles.
Mean +a*, +b*, L* coordinates from different samples (means of 3 - 5 replicates per sample). Pretema reflectance spectrophotometer, illuminant C, 2° standard observer

Fired Clay

Work on the colour effects of clay firing was carried out with Barry Jennings of Norton Priory, Cheshire and with the help of Evelyn Baker. The colour of moderately fired Medieval tiles from four monastic sites was measured. Mean colour coordinates obtained from separate samples from the sites were calculated. Table 1 shows the values of the three coordinates.

An increase of degree of redness is accompanied by an increase in degree of yellowness. This type of colour coordinate change (increasing a* accompanied by increasing b*), for other pigment containing materials, has been found to be indicative of pigment content. That is, the probable order of clay iron content was Warden (lowest),

tiles fired to temp (C)	Lightness L*	degree of redness a*	postulated physical changes	postulated chemical changes
100	51.5	16	particulate	
200	51.5	14	suspension	dehydroxylated
300	49	26	= high L*	clay formation
400	50	44		to 750° C
500	49	56		= increasing a*
600	49	79		to a plateau.
700	49	76		
800	49	76		
900	49.5	86	fusing &	
1000	47.2	92	aggregation	
1100	41	79	= fall in L*	
1150	41	8		haematite +
1200	39.5	2		mullite formed
1250	44.5	-26	structure collapse,	
			surface distortion	
			= higher L*	

Table 2 Model system tiles from Norton Priory, mean L* and a* coordinates. Eel portable colorimeter, illuminant A, 2° standard observer

Newcastle, Warrington, Norton. Clays originating south of Northamptonshire and in south Cambridgeshire have relatively low iron contents.

The main set of measurements was made on tiles fired to different temperatures. Barry Jennings produced these unglazed tiles in a model electric kiln in the presence of air at Norton Priory. Colours were measured using an Eel portable colorimeter. Four measurements were made on each fired disc, which was approximately 50mm in diameter and 8mm thick. Table 2 shows the values of L* and a* obtained.

The results show irregular behaviour as the tile firing temperature is increased. This is to be expected as different mechanisms causing the colour changes occur. As firing temperature is increased to 900 and 1100° C the degree of redness (+a) increases to a peak. As the temperature is further increased, the degree of redness falls with the Lightness (L*) to a dark, slightly green hue (-a*). The mean standard deviation of mean L* values was 1 to 2 units, except for the irregular surfaces at the highest temperatures when the standard deviation increased to 4. The mean standard deviation of a* was 1.5 units.

These different mechanisms are both physically and chemically based. The physical cause is mainly due to the conversion of a high particulate, light scattering clay (hence high values of L*) to a consolidated fused mass. The particulate nature of the matrix is lost, light scattering decreases and L* decreases. At the highest temperature a degree of melting occurs, the surface becomes distorted and misaligned particles reflect specularly into the colorimeter (hence L* tends to increase again). Chemical changes, possibly include the initial formation of dehydroxylated clay, followed by creation of haematite and mullite (Wakamatsu *et al.* 1985). These changes are reflected in the change in a* value. These changes do not occur by accident. They are the direct effect of chemical and physical reactions and can be used to pinpoint changes and quantify the dynamics of colour development.

Glass

The second study occurred in collaboration with David Sanderson, then of Bradford University, and involved an investigation of mechanisms involved in the manufacture of coloured Roman and Saxon glass. Although glass is commonly found on domestic and burial sites from the first millennium AD in Britain, glass of this period is normally excavated from sites where its deposition is several stages removed from its production. However, this does not preclude examination of technological changes over long time spans.

As a preliminary study, 42 samples of lightly tinted glass examined were selected from a larger set of specimens of which the pigments had been analysed by x-ray fluorescence and neutron activation analysis. They spanned the whole of the first millennium AD. All came from British archaeological sites and were in fragmentary condition. Ordinary early Roman domestic glass was represented by ten samples from Castleford. A mixture of late Roman and early Saxon vessels were represented in an assemblage of fragments of the Dark Age (fifth and sixth century AD) hill fort of Cadbury, Congresbury, where they may have been gathered for reworking. Later Saxon period glass fragments from Hamwic (Southampton) and Winchester were examined. Also, late Saxon and early Norman window glass from tenth to early twelfth century contexts at Lincoln Flaxengate were included. All the glasses were of the lightly tinted variety where the colour is almost probably due to impurities in the raw materials. A number of samples of deeply coloured glass were also included in this study.

Analysis of pigments in glass (or any other coloured material) reveals little about the perceived colour. For example, the colour of glass depends partly on the presence of transition metal oxides and partly as a function of the melting conditions (*i.e.* temperature, time, oxygen partial pressure) during manufacture. Hence, colour measurement is complementary to chemical analysis. Taken in combination they provide a means of studying the manufacturing conditions employed in producing the glass within the tradition of soda-lime-silica technology that lasted the whole millennium. This was apparently not disturbed by the departure of the Romans from Britain – although the overall quality of the sands used for glass making may well have changed.

A different technique from that used for the fired clay was used for the colour analysis of these clear and nominally colourless glass samples. Transreflectance spectrophotometry measurements were made to determine the transmission spectra and colour of the samples. Careful selection of the specimens studied minimised effects due to over-thick, undersized, or misshaped samples. It is inappropriate to republish the results in full (they have been reported in detail) but a note of them has been included here.

The use of the combined analytical and colour data brought out a number of new aspects of the colour of ancient glass. The lightly tinted samples, which on visual inspection alone might simply have been dismissed as colourless, possess interesting characteristics, previously unappreciated. It appears that in the Roman and later Saxon periods the lightly tinted glasses were manipulated through controlled furnace conditions and possibly through the use of minor additives. In the early Saxon period a more diverse assemblage of tints may reflect the different level of technology prevalent at the time. The colour of the glass, not its major pigment composition, seems to have been disrupted by the upheavals at the end of the Roman occupation of Britain. The skill with which additives were manipulated in lightly and deeply coloured glasses only adds to the respect that we must have for early glass makers.

Clearly the conclusions from this study must be limited, but it is hoped that the techniques demonstrated here may be further applied to early glass studies to enhance our understanding of the underlying technology (Hutchings and Sanderson 1981; Sanderson and Hutchings 1987).

A current study of glass colour is under way at the Colour and Imaging Institute of the University of Derby. This is a feasibility study involving the use of digital photography to record stained glass windows. It is hoped that this will lead to the generation of colour image archives of sufficient quality for the needs of the art history and conservation communities (MacDonald and Findlater, *pers comm.*).

Flint

A third experiment, that of identifying the causes and dynamics of flint patination, was proposed but never completed. David has observed that flint patination in alkaline conditions (chalk) is fairly rapid, all such prehistoric flints having an all white surface. Patination under acid conditions (for example, sandstone and ironstone), however, is much slower and Bronze Age flints remain black or brown, only Mesolithic material being patinated. Thus, there is potential for a dating method for studying flints from an acid provenance. Measuring the colour of reasonably dated flint tools could yield an approximate calibration curve. This could be applied to undated 'lithic sites' that have waste flakes but no dating material.

Studies of modern flint left for different times at different pHs (acidities) would give values of the rate of patination as a function of pH. If there was a 'sensible' mathematical relationship between the rate of patination as a function of pH, this could be extrapolated to low, real, pHs of, say 9 or 10, and so create a better calibration curve.

Colour Lessons for the Archaeologist

Archaeology is all about the detection of colour difference. We have all heard the digger's statement "I am emptying this pit", followed by the supervisor's "What pit!?", or "Did you find it or did you dig it!?". Some colour differences in the trench are indeed small.

Colour Training for the Archaeologist

We, all of us, tend to see colours differently. This is because what we see is a function of the responses of the light-sensitive rods and cones in the retina. Like all other biological functions vision suffers natural variation within and among populations. Hence, there is a need to define the Standard Observer to whom reference has already been made. Approximately one man in 13 and one woman in 250 perceive colours in markedly different ways from the remainder of the population. Those seeking jobs for which vision quality is important must be screened for colour perception. Such jobs include electrical wiremen, food chemists and meat inspectors. The profession of field archaeology probably falls within the classification where good colour vison is desirable but in which defective colour vision would not necessarily cause a handicap (Fletcher and Voke 1985). On the other hand, good colour vision would be demanded of conservators involved in colour mixing and matching. The Ishihara colour vision charts (Kanehara Shuppan, Tokyo), when correctly applied, are normally sufficient to detect significant abnormality.

The skills of the digger as well of as the fieldwalker depend critically on the ability to detect small colour differences. Sensitivity to small colour differences, such as detection of sherds and flints on the ground and detection of colour continuity in the dig varies among dirt archaeologists. Paul Martin's huge collection of flints (> 100,000) is probably due to his very acute vision – he was always the first to spot the road sign to Wharram Percy. I think that Paul has not been subjected to such indignities, but tests are available to determine the extents of such skills. Matching coloured artefacts, including soils, to colour charts calls for colour matching skills. It would be undesirable to make someone who has failed the Ishihara test responsible for performing such tasks.

Colour is characteristic of period in many aspects of archaeology and history. Modern examples can be found in town refurbishment. In the Art Deco region of Miami pale pastels contrasted with creams are being used to decorate buildings in the regeneration area of the city. In Old San Juan, where the colour spirit of the old Spanish colonialisation is being resurrected, all buildings are being painted with deep pastels contrasted with white. Awareness of colour can only add to the skills of the archaeologist and historian.

Viewing Conditions

When examining coloured artefacts, it is vital to control the ambient conditions. These include the quality of lighting used to illuminate the artefacts. Indeed, it would not be stretching the truth to reveal that the above project on delicately coloured glass would not have taken place had the samples not been removed from their original assessment area and examined under more managed conditions. The examination area should be enclosed with a mid grey surround and all other colours, particularly intense colours, must be removed from the vicinity.

The recommended lighting is the D65 approximation to daylight. This is realised by the Artificial Daylight fluorescent tube and some metal halide lamps. All lamps need to have a colour rendering index greater than 90 and a correlated colour temperature of approximately 6000-6500K. The intensity should be at a reasonable level consistent with that required for critical visual examination.

Conclusions

Training

The archaeologist should be aware of the part played by colour in our lives and in the lives of those living in different periods and under different conditions.

Assessment and training of the prospective archaeologist's colour skills should be part of his/her college education. Individuals would then know their personal colour vision and colour skills, strengths and weaknesses, so decreasing their chances of being asked to perform inappropriate tasks.

The archaeologist demands disciplined viewing in the trench. The archaeologist ought also to demand disciplined viewing during examination and cataloguing of finds. Acuity of vision and sensitivity to colour difference is demanded in the trench, normal colour vision is demanded for the examination of finds and in the conservation laboratory.

Suggestions have been made for the implementation of training for the archaeologist and for the disciplined assessment of finds.

Colour Measurement

We do not yet know fully the colour science of domestic vessels, glass, flint artefacts, decorative materials and possibly other archaeological materials. Pigment analysis is not sufficient to tell the whole story because the perceived colour depends on other properties such as light scattering. Hence, we see colour not pigments and colour measurement ought to occupy a permanent position within archaeological science. Suggestions have been made for further work.

P.S. Lord, please do your best to keep our remaining three country pubs open.

Bibliography

Berlin, B. and Kay, P., 1979, *Basic Color Terms* (Berkeley and Los Angeles, University of California Press)

Billmeyer, F.W. Jr., 1982, 'Identification of organic pigments by solution spectrophotometry', *Color Res. and Appl.* 7, 327

Brain, R., 1979, *The decorated body* (New York, Harper and Row)

Escadafal, A., 1989, 'Munsell soil colour and soil reflectance in the visible spectral bands of Landsat MSS and TM data', *Remote Sens. Environ.* 27, 37-46

Fernandez, R.N. and Schulze, D.G., 1986, 'Calculation of soil colour from reflectance spectra', *Soil Sci. Soc. Am.* 51, 1277-1282

Fernandez, P.L., 1986, 'Measurement and specification of the colors of the polychromatic roof of the Altamira Cave', *Color Res. and Appl.* 11, 43-46

Fletcher, R. and Voke, J., 1985, *Defective colour vision* (Bristol, Hilger)

Hutchings, J., 1997a, 'Living colour and appearance in nature', in Nassau, K. (ed), *Color for science, art and technology* (Amsterdam, Elsevier) 222-246

Hutchings, J., 1997b, 'Color in anthropology and folklore', in Nassau, K. (ed), *Color for science, art and technology* (Amsterdam, Elsevier) 196-208

Hutchings, J., 1997c, 'Folklore and symbolism of green', *Folklore* 1997, 108, 55-63

Hutchings, J., 1998, 'Colour in oral tradition', in Wessel, E. (ed), *Proceedings of the conference Colour between art and science*, Norwegian College of Art and Design, Oslo, 23-31

Hutchings, J. and Sanderson, D., 1981, 'Transreflectance properties of lightly tinted ancient glass', in Richter, M. (ed), *Proc 4th Congress International Colour Association*, Berlin, volume 2

Hutchings, J., Akita, M., Yoshida, N. and Twilley G., 1996, *Colour in Folklore with particular reference to Japan, Britain and Rice* (London, The Folklore Society)

Malinowski, T., 1980, 'A note published with Wrenscher's (1980) paper' *Current Anthropology* 21, 637-638

Merrifield, R., 1987, *The archaeology of ritual and magic* (London, Batsford)

Monger, G., 1991, 'Colour in Marriage', in Hutchings, J. and Wood, J. (eds), *Colour and appearance in folklore* (London, The Folklore Society)

Sanderson, D. and Hutchings, J., 1987, 'The origins and measurement of colour in archaeological glasses', *Glass Technology* 28, 99-105

Simonot, L., Elias, M. and Menu, M., 2000, 'Pigment recognition in works of art thanks to a spectrophotometric database', in conference digest, *Colour and visual scales 2000* (Teddington, National Physical Laboratory)

Sinclair, R.S., 1987, 'The colour specification of Scottish tartans', *Color Res. and Appl.* 12, 202-209

Turner, V., 1967, *The Forest of Symbols* (Ithica, Cornell University Press)

Wakamatsu, M., Takeuchi, N., Maung, O., Ishida, S. and Imai, K., 1985, 'Influence of kiln atmosphere on color and sintering properties of red clay containing iron', *Yogyo-Kyokai-Shi* 93 349-356

Wreschner, E.E., 1980, 'Red ochre and human evolution, a case for discussion', *Current Anthropology* 21, 631-644

Wright, W. D., 1981, 'A mobile spectrophotometer for art conservation', *Color Res. and Appl.* 6, 70-76

10. FENLAND BEAVER

Plate 1 European beaver, *Castor fiber*, swimming in a Breton stream.
Photo: Lionel Lafontaine, Breton Mammal Group

by Bryony Coles

In the Sedgwick Museum in Cambridge, adjacent to a fine skeleton of a beaver which was collected by T.McK. Hughes from Burwell Fen in 1907, there is a card which reads:

> "Castor europaeus
> The common beaver
> Fens, Cambridge
>
> Beaver construct dams across streams thus forming a still water pond where however silts build up in time. The alluvium that this produces is known as a 'beaver meadow'.
>
> Beaver were common in the fenland, but no evidence of a beaver dam or beaver meadow has yet been recorded."

Both before and after this particular skeleton was collected, beaver remains have been recovered from the Fenland of eastern England, from archaeological and natural deposits. Many of the finds are poorly recorded, but there must be at least 140 and probably over 150 individual beaver, from west to east across the southern half of the Fens, and potentially from Mesolithic to medieval times. Compared with the rest of Britain, this is by far the richest region for beaver bones. It is also a region that has been intensively researched in terms of its archaeology and palaeoenvironments. The present paper seeks to draw on this relative abundance of evidence, to consider what can be said of the Fenland beaver and their interactions with contemporary human populations. Details of individual finds, referenced thus '(E31)' in the text, are provided in Table 2 towards the end of the paper.

Castor fiber, the European beaver (Plate 1), became extinct in Britain some centuries ago, and it may be useful briefly to outline its character and ecological requirements. Beaver are large, semi-aquatic rodents, weighing 20-30kg as adults; they have thick waterproof fur, large orange incisors, webbed hind feet and a broad, flat tail. They tolerate a wide temperature range and in Eurasia are known to have lived from the Tigris-Euphrates basin to northern Scandinavia in historic times (Richard 1980,158; Legge and Rowley-Conwy 1986). They live around lakes and ponds, and along streams and rivers, and would appear to colonise almost any sort of water body so long as the water is fresh, not brackish or saline, and food is available. The beaver is vegetarian, eating herbaceous plants such as sedges and Iris, shrubs and trees. They fell trees by gnawing through the trunk with their incisors, mainly to get at the leafy topwood and the bark, which is what they ingest. They do not eat mature wood, but may shred it for bedding. The range of plants known to be eaten by beaver is huge, over 300 herbaceous species according to Macdonald and Barrett (1993, 233), and almost all tree and shrub species of temperate woodland. Their preferred tree species are poplar and willow, with ash, alder, oak, hazel and dogwood being further common food sources. Where winters are cold, beaver store twigs and branches under water in the early autumn, to retrieve and eat the bark when other food is inaccessible due to ice and snow. In more temperate conditions, tree felling also increases in the autumn as herbaceous vegetation dies down, and continues through the winter, as in central Brittany today (Coles, in press).

Beaver build dams, of wood, herbaceous plants, mud and stones (Plate 2), mainly to provide a depth of water sufficient to cover the entrance to their burrows, and where there is a year-round depth of 60-80cm or more, there may be beaver but no dams. The burrow rises from its underwater entrance to an underground but above water den. Where there is insufficient depth of soil to hollow out a dry den, the beaver heap wood, mud, stone and soft vegetation on the ground surface over the inner end of the burrow, and the heap is then hollowed out from inside to make the den. This creates what is commonly known as a beaver lodge. Beaver have a good eye for topography, and frequently make their dens in slight natural rises or, today, in waterside man-made features such as earthen banks. Often, as local water levels rise, an above-ground lodge appears where previously the beaver had only a burrow, and if the water goes on rising, the lodge goes on growing.

From the end of the last glaciation onwards, the beaver's requirements would have been met within the Fenland basin, at least in places if not throughout the region in all periods. It will have coped with all the post-glacial variations in climate. In the dry, pre-Fen period, the rivers and streams of the basin will have provided suitable habitat, just as their upper reaches continued to do as the basin became waterlogged. Even during the intensive drainage for agriculture of recent centuries, had the beaver been around, they could have dammed the drainage channels and burrowed into the banks, but such behaviour would soon have led to their extinction. Throughout the freshwater fen phases, and especially when there was a mosaic of wetland environments, beaver would have flourished. It should be remembered, though, that they will have needed places suitable for burrows, and even lodges are not free-floating but develop from what was once a dry spot on the edge of a watercourse or lake.

Another element of beaver habitats to note is the presence of open water, whether a natural stream or a lake, or a pond behind a dam, or a channel through swampy vegetation cleared by the beaver themselves. These are their swimming routes, for movement between den and feeding areas and for bringing food and building materials back to base. The beaver swim under water, or with their heads emergent. In slow-moving water, a silt-free path eroded through the soft basal deposits represents the beaver's underwater swimming route.

In marshland conditions, beaver may build dams to hold back water locally, for example to keep a depth of water in a swimming channel, or to protect burrow entrances in times of drought. These dams may be built of soft plant materials, and it could be quite difficult to distinguish such a feature from the surrounding *in situ* vegetation when examining peats.

One notable characteristic of beaver habitats today is the increase in biodiversity consequent on the beavers' presence. They diversify the wetland environment, and the fringing woodland areas where they feed. This in turn increases the variety of both fauna and flora. Whether the effect would have been quite as marked in the past as in the impoverished environment of today is uncertain, but at least we should be aware that a beaver presence indicates a probable abundance of wildlife.

Beaver in the Archaeological and Palaeoenvironmental Record: The Potential Record.

The former presence of beaver in a region is signalled by skeletal remains, beaver-gnawed wood, beaver dams and lodges, beaver channels

Plate 2 A beaver dam in the Roudoudour valley, Central Brittany.
The dams in this marshy territory are built of wood, tussocks of uprooted vegetation such as rushes and flag iris, mud, and occasional stones. They withstand floods, and provide a safe crossing of the watercourse for humans.
Photo: Beaver Works Project, Exeter

(though these may be difficult to recognise), place-names with a beaver element, pictorial representations and carvings, and written records. In the Fenland basin, some of these categories of evidence will have had a restricted distribution in time and space, quite apart from the obvious limitation of documentary evidence to the more recent times. For example, woody dams are likely to have been built across the streams and smaller rivers of the pre-Fenland basin whereas later where reed swamp and carr woodland predominated, dams were probably less frequent and, as noted above, built of materials that made their subsequent recognition more difficult. Where brackish or saline conditions prevailed, evidence for beaver living locally should not be expected.

Skeletal evidence from natural deposits (*i.e.* not associated with archaeological deposits) may result from deaths from old age or disease, or from beaver wounded but not retrieved by predators, notably humans and wolves, or indeed beaver wounded or killed by fellow beaver. The young leave their parents at about two years old and they are then very vulnerable to attack by strange beaver, whose home ranges they pass through in the search for a mate and somewhere to settle. Adults on the move, perhaps through loss of habitat or loss of mate, will also be attacked. Disease may have caused deaths in the past as now (Novak 1976). Sudden flooding can drown the very young in their den, and flooding under ice can drown adults as well, but neither event is likely to have been a major cause of beaver deaths in the Fens in the past. Mayhew (1978) aged a number of the Fen beaver skeletons, and his results do not show a peak for juveniles and young adults as might be expected. Further measurement of incisor width in the course of the present research confirms that the recovered skeletons are predominantly those of adults (Fig. 1). The reasons for this are unclear: there may have been a bias to the survival and collection of adult skeletons, due to their more robust bones, or adult beaver may have commonly died out in the open following wounding but not capture by a predator, following a fight with another beaver, or due to disease. In most instances where a complete or near-complete skeleton has been found, death probably occurred

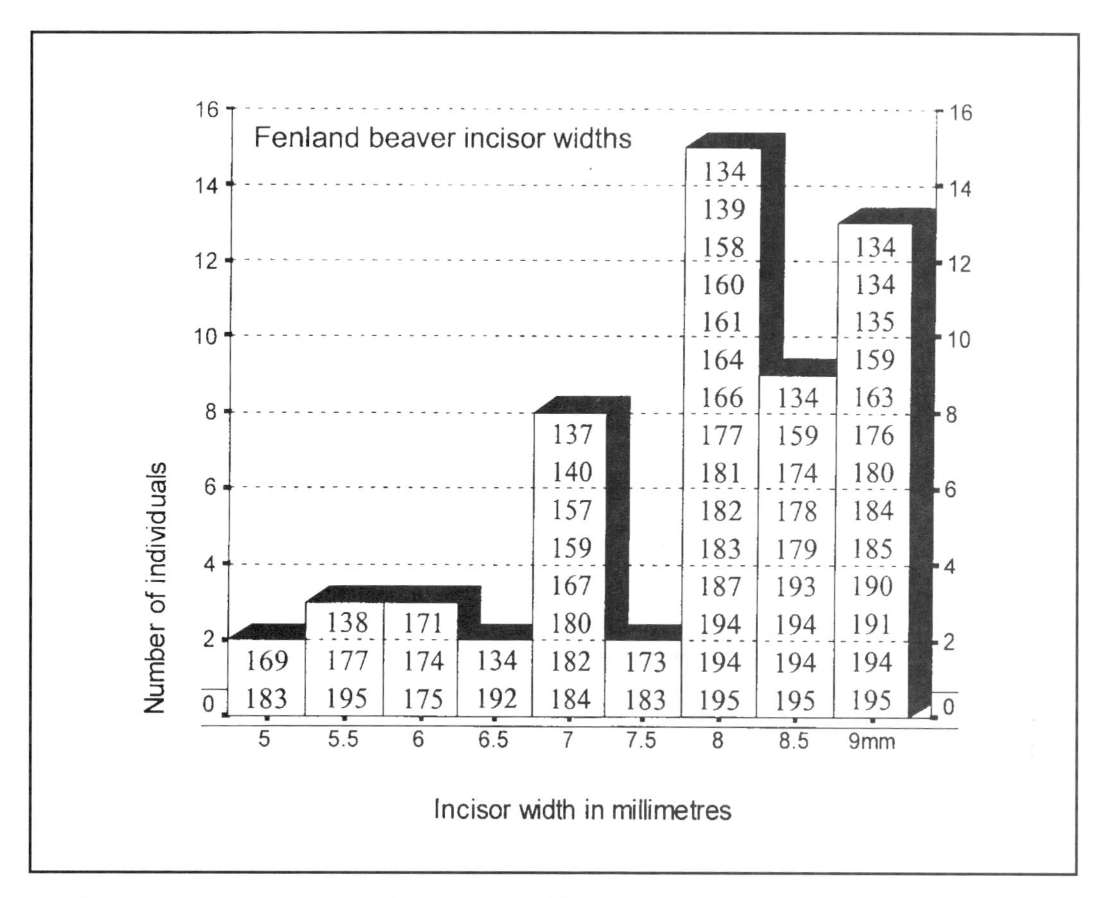

Figure 1 Measurement of incisor width of Fenland beaver specimens in the Sedgwick Museum and the University Museum of Zoology, Cambridge. Incisor width increases with age, and the measurements thus provide a rough guide to the age at death of the Fenland beaver population. The catalogue number of each beaver measured is given in the relevant column; for total of individuals in each width band, see vertical axis. The majority of skeletons recovered are from older beaver

when a weakened animal drowned in relatively still waters, or died in its den. These questions are considered again below.

Evidence Lacking in the Fenland Record

Although the Fenland basin provided good habitat for beaver, which were hunted, skinned and eaten by people in England into historic times (Coy 1980), no beaver place-names have been recognised from the region, nor is any pictorial or documentary evidence known. It will be argued below that this does not necessarily stem from a total absence of beaver during the historic period.

Beaver dams are also absent, or almost entirely so. Skertchly noted the absence, and attributed it to the 'abundance of still water' (Miller and Skertchly 1878, 348). Godwin (1978, 166) writes that Fowler reported a beaver dam, but gives no further detail. There may be dams at the base of the lower peats, built across streams and rivers of the earlier Holocene, and flooded as the water table rose, but very little is yet known of these buried channels. As discussed above, during the various freshwater fen phases dams were perhaps rarely built, or built of material which is now hard to distinguish from the surrounding peat matrix. Some dams may have been used by people as the base for causeways. Skertchly's description of timber on the edge of the Crowland island, with pointed sallow stakes and brushwood overlain by gravel, suggests a possible beaver dam or lodge adapted by humans, and Skertchly wrote that it looked like a causeway (1877, 247). There was much bone associated, and beaver teeth (E31), and a jet intaglio, and elsewhere this evidence has been interpreted as a possible Roman causeway (Hall and Coles 1994), none of which need preclude a beaver dam foundation.

Beaver burrows and lodges may also have been present but unrecognised. Many of the heaps of brushwood and 'platforms' found in wetlands throughout England, especially those associated with palaeochannels, could be the remnants of lodges and, like dams, some may have provided a base for human activity.

Curiously, there may be indirect evidence for beaver dams hidden in the place-name evidence. In Cambridgeshire, the place-names 'Landwade' and 'Fordham' can be interpreted as 'long ford' and 'village (or homestead) by the ford' (Reaney 1943). These two places lie about 1 km apart on the southwestern fen edge, just north of Burwell, and the river Snail flows between them into the Fenland basin. Speculatively, one might suggest that in this area a long relict beaver dam provided the basis for a safe crossing between the two settlements. Beaver bones have been found from Fordham (E122) in addition to the numerous examples from Burwell Fen (E92,96,120,134,161-180). Only one of the Burwell beaver has a date, in the Bronze Age and probably long before the place-names came into being. But there is also a beaver incisor pendant (E72) from the Anglo-Saxon cemetery at Burwell, potentially coeval with the naming of the 'ford' settlements. The likelihood of beaver living in the Fens during the Anglo-Saxon period is discussed further below, and perhaps a search for other 'ford' and 'causeway' place-names would identify some other pairings suggestive of former beaver dams.

The Fenland Beaver Evidence

The majority of beaver skeletons found within the Fenland basin have come from natural contexts, or more precisely from contexts with no record of associated archaeological evidence. A great many are poorly recorded finds made during the second half of the nineteenth century, with no more provenance than 'Fens, England' (E129) or the slightly more precise 'Fens, Norfolk' (E126). Sometimes, a little more detail has been recorded, as for one of the skeletons bought by the University Museum of Zoology, Cambridge (UMZC E1790; E136) which came from 'Littleport Fen. 1896'. In this case, an approximate findspot can be placed on the map (Fig. 2).

Two beaver skeletons from the Fens have been dated by radiocarbon. Bones from a skeleton from Burwell Fen (UMZC E1797; E134) were dated to 2677±123BP (BM-722), or about 1100-450 cal BC. An unprovenanced skull (BMNH 1956.7.10.3; E128) from the Natural History Museum's collections dates to 3079±99BP (BM-723), or about 1500-1050 cal BC. Burleigh *et al.* (1976,30) commented of BM-722 'Brown colouration of original bones suggested possible humic contamination; age should be considered minimum'. In a discussion of the radiocarbon dates and the possibility that the Fen beaver skeletons all belong to the Bronze Age, Mayhew (1975,14) reports that Gibbard examined pollen from the peat found in beaver skulls, and attributed it to 'late zone VII (Fl II)', *i.e.* consonant with a Bronze Age date. On the whole, the evidence available today indicates a much longer timespan for the Fen beaver, and some of this evidence is detailed below, but only further direct dating can resolve the issue.

During the several millennia before the Fenland basin became a wetland, beaver could have lived along all the watercourses of the region. Paradoxically, there may have been as many if not more beaver during the Mesolithic and earlier Neolithic than in later periods; the reason being the ample suitable habitat in the form of watercourses with dry banks for burrows, and nearby wooded land where trees and shrubs grew for food and building materials. A reminder of these conditions is provided by a beaver from just outside the Fens, from the bed of the Great Ouse at Brampton near Huntingdon (E54). This find is undated, and could be of any period from the early Mesolithic onwards.

The majority of Fenland beaver skeletons are similarly undated. When the bones are still peaty, or recorded as having come from peat, they must date to periods when peat formation occured, or to subsequent periods. Beaver, unlike rabbits, burrow upwards, but usually from a watercourse cut through earlier deposits so, like rabbits, a natural death may occur within earlier deposits as well as in coeval ones. But knowing this does not necessarily narrow the date range in any useful way, as the Burwell Fen beaver illustrate.

The Burwell skeletons, numbering at least 40 individuals, are by far the largest group of beaver remains with some degree of provenance (see Catalogue). Most now reside in Cambridge, at the Sedgwick Museum and the University Museum of Zoology, both of which have a Burwell Beaver on display. A few, rather in the manner of the prolific finds from the Swiss Lake Villages, were given to or acquired by other museums, and there are now Burwell beaver in Manchester (E96), Brighton (E92), and the Natural History Museum in London (E120). Many of the bones clearly were found in peat, and so must date from the onset of peat formation in this part of the Fens, which Waller places at about 2000 cal BC or soon thereafter (Waller 1994, Maps 7 and 8). But they do not necessarily all belong to the Bronze Age, as seemed likely to Mayhew using the evidence available in the early 1970s. Burwell Fen lies in the peri-marine zone, defined by Waller as the area beyond marine influence throughout

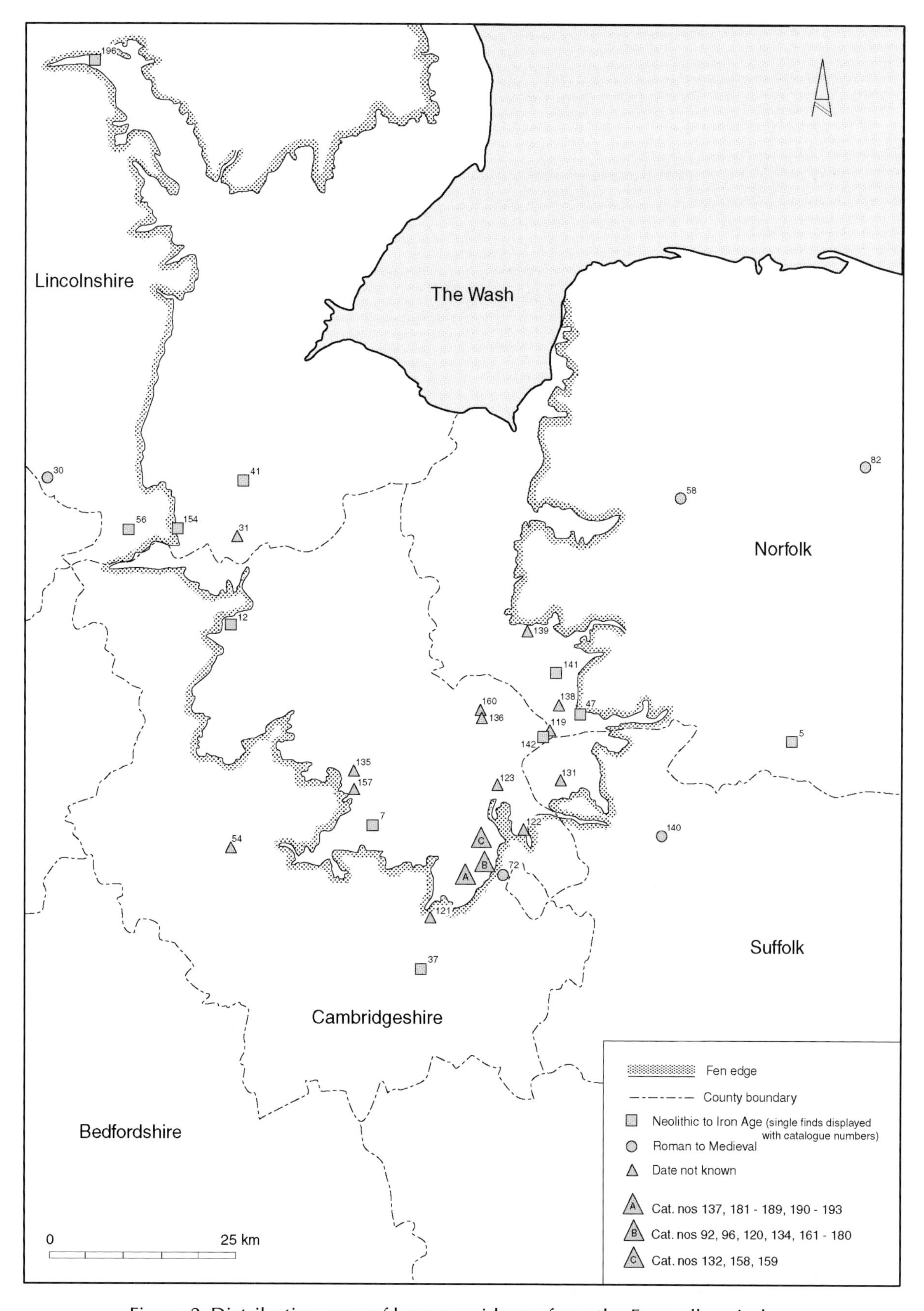

Figure 2 Distribution map of beaver evidence from the Fens, all periods

the Holocene where peat formed without any intercalated layers of silts and clays. Thus the peaty Burwell beaver could date to any period from the onset of freshwater wetland conditions to the local extinction of the species, and the question of their age can probably only be resolved by more extensive radiocarbon dating. One example that might be relatively recent is a skull from peat found in 1909 (E176), which is unusual in retaining patches of orange-brown colour on its incisors, whereas most incisors from peat have turned to a dark blue-grey or to a dirty ivory colour. The millennia of suitable conditions for beaver may be one reason for the number of skeletons retrieved from Burwell Fen, and a second reason lies in the absence of marine silts and clays which facilitated peat cutting and thereby brought the skeletons to light.

The palaeoenvironmental researches carried out for the Fenland Project have been important in demonstrating that the onset of peat formation was not synchronous across the Fens, nor was the sequence of wetland change identical. The relevance of this to the beaver evidence is illustrated by a find from Swaffham Prior Fen (E137), just to the west of Burwell Fen, where the onset of peat formation is dated to 4100BP, or about 2800 cal BC (Waller 1994, Map 5). The Swaffham Prior beaver bones are peaty, so could date up to about 800 years older than those from Burwell Fen.

In one instance, it may be possible to narrow the likely time span for one of the 'natural' beaver skeletons. In June 1896, the University Museum of Zoology, Cambridge, acquired a beaver skeleton from H.F. Fryer (UMZC E1789; E135). The entry in the Museum Register reads 'Found below peat on surface of clay, 5 feet below surface, in land belonging to Christ Church, Oxford, at Chatteris, within borders of Hunts.' In 1690 the Bishop of Coventry and Lichfield had bequeathed Holwood Farm, Chatteris to Christ Church, and Herbert Fortescue Fryer was a tenant from 1876 (J.Curthoys, Christ Church archivist, *pers comm.*). The farm is indicated on modern maps, and comparison with a 1780 map of the college holding puts the centre of the block of land at TL390795. Waller (1994, 182-3) suggests that this area of the fenland basin was relatively dry throughout the Mesolithic and much of the Neolithic, followed by a marine incursion and, from the Late Bronze Age or Early Iron Age a fen with willow carr. The beaver skeleton, found on the surface of the clay, probably dates to the onset of fen conditions in the earlier first millennium BC.

Moving eastwards to the former course of the Little Ouse, to the area of Shippea Hill well known for archaeological and environmental investigations, there are beaver finds from both natural and archaeological contexts. In 1871, 4 bones, probably from one individual (E119), were collected from Burnt Fen, near Plantation Farm, and later donated to the Natural History Museum by the Hon. Walter Rothschild. Nothing more is known of their context. In the early 1930s, Grahame Clark excavated at Plantation Farm, and found beaver bone (E142) among the debris which had spread from Early Bronze Age occupation on the sandy island into the adjacent, peat-forming wetland (Clark 1933). The beaver was most probably living in these wetlands until it fell prey to the people, and it can be dated with a fair degree of confidence to the Early Bronze Age. As for the nearby Burnt Fen bones, they have no date but it may be assumed that there were no beaver living in this part of the Fens from about 3000 cal BC to about 2400 cal BC, during which time brackish or marine conditions prevailed (Waller 1994, 119; Healy 1996, 9) and the 'Buttery Clay' was deposited. Below this clay, there is peat which began to form in the earlier Holocene (Clark and Godwin 1962; Smith *et al.* 1989); the evidence suggests complex minor local variations in the peat sequences which could well be due to the presence of beaver in the former Little Ouse valley. In particular, the pools and channels, erosions and infillings, and local variation in lithostratigraphy described by Smith and Whittle (Smith *et al.* 1989, 236ff) could be the products of beaver activity within the valley. The Burnt Fen bones which prompt this consideration remain undated.

Several finds have come from the Norfolk Fens. A young beaver from Feltwell Fen (E138) is represented by an incomplete lower jaw with well preserved incisors. The cutting facets on the incisors are intact, and measure half the size of those found on an adult: this juvenile was nibbling willow twigs, dogwood shoots, iris rhizomes and sedge stems, and had yet to graduate to tree felling. A skull from Poppylot Farm, Methwold (E141), was found in 1883 and lost by 1923 when Rainbird Clarke made out a record card for it (Jan Allen, *pers comm.*). This beaver was one that went missing in earlier times too, for a barbed and tanged arrowhead was found with the skull, suggesting that a wounded beaver had escaped the hunter but drowned soon thereafter or died in its burrow from weakness.

If the Poppylot beaver got away, one from the fen edge at Hockwold cum Wilton (E47) did not. Here,

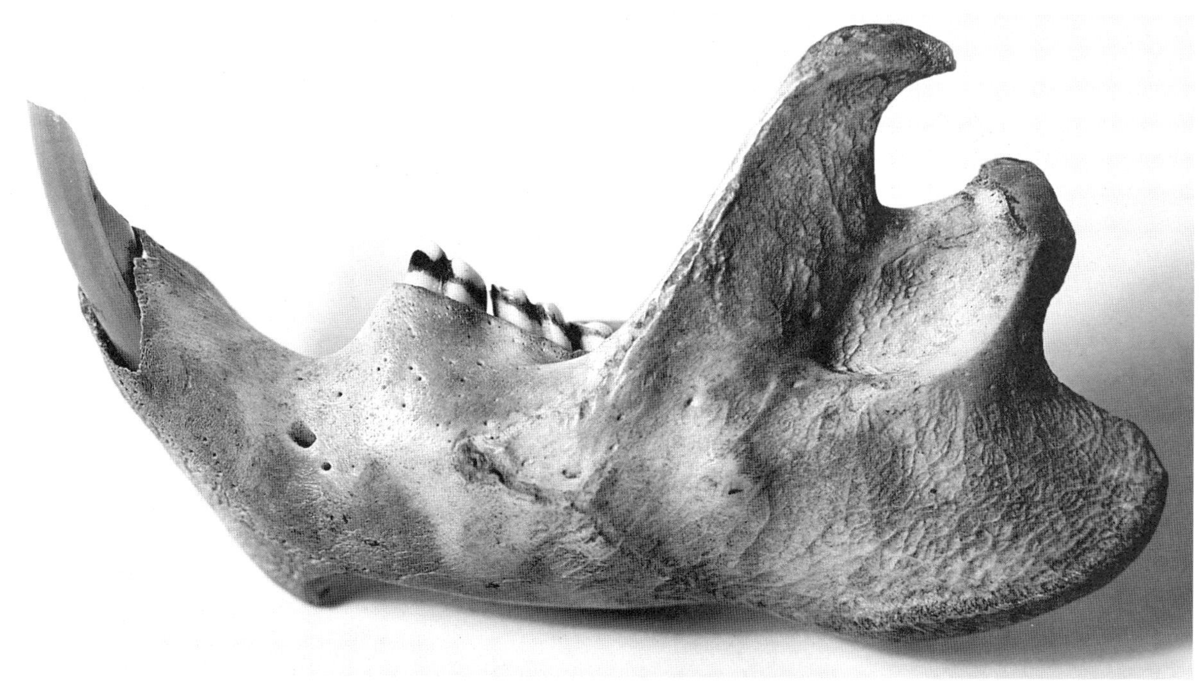

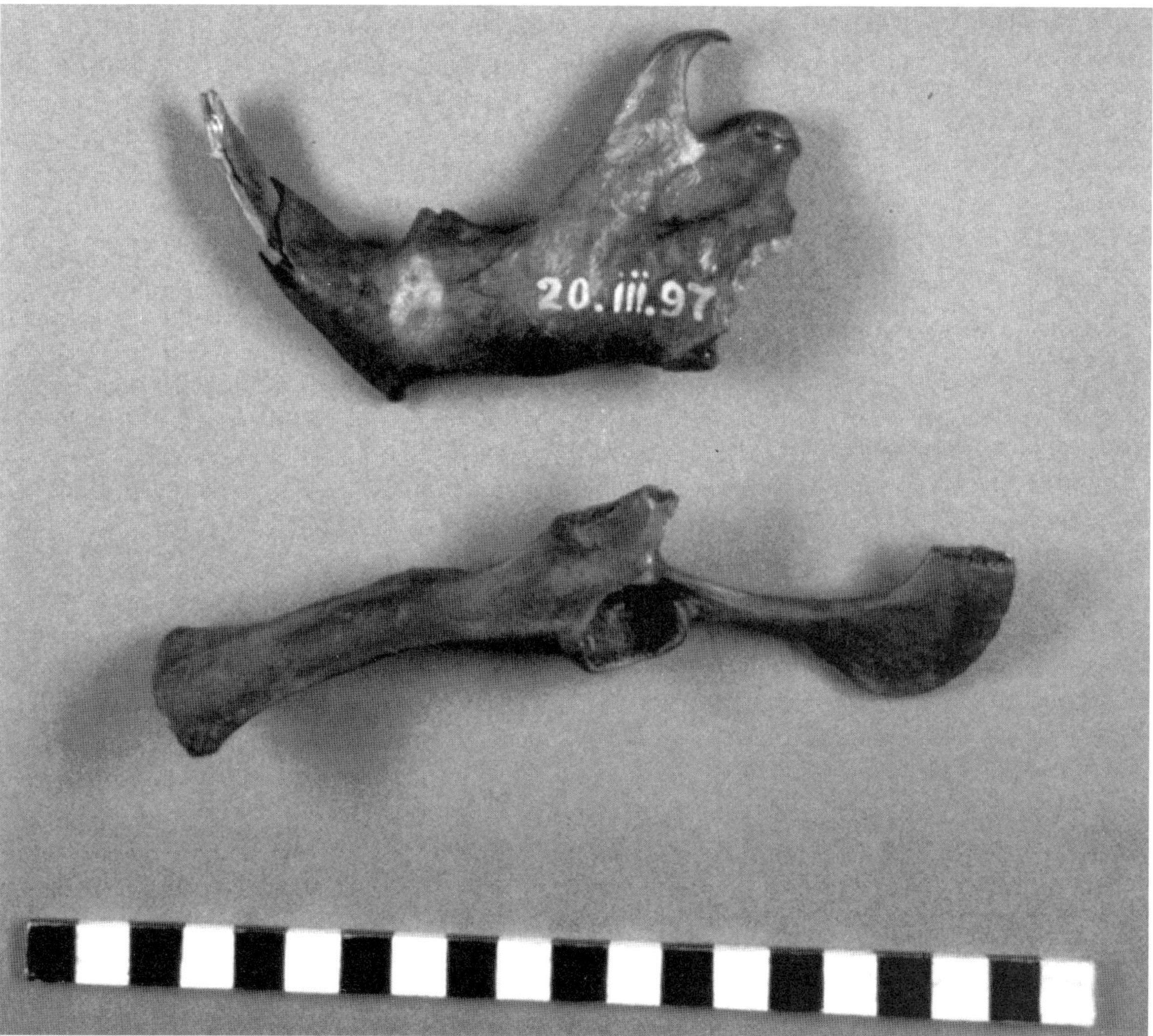

Plates 3a and 3b A modern, unaltered beaver jaw, and a trimmed jaw from the University Museum of Zoology collections (20.iii.97: E140). Photos: Beaver Works Project, Exeter

beaver bone was collected from a ploughed field, from amongst a dense spread of animal bone and artefacts which are dated to the end of the Early Bronze Age (Healy 1996,11ff). The bone includes a beaver mandible collected by Frank Curtis in 1959 when the field was first ploughed. Curtis made a sketch map (Healy 1996, Plate III) on which he recorded 'beaver teeth' from the edge of the field, which may refer to the mandible as suggested by Healy but, given the dramatic appearance of beaver incisors, this was quite possibly a separate find which did not remain with the main collection (it is perhaps less likely that molars would be recognised to species and recorded separately in the field). The other animal bone from the site consisted mainly of domestic cattle, pig and sheep or goat, with a few wild animals including otter and duck in addition to the beaver. The material probably derives from a fen edge settlement looking south over the valley of the Little Ouse, and inhabited by people who lived in the main off their domestic animals and crops but also hunted in the wetlands. They or their neighbours may have included the hunter who lost the Poppylot beaver, since the artefact scatter included barbed and tanged arrowheads (Healy 1996, fig. 44). Other possibly contemporary beaver hunters were the people at Plantation Farm, just a short paddling distance down the Little Ouse. The beaver may have facilitated their own death: during the fen phases, the rivers flowing through the basin are likely to have spread into multiple, amorphous, interconnecting channels and seeps of water through swamp vegetation, where beaver and the larger waterfowl created and maintained clear water paths wide enough for people to pass in a coracle or small dugout.

One of the unprovenanced finds of beaver bone, known only as '20.iii.97' in the UMZC Register (part of E140), consists of a hind leg bone, a right pelvis and a left lower jaw. The pelvic bone may have been cut or broken, and the jaw has had the lower back corner trimmed off with a sharp blade, leaving a denticulate edge (Plate 3). The incisor and two of the molars are still in place, and the trimmed jawbone is reminiscent of a Bronze Age example from Ulrome in Holderness, published as a probable implement by Clark (1971). Clark compared the Ulrome beaver jaw with hafted jaws described and illustrated by Osgood (1940) in his account of the material culture of the Ingalik of northern North America. The Ingalik used a hafted jaw complete with teeth, to scrape spruce roots with the molars, and to gouge out irregularities in the roots with the incisor.

Several of the beaver jaws from the Sedgwick collection show signs of possible human trimming or cut marks. They include a jaw from Burwell Fen found in 1886 (E162) which has had the lower back corner trimmed off and the incisor has been worn to a most unbeaverlike rounded blunt tip, perhaps through long use as a gouge for hollowing out small confined spaces. Two further Fenland jaws (part of E195) appear to have similar trimming of the lower corner, and they also bear vertical cutmarks on the outer surface just below the central molar. In addition, a tibia found in Burwell Fen in 1907 (E174) has two definite chop marks, executed in antiquity, near its lower end which may have occured when someone chopped the foot from a beaver carcase, perhaps during skinning.

Whereas the majority of beaver skeletons from natural contexts have come from the southeastern fens, those from archaeological sites are more widely distributed. In addition to the southeastern examples discussed above, there are finds of beaver from the southern and western fens, and from around the Fen edge. As yet, there are none from the Silt Fens to the north, a lack which is not unexpected, given the brackish and marine conditions which the silts represent, and the saltmaking which at least some of the human occupants pursued.

The earliest dated archaeological site with beaver remains is that of Barholm in Lincolnshire, in the lower Welland valley on the north side of the river. Here, a number of pits and post holes and 'working hollows', excavated in 1965, were found to contain Late Neolithic debris and animal bone (Simpson 1993). The latter came mainly from domestic animals, with a few from red deer, brown bear, fox, cat and some beaver teeth (E56). Harman (1993) suggests that the beaver, fox and cat were hunted for their pelts. Quite possibly the bear was too, and both beaver and bear were probably eaten. Two radiocarbon dates were obtained for the site: 4305±130BP (UB-457) from charcoal from the base of pit 4 and 4255±135BP (UB-548) from charcoal from the upper fill of Pit 13 (Simpson 1993). These dates calibrate to about 3350-2450 cal BC. At this time, the Barholm site was probably 5 - 10 km inland of the fen edge (Waller 1994, Map 5); the beaver could have found closer suitable habitat in the Welland and its tributaries, as well as out in the Fens, while the humans who hunted and trapped them probably ranged over both environments.

Further beaver remains of late Neolithic date come from the recent excavations at the Babraham Road site, Cambridge. The site lies at the foot of the Gog

Magog hills, near to springs which probably fed small streams flowing to the Cam a few kilometres to the west; the contemporary fenland edge was a similar distance to the north. The Neolithic phase of activity is dated to 2619-2345 cal BC (GU-9018), a date consistent with the presence of Grooved Ware and with the lithic typology (Hinman, in press.). The beaver bones (E37) come from pits and a natural hollow, and consist of teeth fragments and a mandible, with fragments of scapula and tibia of uncertain but possible beaver origin (Ian Baxter, *pers comm.*). Baxter has also identified a number of pine marten bones, including limb bones, from the Babraham pits. This evidence suggests that small mammals were being hunted for their pelts, and processed at the site. The marten carcases appear to have been discarded, whereas the beaver may have been cooked and eaten. From a beaver perspective, the Babraham and Barholm sites are quite similar and suggestive of hunters and trappers with a base near to fen and forest, from where they could exploit a diversity of fur-bearing mammals. The earlier Bronze Age people of the eastern fen edge, discussed above, would seem to have continued this tradition.

In the western Fens, there appear to be no beaver from Early Bronze Age contexts. The explanation may lie both in the prevailing environmental conditions and in the character of the known archaeology of the period (summed up in Hall and Coles 1994, fig. 39). While the southwestern fens were a freshwater, beaver-friendly, peat-forming wetland, the eastern half of the basin was dominated by brackish and marine conditions inimical to beaver. The archaeology of the southeast includes much evidence for settlement and a number of burial sites, including burial in the wetlands (Roberts 1998). In the west, burial sites predominate and fewer settlements are known. Since settlements seem to provide the context for beaver finds of this period in the Fens, the chances of discovery in the west are slight. There are some indications that settlements of the period may survive under later sediments (Hayes and Lane 1992,112; Hall and Coles 1994,67-68), but whether local conditions were suitable for beaver to live in the area remains uncertain.

In the Later Bronze Age, the beaver evidence becomes more varied, with beaver wood reported for the first time, from the lower levels of the Flag

Plate 4 Modern wood gnawed by European beaver, compared with wood cut using stone and bronze axe-blades. The beaver wood is at either end of the row.
Photo: J.M.Coles

Fen platform (E12; Maisie Taylor, *pers comm.*). Topography in the area of Flag Fen, where the Northey-Whittlesey island lies about 1km off the fen edge and to some extent blocks the emergence of the river Nene into the fen basin, suggests multi-channelled watercourses with sluggish drainage and perhaps easy reversal of flow. The massive timber platform lies closer to Northey island than to the western fen edge, with a line of massive posts, sometimes several rows deep, running from the island, through the Platform and over to the western fen edge where it is aligned upon an earlier field system (Pryor 1992).

The beaver-gnawed wood is a rare find for the Fens. It is likely that there have been other occurrences which went unrecognised by the excavators: people who have seen and handled freshly-gnawed beaver wood (Plate 4) are more likely to recognise ancient and perhaps eroded or desiccated pieces during an excavation, as both Taylor (1993) and the author have found. One of the several pieces of beaver wood from Flag Fen had been chopped by a person using an axe, probably after the beaver had gnawed it (Taylor 1993 and in press), suggesting the opportunistic but deliberate exploitation of the beaver's effort, and not merely beaver-gnawed driftwood washing up on the timber platform. Moreover, the wood was alder, and from a coppiced stool, and it would be typical of beaver to create over the years a 'coppice' or 'beaver pasture ' from the trees along the water's edge, simply through repeated feeding (Coles 2000). They may, therefore, have been in the area for some time before this particular piece of wood was cut. One wonders whether, under the extensive, humanly-built heap of wood there lies perhaps a smaller beaver-built heap, the remains of a lodge which began life on an old shore-line, and just possibly in the bank of a field-system abandoned by people as the local water levels rose.

At Welland Bank, to the north of Flag Fen, part of another Bronze Age fen edge field system has been excavated, on the northern edge of the Welland flood plain. Occupation was broadly contemporary with that at the Fengate-Flag Fen complex, from the earlier Bronze Age to about 500BC. In this part of the Fens, conditions were brackish or marine from about 2500 cal BC, followed by a retreat of the sea and extension of freshwater wetlands in the earlier first millennium BC (Waller 1994,221-226). Preliminary assessment of the animal bone shows beaver were brought into the site, and their bones (E41) include several mandibles with cut marks, as well as some post-cranial pieces (Albarella, *pers comm.*). Much of the beaver bone came from a pit which also contained Late Bronze Age pottery and shale bracelet pieces (Lane, *pers comm.*; Scurfield, *pers comm.*). As from sites of earlier periods, it looks as though people were skinning beaver and probably eating them too. There is evidence for saltmaking from the site, probably contemporary with the earlier Bronze Age period of marine incursion, when it is likely that the local beaver populations moved away up the Welland valley. When they moved back down again, some at least fell victim to humans.

At Fiskerton in the Witham valley, where a timber causeway was built in the earlier Iron Age, and artefacts deposited in the watery conditions, the animal remains included beaver bone (E196. Mulville in press; Hall and Coles 1994). A left foreleg and two caudal vertebrae have been identified, the latter having been chopped. Mulville has suggested that people may have detached the tail for its meat and fat, and to get at the castoreum glands, which are situated just behind the anal glands of both males and females, and which can be 10cm or so across in size. Castoreum is a secretion similar to runny honey in its colour and viscosity (but not smell), which the beaver uses in territorial marking. When deposited, it oxidises rapidly to a tarry colour and it has a smell slightly reminiscent of creosote. It was used in folk medicine as a febrifuge and cure-all, and as its composition is akin to aspirin (from the willowbark which the beaver eat), it was probably effective. Certainly, it was much sought after. Castoreum has also been used in perfumery. There is no evidence, as yet, to show what uses, if any, people made of castoreum in the Iron Age.

Fiskerton, like Flag Fen, has been dated by dendrochronology, with felling dates for the timbers ranging from 456BC to 375BC with a concerted episode at 406BC (Hillam 1992). However, material was deposited in the wetland for several centuries after this, and the beaver bones are not as closely dated as the timber structure.

One of the most prolific archaeological sites for beaver remains, and generally in terms of evidence for the exploitation of wetland fauna, is the Iron Age settlement known as Haddenham V (Evans and Serjeantson 1988; Evans and Hodder in press). The site consisted of a small enclosed settlement on the edge of a gravel terrace on the southwestern fen edge. A similar and probably contemporary settlement, Haddenham VI, was only some 150m away. Careful excavation and sieving at Haddenham V during the mid-1980s investigations produced a range of wetland animals, including pelican, crane, heron and swan as well as beaver. The beaver bones (E7), which were mainly post-cranial elements, came from a minimum of 19 animals, and several of the bones showed cut marks due to skinning and butchery (Evans and Serjeantson 1988, fig 4). Few phalanges were retrieved despite the sieving, which Serjeantson suggests could be due to the export of pelts from the site with paws still attached, The near-absence of skulls and teeth suggest that heads too were exported, or left at the kill site, since on other sites these elements have proved very durable. Evans and Serjeantson discuss the exploitation of wetland animals in general and the beaver in particular, and point out that beaver hair, which sheds water, could have been felted if not left on the skin to use as a waterproof fur. They also discuss the possible exploitation of castoreum, for reasons similar to those noted for Fiskerton.

There is an absence of beaver and other wetland animals from the nearby Haddenham VI, which raises the interesting possibility that the two communities pursued separate economic specialisations in addition to farming (Evans and Serjeantson 1988,369-69). The inhabitants of Haddenham V were probably well versed in the use of nets and snares, and may have used underwater wooden traps such as those reported by Munro (1891) and interpreted as beaver or otter traps, although the actual use of these objects has not been determined for sure.

Less abundant evidence, but of a similar character to that from Haddenham V, has been identified from the Fenland Management Project evaluations at Outgang Road, Market Deeping, on the western fen edge north of Peterborough (Crowson *et al.* 2000). Although evidence for saltmaking has been found on the site, preliminary analysis of the deposits points towards a freshwater environment. Beaver (E154), swan, goose and duck bones were found amongst wood and other debris in the fill of a palaeochannel, and two swan wing bones had cut marks as if for the removal of the feathered tip (Albarella, *pers comm.*). On the western fen edge as in the south at Haddenham, the Iron Age people appear to have been culling wild animals to make and decorate clothes and other articles, as well as to enjoy the sort of food that we now associate with winter feasting, and perhaps to acquire the medicine to deal with the consequences.

No Fenland beaver remains have yet been securely dated to the Romano-British period, but this is consonant with the picture from Britain as a whole where little beaver evidence is unambiguously Romano-British (Coles, in prep.). The find from Crowland might, as noted above, belong to the period, but nothing remains to check the possibility. The Fenland people of these few centuries, and there were apparently many of them, had extensive areas of freshwater wetland to exploit (Hall and Coles 1994, fig. 68). But their means of doing so was largely through the rural industries of saltmaking and peat-cutting, not hunting, fishing and fowling. To some extent, the picture may be biased by the character of archaeological investigations of the period, but the lack of beaver evidence seems genuine enough to suggest that either the species was locally extinct, or people were simply not interested in it. Possibly the intensive exploitation of wetland fauna in the Iron Age, as seen at Haddenham V, had led to the elimination of beaver from the region. One could also argue that people of the Romano-British period, who needed to control water levels for navigation and for peat extraction, had got rid of the pesky dam builders who blocked waterways and burrowed into canal banks. However, if beaver had been deliberately hunted to extinction by Romano-British people, some bone evidence might be expected at occupation sites for beaver are good to eat. The recent history of beaver in France suggests an alternative explanation, that under increasing human persecution in the later Iron Age the beaver abandoned fen edge habitats and retreated to the deep marshes, where they no longer felled trees or built dams and lodges with wood, becoming so inconspicuous that few people saw any signs of their presence. This is how beaver survived in recent centuries in the Camargue, from where they eventually recolonised the Rhône catchment when human pressure lessened (Richard 1967; 1980; Rouland 1990).

The majority of beaver remains from archaeological sites of confirmed Anglo-Saxon date come from fen edge sites rather than from within the fenland basin, a situation comparable with earlier periods. There are beaver incisors (E143) from West Stow beside the river Lark, where occupation is dated to the fifth to seventh centuries AD (West 1985). At Burwell, on the dry land adjacent to the fen which has been so prolific of beaver bones, late nineteenth century investigations of an Anglo-Saxon cemetery revealed a number of graves. In one, where a woman and infant were buried, the artefacts included a beaver incisor bound with bronze (E72). The burial is dated to the late sixth century AD or a little later (Meaney 1964, 1981). A similar find of a beaver incisor set in metal was made at Castle Bytham near Stamford (E30). It was published in 1853 by the Reverend J.Birch

Plate 5 A beaver dam in wet woodland, upstream of the dam shown in Plate 2.
Photo: Beaver Works Project, Exeter.

Reynardson, who wrote that the identification of the object as a beaver tooth was confirmed by comparison with a beaver skull in the Museum of the Royal College of Surgeons in London. He noted that 'the peculiar orange-brown streaks upon the outer surface of the tooth are still distinctly preserved' (Birch Reynardson 1853, 81). The orange colour may have been part of what attracted people to the incisors for use as pendants, which were probably worn as amulets (Meaney 1981) and which could have been imported as such rather than being made from the incisors of local beaver. However, beaver were probably still present within the broader East Anglian region, since fragmentary limb bones (E82) have been identified from a contemporary cremation burial at Spong Hill, Norfolk (McKinley 1994).

The most recent beaver evidence from the Fenland Basin catchment comes from Castle Acre on the river Nar, upstream of King's Lynn. Excavations in the early 1970s (Coad and Streeten 1982) produced, amongst many other finds, two beaver mandibles (E58) from a twelfth century context. The bones came from the make-up associated with a late phase of re-building of the castle, together with quantities of bone from domestic animals and a few from other wild or feral species such as fallow deer, rabbit, rat and water vole (Lawrance 1982). In discussing the beaver mandibles, Lawrance suggests that they could be residual or imported, rather than coming from contemporary indigenous beaver. It seems reasonable to suggest that the make-up material consisted of occupation debris dug from nearby, and given the quantity of animal bone, it could have derived from a midden associated with an earlier phase of the castle. The inclusion of rabbit bones, together with the dating of the castle itself, suggest it was a post-conquest midden and their residuality only moves the beaver jaws back a century at most. The possibility of import from the continent cannot be ruled out, but neither can a local provenance since there is other post-conquest evidence to suggest the continuing presence of beaver in England (Coles, in prep.). In remote parts of the Fens, a beaver population may well have survived into the second millennium AD, in a manner similar to that suggested above for the Romano-British period.

Some General Considerations

In cataloguing the beaver evidence from the Fens, it is clear that there is little or no provenance for most finds, and the majority are undated. Many of

Cat. No.	Site	Period	Skull	Mandible	Teeth	Postcranial	'Bones'– not identifiable to skeletal element	Site Type
			Skeletal Elements					
E 56	Barholm	LN	—	—	✔	—	—	Occupation
E 37	Babraham	LN	—	✔	✔	(✔)	—	Occupation
E 142	Plantation Farm	EBA	—	—	—	—	✔	Occupation
E 141	Poppylot	EBA	✔	—	—	—	—	Stray find
E 47	Hockwold-cum-Wilton	EBA	—	✔	✔	—	—	Occupation
E 41	Welland Bank	LBA	—	✔	—	✔	—	Occupation
E 196	Fiskerton	IA	—	—	—	✔	—	Causeway
E 7	Haddenham	IA	—	—	—	✔	—	Occupation
E 154	Market Deeping	IA	—	—	✔	✔	—	Occupation
E 143	West Stow	AS	—	—	✔	—	—	Occupation
E 72	Burwell	AS	—	—	✔	—	—	Burial
E 30	Castle Bytham	AS	—	—	✔	—	—	Burial
E 58	Castle Acre	M	—	✔	—	—	—	Occupation

Table 1 Beaver skeletal elements from Fenland archaeological sites

the finds which do have a secure or reasonably secure archaeological context were made during the recent excavations and evaluations of the Fenland Survey and the Fenland Management Project, a reminder of the way in which these programmes have extended our knowledge and understanding of the region's past. But neither recent excavations nor earlier ones have necessarily had complete faunal analyses. For example, at the time of writing only a partial picture is available for Market Deeping, where excavation has been limited to evaluation trenches and faunal analyses to a preliminary assessment. These factors restrict the possibilities of a chronological analysis of the beaver evidence, and what follows should be regarded as provisional suggestions rather than positive interpretations.

Many skeletons are from 'natural' contexts, although the beaver from Poppylot perhaps only narrowly escaped finishing up on an archaeological site. It may be that a number of the other 'natural' deaths are similar escapees, since humans would have been the beavers' main enemy in the watery fen conditions, and many may have been trapped or snared underwater and drowned without being retrieved.

The sheer number of finds from Burwell Fen, a few of which show evidence of human activity in the form of cut marks, suggests that year-by-year in the late nineteenth and early twentieth centuries peat cutting by hand may have exposed the refuse dump of ancient fur-trappers. To further our understanding of the natural and human agencies involved in this concentration of beaver skeletons, further research is required into associated animal species, if any are known, together with a more thorough analysis of the beaver bones than has yet been possible, and a series of radiocarbon dates.

On archaeological sites, mandibles and teeth (incisors and molars) predominate for the Later Neolithic and Earlier Bronze Age contexts, in the Iron Age post-cranial elements are more common, and incisors in the Anglo-Saxon period, with mandibles from the one post-conquest site (Table 1). It is probable that these differences reflect differences in the human exploitation of the beaver, which offered such varied resources to their predators. In most periods, it is likely that good use was made of as much as possible: the pelt taken for fur or to make felt, castoreum removed and stored for medicine, body and tail cooked and eaten, and jaw complete with teeth saved for hafting. However, which of these uses left behind the bones that have been recovered is less than clear.

The evidence from Babraham indicates that most of the beaver were treated in a way that left fragmentary, friable bone, whereas the pine marten is in better condition and more of the skeleton is present (Baxter, *pers comm.*). As the pine marten is a carnivore weighing up to 2kg, in contrast to the vegetarian beaver that weighs up to 30kg as an adult, it seems plausible to suggest that the latter were skinned, cooked and eaten in preference to the former which were simply skinned and discarded.

The emphasis on beaver mandibles at the earlier sites may reflect a habit of saving them to make tools, as described by Osgood (1940). This fits with the apparent end of the practice in the later Bronze Age, a time when metal was coming into more common use for everyday tools. However, the stray finds of mandibles which do seem to have been used for tools have yet to be dated.

The three Iron Age sites, Haddenham in particular, show greater representation of post-cranial elements. This may be a reflection of new cooking practices, perhaps linked to a more specialised exploitation of wild animals. If there was an external demand for furs and feathers, and for castoreum, this could have led to more beaver being trapped than were needed locally for food, but there is no evidence to suggest that whole carcases were discarded like the Babraham pine marten. Possibly, joints were preserved by salting and smoking, for later use locally or for export.

At Welland Bank and Market Deeping, the evidence for saltmaking may have a further bearing on the beaver presence. Beaver alive avoid salt water. But humans with dead beaver might well use salt, or salty earth or ashes, to cure beaver pelts so that they could be stored up during a trapping season, and later taken to a more central place for careful tanning or even for immediate trade. Salt rubbed into the fresh skin delays bacterial action and draws out water, and a compact pile of skins treated in this way is an efficient means of temporary storage (Reed 1972,49-50).

The lack of beaver bones from Romano-British sites has already been commented upon, as has the question of local extinction and Anglo-Saxon recolonisation. The presence of beaver elsewhere in England during the first millennium AD suggests that a population was probably present in the Fens too at this time, given the expansion of wetland conditions where the beaver would have felt much more at home than humans. But the incisors which dominate the Anglo-Saxon finds make it difficult to resolve the question, since they could so easily have been imports to the region.

The metal-bound incisors are usually considered to have been pendants, worn as amulets (Meaney 1981), but the Ingalik artefacts made from beaver jaws and incisors show that the latter can be put to a variety of uses, mostly to do with scraping or chiselling in small confined areas (Osgood 1940). It might therefore be worthwhile considering the context and associations of the Anglo-Saxon incisors with this in mind.

The Extinction of Beaver from the Fens

The Holocene beaver population in the Fenland basin must have responded to the changing environmental conditions, which the Fenland Survey and other research has now documented in some detail (Waller 1994). Beaver numbers will have increased or decreased as favourable habitat expanded or contracted, and here one should remember that dry land with streams and rivers is favourable, whereas salt marsh and brackish water is not. Numbers may also have fluctuated as a consequence of disease. A few decades ago, one might have assumed that there were periods of human absence which also favoured the beaver, but another result of the Fenland Survey has been to demonstrate that humans were usually present, although the character of their activities altered as they adapted to changing conditions.

The change in human activity which probably marked the beginning of the end for the beaver, was something which initially protected their freshwater habitat. It was the building of the medieval sea banks, which lessened marine incursions sufficiently to make management of the freshwater environment a viable proposition for the human communities of the Fens (Lane 1993; Hall and Coles 1994, ch.9; Silvester 1999). When people began to turn the Fens into hay meadows, they turned their former predator-prey relationship with beaver into one of competition and conflict over water control, and this is when people will have sought to wipe out the animal which had previously been a valued resource.

Acknowledgements

The research for this paper forms part of a larger project funded by the AHRB and the Leverhulme Trust, and research on beaver environments and structures has been funded by the British Academy, NERC and the AHRB. Staff at the Natural History Museum in London and at the Sedgwick Museum and the University Museum of Zoology in Cambridge have provided much help for the examination of beaver skeletons, and staff from a number of other museums with Fenland collections and from SMRs and Units have assisted in the search for evidence.

Umberto Albarella, Ian Baxter, Mark Hinman, Tom Lane, Jacqui Mulville, Dale Serjeantson and Maisie Taylor have kindly provided information ahead of publication of excavation reports, whilst Stanley West and Pamela Crabtree enlarged on the West Stow details.

Much of the information about the habits and habitats of European beaver is based on fieldwork in Brittany and the Drome, France, and I am grateful to French colleagues for their advice and assistance, and to the Exeter team who carried out the work, especially Mike Rouillard and Sean Hawken, who also assisted with the illustrations and analyses. Ralph Fyfe assisted with checking and calibrating the radiocarbon dates and Kit Patrick with text preparation. The Planel family kindly loaned the modern beaver jaw shown in Plate 3. My thanks go also to John Coles for his assistance throughout.

Catalogue on pg 122

CATALOGUE NUMBER	SITE	DATE	NUMBER OF INDIVIDUALS	NOTES
E7	Upper Delphs, Haddenham	Iron Age	19	97 post-cranial bones, at least 9 with cutmarks
E12	Flag Fen, Peterborough	Bronze Age	1	beaver-gnawed wood, at least 8-10 pieces
E30	Castle Bytham	Anglo-Saxon	1	lower incisor with metal mount
E31	Crowland, NE of Peterboro'	?	1	teeth
E37	Babraham Road, Cambridge	Neolithic	1	c. 7 teeth, mandible and 2 poss post-cranial bones
E41	Welland Bank, nr Peterborough	Bronze Age	'abundant'	detail not yet published
E47	Hockwold-cum-Wilton	Bronze Age	1	mandible and teeth
E54	Brampton, nr Huntingdon	?	1	mandible
E56	Barholm, nr Peterborough	Neolithic	1	2 teeth
E58	Castle Acre, nr Swaffham	Medieval	1	2 mandibles
E72	Burwell, NE of Cambridge	Anglo-Saxon	1	incisor set in bronze
E92	Burwell Fen, NE of Cambridge	?	1	incomplete skull and mandible
E96	Burwell Fen, NE of Cambridge	?	1	skull
E119	Burnt Fen, NE of Ely	?	1	2 pelvic bones, femur and tibia
E120	Burwell Fen, NE of Cambridge	?	1	juvenile mandible with incisor
E121	Fen Ditton, nr Cambridge	?	1	skull and mandible, both with teeth
E122	Fordham, N of Newmarket	?	1	2 mandibles, with teeth
E123	Fens near Ely	?	1	2 mandibles, with teeth
E124	Cambridgeshire Fens	?	2	3 mandibles, with teeth
E125	Fens near Cambridge	?	1	16 post-cranial bones (nt nec. one find)
E126	Norfolk Fens	?	2 ad, 1 juv	34 post-cranial bones,
E127	Lincolnshire Fens	?	1 ad, 1 juv	part skull, 3 mandibles and post-cranial bones
E128	Fens, ?Cambs ?Car Dyke	BM-723	4 ad, 2 juv	6 skulls, 12 mandibles, 10 teeth, 23 postcr.
		3079+/-99BP		
E129	Fens, England	?	1 ad, 1 juv	part skull with molars, femur
E130	Fens	?	2	3 mandibles with teeth
E131	Mildenhall	?	1	adult skeleton, incomplete
E132	Wicken Fen, Cambs	?	2	1 skull, 1 mandible and 1 incomplete skel
E134	Burwell Fen, Cambs	BM-722	9	9 skulls and assoc. post-cranial bones
		2677+/-123BP		
E135	Chatteris Fen, Holwood Farm	?	2	1 incompl. skel and additional scapulae
E136	Littleport Fen, N of Ely	?	1 young ad	1 incompl. skel
E137	Swaffham Prior Fen, nr Cambridge	?	1	mandible with teeth
E138	Feltwell Fen, NE of Ely	?	2	juv mandible, and tibia
E139	Hilgay Fen, nr Downham Mkt	?	1	mandible with teeth
E140	Fens, Cambs	?	2 ad, 1 juv	2 adult pelvic bones, 1 juv p.b., 2 tibia
E140A	Fens, Cambs	?	1	mandible with cutmarks, pelvic bone and tibia
E141	Poppylot, Methwold	Bronze Age	1	skull with arrowhead
E142	Plantation Farm, NE of Ely	Bronze Age	1	?
E143	West Stow, SE of Mildenhall	Anglo-Saxon	1	one incisor
E154	Market Deeping, N of Peterborough	Iron Age	1	teeth, radius, other frags
E156	West Norfolk	?	1	skull
E157	Sutton Fen, nr Somersham	?	1	2 mandibles
E158	Upware, NE of Cambridge	?	1	skull, 2 mandibles and assoc post-cranial bones
E159	Wicken Fen, NE of Cambridge	?	2	2 mandibles and 2 upper incisors
E160	Littleport, Cambs	?	1	2 mandibles and post-cranial bones
E161	Burwell Fen, 1885	?	1	skull
E162	Burwell Fen, 1886	?	1	R mandible, ? artefact
E163	Burwell Fen, 1890	?	2	Skull, assoc. mandibles, post-cranial bones
E164	Burwell Fen, 1891	?	1	Battered and fragmentary skeleton
E165	Burwell Fen, 1892	?	1	Skull, vertebrae, limb bones
E166	Burwell Fen, 1893	?	1	Incisor
E167	Burwell Fen, 1894	?	1	Skull frags and ulna
E168	Burwell Fen, 1895	?	1	R mandible
E169	Burwell Fen, 1898	?	1	Tibia, 7 molars, one incisor
E170	Burwell Fen, 1900	?	2	Skull frags, vertebrae, pelvic girdle; Pelvic bone and 2 femurs

cntd.

Table 2 Beaver evidence from the Fenland basin (bone and wood)

CATALOGUE NUMBER	SITE	DATE	NUMBER OF INDIVIDUALS	NOTES
E171	Burwell Fen, Nov, 1901	?	2 (1ad,1juv)	Skull and mandible, juv; Tibia, ad.
E172	Burwell Fen, 1903	?	1	Pair pelvic bones
E173	Burwell Fen, 1906	?	3	I femur, 1 tibia, calc.; 1 tibia; Skull, 2 mand., 2 vert.
E174	Burwell Fen, 1907	?	2(1ad,1juv)	Frags juv skull, mand, hum; Cut tibia, mand, incisor
E175	Burwell Fen, 1908	?	1	Skull, mandibles, humerus
E176	Burwell Fen, 1909	?	1	Skull, mandibles, vert, limb bones
E177	Burwell Fen, 1911	?	3 (Juv, young ad and ad)	Part juv.skull; Skull frag; Lower incisor
E178	Burwell Fen, 1912	?	1	Skull and post-cranial bones
E179	Burwell Fen, 1913	?	1 large ad	Skull and post-cranial bones
E180	Burwell Fen, no date	?	2	Skull, 2 mandibles; 2 mandibles
E181	Swaffham Fen, 1892	?	1	2 mandibles
E182	Swaffham Fen, 1904	?	2	Frag skull and 1 mand; Frag skull and 2 mand
E183	Swaffham Fen, 1904/1910	?	2(1ad,1juv)	2 upper incisors; 2 mandibles
E184	Swaffham Fen, 1905	?	1 large adult	Skull and post-cranial bones
E185	Swaffham Fen, 1911	?	1	3 limb bones, 1 inc
E186	Swaffham Fen, 1912	?	1	calcaneum
E187	Swaffham Fen, 1921	?	1	Skull, 2 mand, post-cranial bones
E188	Swaffham Fen, 1924	?	2	Skull and post-cran.bones; Humerus
E189	Swaffham Fen, no date	?	2-3	2 mandibles; Skull, pelvic and limbs; Skull frag and vert
E190	Reach Fen, 1885	?	1 large adult	2 mandibles
E191	Reach Fen, 1921	?	1	Skull and 2 mandibles
E192	Reach Fen, 1922	?	2	Left mand and incisor; Lower L incisor
E193	Reach Fen, 1924	?	1	Skull, 2 mandibles, pelvis, femur, tibia
E194	Fens, Cambridge	?	4	4 skulls, 4L & 3R mand, numerous post-cr.bones
E195	Fens, loc. Unknown	?	4	4 skulls, 4L & 3R mand, numerous post-cr.bones
E196	Fiskerton, Lincs	Iron Age	1	humerus, ulna, 2 caudal vert.

Table 2 Beaver evidence from the Fenland basin (bone and wood)

Bibliography

Birch Reynardson, J., 1853, 'Antiquities and Works of Art Exhibited', *Archaeological Journal* 10, 81-86

Burleigh, R., Hewson, A. and Meeks, N., 1976, 'British Museum Natural Radiocarbon Measurements VIII', *Radiocarbon* 18 (1), 16-42

Clark, G., 1933, 'Report on an Early Bronze Age site in the south-eastern Fens', *Antiquaries Journal* 13, 266-296

Clark, G., 1971, 'A shaped and utilized beaver jaw from Ulrome, Holderness, Yorkshire (E.R)', *The Antiquaries Journal* 61, 305-307, Pl. LXIII

Clark, J.G.D. and Godwin, H., 1962, 'The Neolithic in the Cambridgeshire Fens', *Antiquity* 36, 10-23

Coad, J.G. and Streeten, A.D.F., 1982, 'Excavations at Castle Acre, Norfolk, 1972-77', *The Archaeological Journal* 139, 138-301

Coles, B., 2000, 'Beaver Territories: the resource potential for humans', in Bailey, G., Charles, R. and Winder, N. (eds), *Human Ecodynamics*, 80-89 (Oxford, Oxbow)

Coles, B., in prep, *Beaver in Britain's Past*

Coles, B. in press, 'Beaver structures and the archaeological record' in Raftery, B. (ed), *Recent Work in Wetland Archaeology,* WARP Occasional Paper No. 14

Coy, J., 1980, 'The animal bone', in Haslam, J. 'A Middle Saxon Iron Smelting Site at Ramsbury, Wiltshire', *Medieval Archaeology* 24, 41-45

Crowson, A., Lane, T. and Reeve, J. (eds), 2000, *Fenland Management Project Excavations 1991-1995*, Lincolnshire Archaeology and Heritage Report Series No.3

Evans, C. and Hodder, I., in press, *Marshland Communities and Cultural Landscape,* Cambridgeshire, McDonald Institute Research Series

Evans, C. and Serjeantson, D., 1988, 'The backwater economy of a fen-edge community in the Iron Age: the Upper Delphs, Haddenham', *Antiquity* 62, 360-370

Godwin, H., 1978, *Fenland: its ancient past and uncertain future* (Cambridge University Press)

Hall, D. and Coles, J., 1994, *Fenland Survey: an essay in landscape and persistence*, English Heritage Archaeological Report 1 (London)

Harman, M., 1993, 'The mammalian bone', in Simpson, W.G., Gurney, D.A., Nene, J. and Pryor, F.M.M., *The Fenland Project Number 7: Excavations in Peterborough and the Lower Welland Valley 1960-1969*, East Anglian Archaeology 61

Hayes, P.P. and Lane, T.W., 1992, *The Fenland Project, Number 5: Lincolnshire Survey, The South-West Fens*, East Anglian Archaeology 55

Healy, F., 1996, *The Fenland Project, Number 11: The Wissey Embayment: Evidence for pre-Iron Age Occupation accumulated prior to the Fenland Project*, East Anglian Archaeology 78

Hillam, J., 1992, 'The dating of archaeological sites in the United Kingdom', in Bartholin. T., Berglund, B., Eckstein, D. and Schweingruber, F. (eds), *Tree-rings and environment*, 146-9, Lund

Hinman, M., in press, 'Ritual Activity at the Foot of the Gog Magog Hills, Cambridge' (*Space and Place*)

Lane, T.W., 1993, *The Fenland Project, Number 8: Lincolnshire Survey. The northern fen-edge*, East Anglian Archaeology 66

Lawrance, P., 1982, 'Animal Bones', in Coad, J.G. and Streeten, A.D.F., 'Excavations at Castle Acre, Norfolk, 1972-77', *Archaeological Journal* 139, 275-96

Legge, A.J. and Rowley-Conwy, P.A., 1986, 'The Beaver (Castor fiber L.) in the Tigris-Euphrates basin', *Journal of Archaeological Science* 13, 469-476

Macdonald, D. and Barrett, P., 1993, *Mammals of Britain and Europe*, (London, Harper Collins)

Mayhew, D.F., 1975, *The Quaternary History of some British Rodents and Lagomorphs* (Unpublished, D.Phil., Dept. Zoology, Cambridge)

Mayhew, D.F., 1978, 'Age structure of a sample of subfossil beaver (Castor fiber L.)' in Butler, P.M. and Joysey K.A. (eds), *Development, Function and Evolution of Teeth*, 495-505 (London, Academic Press)

McKinley, J., 1994, *The Anglo-Saxon Cemetery at Spong Hill, North Elmham. Part VIII: The Cremations*, East Anglian Archaeology 69

Meaney, A., 1964, *Gazetteer of Early Anglo-Saxon Burial Sites* (London, George Allen and Unwin)

Meaney, A., 1981, *Anglo-Saxon Amulets and Curing Stones*, Brit. Archaeol. Rep. British Series 96

Miller, S.H. and Skertchly, S.B.J., 1878, *The Fenland Past and Present* (Wisbech)

Mulville, J. with Bramwell, D. and Harman, M., in press, 'The mammalian and bird bone' in Field, N. and Parker Pearson, M. (eds), *Fiskerton: an Iron Age Timber Causeway with Iron Age and Roman votive offerings* (Oxford, Oxbow Books)

Munro, R., 1891, 'On supposed otter and beaver traps from peat bogs', *Proceedings of the Society of Antiquaries of Scotland* 25, 73-89

Novak, M., 1976, *The Beaver in Ontario* (Ontario, Ministry of Natural Resources)

Osgood, C, 1940, 'Ingalik Material Culture', *Yale University Publications in Anthropology* No.22

Pryor, F., 1992, 'Current research at Flag Fen, Peterborough', *Antiquity* 66, 439-457

Radclyffe Dugmore, A., 1914, *The Romance of the Beaver* (London, William Heinemann)

Reaney, P.H., 1943, *The Placenames of Cambridgeshire and the Isle of Ely*, English Place-names Society vol.19 (Cambridge University Press)

Reed, R., 1972, *Ancient Skins, Parchments and Leather* (London and New York, Seminar Press)

Richard, P.B., 1967, 'Le determinisme de la construction des barrages chez le castor du Rhône', *Revue d'Ecologie – La Terre et la Vie* 114 (4), 339-470

Richard, B., 1980, *Les Castors* (Poitiers, Balland)

Roberts, J., 1998, 'A contextual approach to the interpretation of the early Bronze Age skeletons of the East Anglian Fens', *Antiquity* 72, 188-197

Rouland, P., 1990, *Essai de synthese sur la reintroduction du castor en France et perspectives*, Office National de la Chasse

Silvester, R., 1999, 'Medieval reclamation of marsh and fen', in Cook, H. and Williamson, T. (eds), *Water Management in the English Landscape*, 122-140 (Edinburgh, University Press)

Simpson, W.G., 1993, 'The excavation of a Late Neolithic settlement at Barholm, Lincolnshire', in Simpson, W.G., Gurney, D.A., Nene, J. and Pryor, F.M.M., *The Fenland Project, Number 7: Excavations in Peterborough and the Lower Welland Valley 1960-1969*, East Anglian Archaeology 61

Skertchly, S.B.J, 1877, *The Geology of the Fenland* (Mem. Geol. Survey, London)

Smith, A.G., Whittle, A., Cloutman, E.W. and Morgan, L., 1989, 'Mesolithic and Neolithic activity and environmental impact in the south-east fen-edge in Cambridgeshire', *Proceedings of the Prehistoric Society* 55, 207-249

Taylor, M., 1993, 'Notes', *Fenland Archaeological Trust Newsletter* 54, 2

Taylor, M., in press, 'The waterlogged wood: Woodworking', in Pryor, F.M.M., *Flag Fen* (London, English Heritage)

Waller, M., 1994, *The Fenland Project, Number 9: Flandrian Environmental Change in Fenland*, East Anglian Archaeology 70

West, S., 1985, 'West Stow. The Anglo-Saxon Village', *East Anglian Archaeology* 24

Wilsson, L., 1968, *My Beaver Colony* (London, Souvenir Press)

11. HOMES FOR THE PEAT DIGGERS?

by Rog Palmer

My title is not the beginning of a protest movement but will be explained later in this paper. The question mark, however, remains with us beyond the end of this brief review, as what follows is little more than a developing line of thought.

Most of my archaeological work has come from playing with aerial photographs and I feel a relative beginner in Fenland archaeology. This started, as did my association with David Hall, when I replaced Tim Malim as 'Fenland Assistant' in 1986. Work included drawing maps for David's Fenland volumes, boring the fens with Martyn Waller, and taking the boss for a pint on the one day a week he was in Cambridge. From my point of view, David was a great boss as he left me alone to get on with things. When I asked what was going to be done about incorporating the evidence from air photos into the Cambridgeshire volumes his reply was that I could do whatever I wanted providing it did not slow down the other work. I knew that the Cambridgeshire SMR, although recently remapped from CUCAP (Cambridge University Collection) aerial photographs, was not at its best in the Fens where the photo interpretation had been done by an over-confident anthropologist working on an MSC (Manpower Services Commission) scheme under my supervision in 1983-4. If the aerial photos could be re-interpreted, adding in information from the RCHME collection (now part of the National Monuments Record), it meant that for the then forthcoming volumes we would be able to present as complete a picture of the known evidence as was then possible. This could combine David's fieldwalking and documentary research, with information more thoughtfully interpreted from air photos. We were aware that each source was subject to a range of factors that affect recovery and reliability, but the Fenland Survey provided us with a couple of thousand fieldwalked sites of all periods and, in places, the landscape of ditched boundaries that accompanied them (see, for example, Hall 1996, Figs 67, 95-96, 102).

My intention for this paper *was* to look at the turbary sites which, from the air, dominate the Romano-British landscape between March and the Old Croft river (Hall 1996, Fig 96). I hoped to be able to examine those alongside surface and air photograph evidence and reach some worthwhile conclusions. So much for theory!

Photo interpretation has considerably extended the distribution and numbers of known turbaries, and the fieldwalked sites provide us with roughly dated settlements and salterns in the same area. Would it be possible to link, or try to link, the dwellings of the peat diggers with their workplaces? This was the origin of my title but the limitations of the evidence may not allow us to reach any useful conclusions. There has also been a certain reticence on my part because I can't help thinking that David will have found the answers to most Fenland questions long before I even think of the questions.

Let's begin with a few definitions.

Turbaries are the cuttings from which peat has been extracted. They now survive as silt mounds which can be clearly (Plate 1), or less clearly, visible from the air, especially in winter. Their edges can be indistinct and they give the impression – to me at least – that they are still emerging from the peat. I like the things because they are never likely to attain the glamorous status of the ditched features that are hunted by most aerial photographers and they provide indications of the tremendous amount of work, or muck shifting if you like, that was carried out locally. Peat, when dried after extraction, was likely to have provided the major source of fuel in the central Fenland. Fuel would be needed for domestic purposes and for salt making which, field and excavation evidence shows, was undertaken at domestic and industrial levels.

Romans are responsible for the various activities discussed in this paper. Environmental and artefactual evidence show us that this part of the Fenland was settled only in this short 4-500 year period. As a student I avoided the Romans whose study I saw as immersed in discussion of inscriptions, statues, pottery, and other 'junk' – all far too civilised for me. But air photos show us that during the Roman period there were some wonderful holes cut in the ground which now can be recorded on, and interpreted from, aerial photos. These holes, rural civil engineering done by peasants of that period, have provided the main content of this paper. My own apolitical existence makes me wonder how much any change in the management of the country would have affected the daily life of the average peasant: and my conclusion, also based on a few years spent

Plate 1 Turbaries south of the Fen Causeway at TL4697 (Cambridgeshire).
The photograph shows them as light-toned silt-filled ridges, the height of which can be seen by undulations in those modern field boundaries and tracks that cross them.
Photo: Rog Palmer: 93.24/12

mapping those landscapes, is not at all. The tax collector may change (from Cockney to Italian if you like) and demands for specific products may vary but I cannot imagine that much else would change. I see the Fenland landscape of this period as that largely created and used by the natives although here and there we can see obvious non-local influence, as for example, in the great stone buildings at Stonea (TL450936) and Langwood (TL418852) and the regular field system at Christchurch (TL4997: see Figure 4).

The Fen Causeway is one actual Roman-made feature in the central Fenland (Fig. 1). The route crosses the fens from – as relevant to this paper – Denver to March, although we might ask if this may have enhanced an existing high-ground communication route. From Denver, the route follows a silt ridge to the Old Croft river and from there – if we look at a map showing 'topography' (*i.e.* roddons) it appears to cut across the highest ground to March. It can be seen that the roddons north of the route flow to the north while those on the south go south. So the route actually does not cut many tidal watercourses other than the Old Croft river at the east and the Flaggrass Waterway flanking March island, which may have been the major factors in silting of what is thought to be the 'canal' phase. May we ask again, whether native Fenlander lore was a key factor in cutting this feature in the knowledge that its silting could be encouraged and would provide a firm surface for access? We know little about water management during this period but the air photo evidence shows it to have been ubiquitous and it must have been an important aspect of daily life in the Fens. My question – another question! – is to ask whether we are correct in identifying these 'broad ditches' crossing the peat fen as canals? May they have been cut so that they would fill with silt?

As roads will, it attracted nearby settlements as shown mainly by the field-collected evidence. Dating shows these, with minor shifts in location, to continue through the Roman period and to be mainly settlement + saltern with some non-saltern settlements. Purely saltern sites – possibly industrial – are mostly set away from the Fen Causeway (Fig. 4).

So much for setting the scene.
Now to some evidence.

The period covered by this discussion is one when the sea level had been falling, there was an expansion of dry land areas and, with the lowering of the water table, the peat fens would have been more readily accessible. Access would have been facilitated by use of the partly silted watercourses, as is clearly indicated by the widespread presence throughout the Fens of ditch-defined tracks on them (as, for example, at TF4503: Hall 1996, fig 96). Roddons which formerly provided a network of

Figure 1 The study area showing natural features and the Fen Causeway. March is the blank area on the left, the Old Croft river – the Cambridgeshire-Norfolk boundary – is centre, and Denver Sluice is at the far right. The watercourses suggest that the Fen Causeway in Cambridgeshire follows a ridge of higher ground

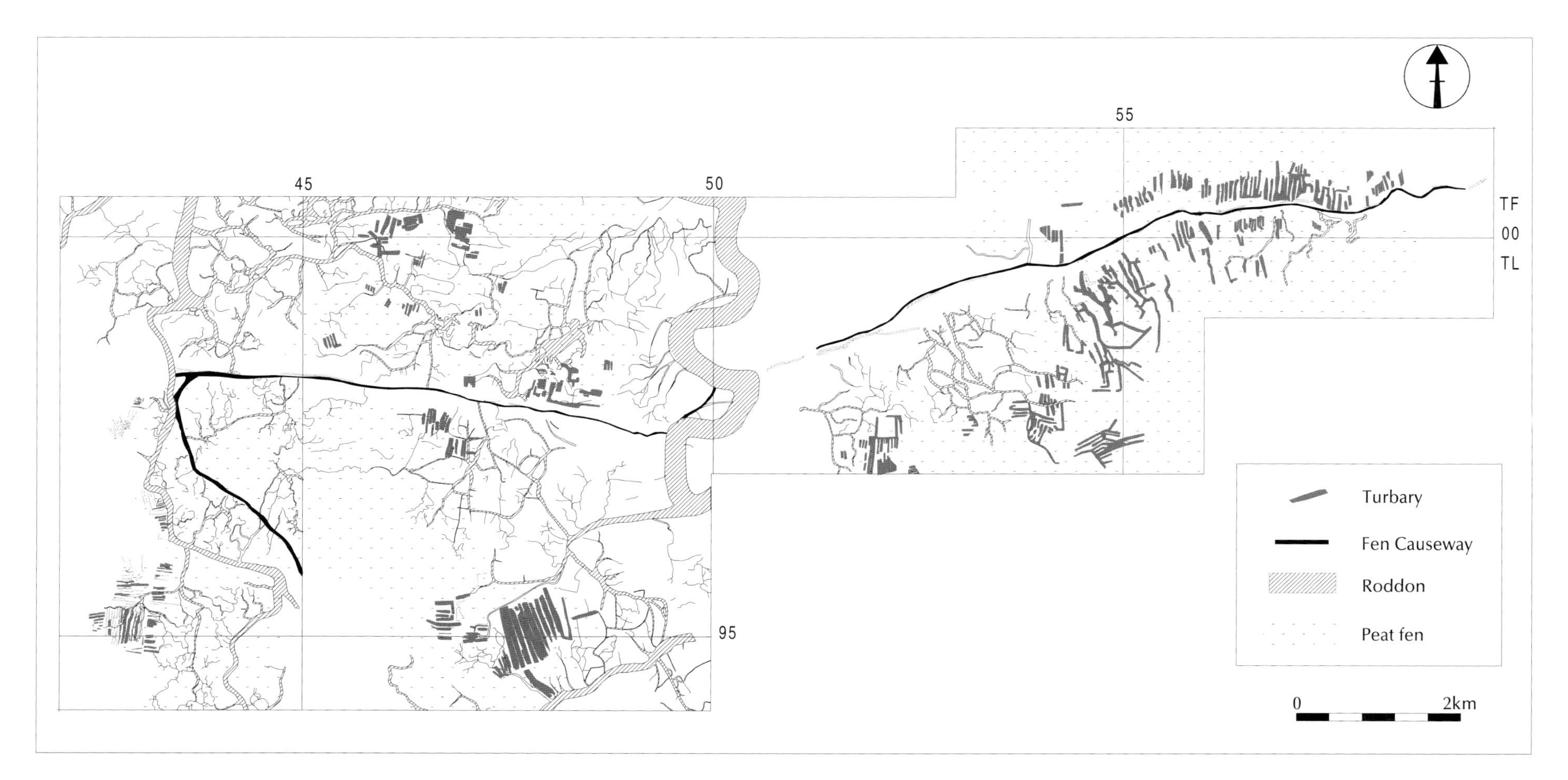

Figure 2 Study Area with turbaries added to the natural background. This map illustrates the extent of currently recorded peat extraction that took place in this part of the Fenland

waterways had now become dry roads – providing an interesting example of 'continuity'.

Settlements show a preferred location on high, dry, ground. Peat, and therefore peat cuttings, will be found in wetter areas. The two are mutually exclusive, but could be adjacent. It is also reasonable to assume that a walk to work of a few kilometres would have been acceptable.

Dating of surface collections can be used to divide sites into *early* (second to third century AD) and *late* (third to fourth century AD) with some sites continuing throughout. This dating equates with that used by Bob Silvester in his analysis of Fen Causeway sites (1991, 103-115) and can help define the phase of 'mid third century' flooding which is reckoned to be responsible for the silting of turbaries and other contemporary holes in this part of the Fenland (Churchill 1970, 135-139; Silvester 1991, 101).

Martyn Waller's environmental research can be used to show that the peats in this area, which would have formed a surface in Roman times, began forming at about –1.5m OD at Welney Washes (Waller 1994, fig 7.25) while at Hobbs Lot the depth was –0.9m (*ibid.*, fig 10.10). With a Roman fen edge at +2.0m (Hall 1987, 11) this allows a depth of 3.5m of extractable peat above marine sediments. My encounters with the peat-clay interface when digging for John Coles in the Somerset Levels showed it to be extremely wet and unpleasant with the clay acting as an impermeable bottom for the wet sponge-like peat. Cut a hole to the clay and it rapidly filled with water.... Similar occurrences in the Fenland turbaries may have led to their abandonment or certainly created a logical bottom level.

The surface area of mapped peat cuts (Fig. 2) is 246 hectares (or for David 608 acres, which is close to one square mile). Using our 3.5m depth we have an estimated volume of 8.6 million cubic metres of extracted peat or, using figures from Godwin (1978, 121: a 25cm^3 block weighing about 8kg) around 4500 tons. Godwin notes variations in the size of hand-dug turves from which an average block of 24 x 16 x 10 cm can be calculated. A good digger, he says, can cut 8-10,000 turves in a 14 hour day (*ibid.*, 119). Tools in the Roman period would have allowed a similar rate of work and provide us with a daily extraction rate of 30m^3 per person. Put another way, in medieval times one week's peat cutting could produce fuel sufficient for a year (Darby 1983,139).

Therefore, the turbaries in my study area would provide 287,000 days work, or 786 man-years.

On a more local scale we can look at the Upwell turbaries, which amount to about half the area of those in this part of Cambridgeshire. At Upwell we also have adjacent settlement, perhaps the peat-cutters' village, (Fig. 3) which has been recorded in considerable detail from the air and for which fieldwalking has provided evidence of what may be a large and long-term saltern industry (Upwell sites 12, 13, 14) and an associated settlement with possible early second to late fourth century pottery (Upwell site 15). The context of the Upwell features can be seen on Fig. 3.

Retaining the 3.5m depth, the Upwell turbaries would have provided 2,068,000m^3 of peat. This could have been extracted in 68,900 days. Although the ditched boundaries of the adjacent village are clear, we lack evidence for houses and, for the sake of discussion, will assume a working group of ten families which, by coincidence, equals one to each of the major peat 'fingers'. If all were worked together that would have reduced the extraction time to 6890 days.

We move further into hypothesis now. Peat has to dry before it is useful as fuel and this, plus general Fenny wetness, may restrict the cutting season to one which I suggest may be of 70 days per year (say May to mid-July, after which harvest takes priority while the turves dry out and are occasionally turned). This guessed cutting period is supported by Darby (1974, 84) who noted that in medieval times the cutting period was between the Feasts of St Philip and St James – May 1 to August 1. At that rate, our 6890 days become 98 years which – if it is not too circular an argument – may fit quite nicely into the duration between the spread of occupation into this part of the Fenland (say, after things quietened down after the Boudiccan rebellion of AD 60-61) and up to the period of flooding (mid third century). It is, in fact, about half that time-span.

However, peat cutting at that intensity suggests industrial use rather than the 'one week's cutting provides a year's domestic requirements' noted above. The scale and planning of the turbaries supports the industrial concept with, perhaps, the rest of the year spent in transporting, tool-making and performing whatever agricultural activities were necessary to stay alive in the Roman Fenland. Most of the recorded turbaries suggest, to me,

Figure 3 Upwell, Cambridgeshire, area TL4795. An enlargement from the area map showing the most detailed area of settlement that has been recorded in close association with turbaries. The channel immediately north of the turbaries appears to have been canalised and may have combined functions of drainage and transport, linking the peat cutting area to other watercourses. More detailed plans of the 'village' have been published elsewhere (Palmer 1990; Palmer and Cox 1993, fig 1) and the symbols show and identify 'sites' found by fieldwalking (Hall 1996). Conventions as Fig. 4

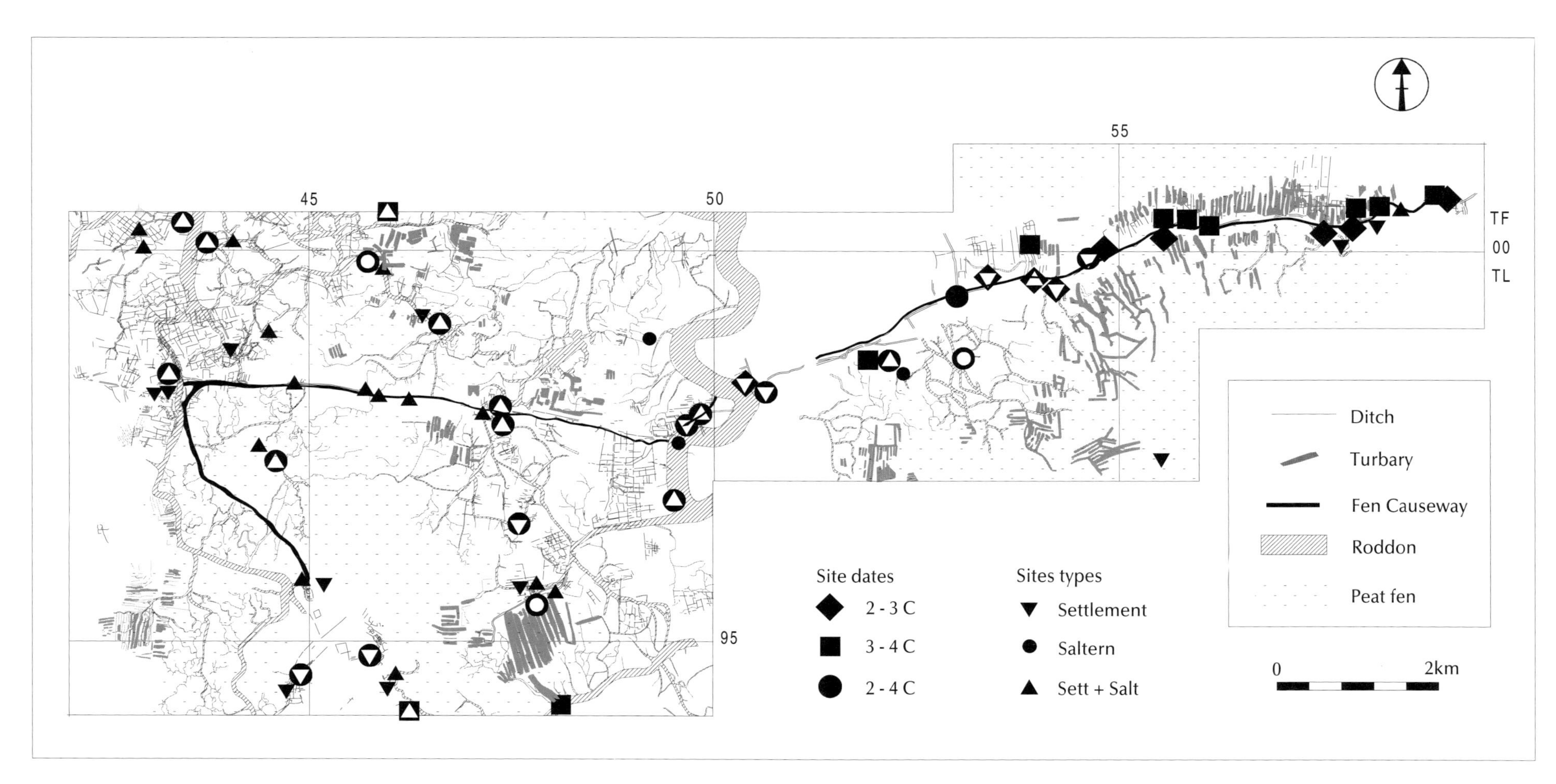

Figure 4 Information has been added to show the known pattern of settlement in the area. Symbols identify types and date ranges of fieldwalked 'sites' while the landscape of ditched fields, tracks and enclosures mapped from aerial photographs can be seen – murkily – in the background

long-term and well-planned peat cutting. Any repetitive cutting has to be organised to provide staged lowering of the surface so that each removed layer provides the surface on which to stack, turn and dry peat cut from the next series of trenches and to provide access for their removal. This, I suggest, is what is recorded at Upwell and over much of the central Fenland. If there were single-year or single-use cuts I doubt that we could now recognise them from surface or aerial evidence.

Let us now return to the larger area and use the Survey data to show the settlement pattern (Fig. 4). Pottery from the majority of sites covers the second to fourth century range and *may* indicate continuous occupation. Among these is a scatter of early sites – in Norfolk most flank the Fen Causeway, in Cambridgeshire they lie well away from it, and similarly in later periods. Make what you like of that – but remember that survey in this part of Norfolk did not extend much beyond the edges of my mapped area. Add the evidence from air photos (Fig. 4) and we can see the pattern of that settlement with extensive field systems northeast of March and at Christchurch and traces of regular fields north of the Fen Causeway in Norfolk. Bob Silvester's work in Norfolk has shown that many of the fields date to the late phase of occupation and overlay the turbaries (Silvester 1991, fig 60d).

Now we come to a dilemma. Returning to our earlier landscape we can see a hive of activity in which turbaries and settlements + salterns predominate. The mid-third century marine incursion is the only observed event that could be responsible for the silting of turbaries. Later wetness due to rising water tables in post-Roman times was freshwater and resulted in the peat growth that provided fuel for medieval Fenlanders. It is difficult to avoid the conclusion that the mapped turbaries have to be those of the earlier Roman period which were 'closed' by the mid-third century flooding.

So – another question – why does the later landscape retain a similar picture of salt-making activity? Sites producing salt on an apparently industrial scale appear to continue, as for example at Upwell (Fig. 4: TL4795), northeast of March (Fig. 4: TL4599) and at Denver in Norfolk (Fig. 4: TF5800) and domestic settlement + salterns continued and were founded (e.g. at Upwell: TL4795 and Denver TF5700) in the later period. Where did the fuel come from?

The only logical answer seems to be that the source of peat was from a second set of turbaries in the same area. Because they did not fill subsequently with marine silts they are no longer visible. In fact they are most likely gone for ever, having been 'backfilled' by post-Roman peat growth and cut during medieval extraction, which we know by comparison of documentary records and the ground to have left no trace, to have removed a layer from the surface. All we can do now is reverse my original question and turn *homes for peat cutters?* into *peat cuttings for homes?* and propose that the apparently open spaces in which fieldwalking and aerial photography now reveal nothing but peat could have once included the later phases of Roman-period peat cutting. This suggestion may help explain the apparent absence of peat cutting in other parts of the Fenland – as would have been required, for example, to serve the salt making industry that has been identified recently near Grandford on the west side of March island.

If negative evidence and guesswork are correct, may I have deduced another square mile of peat cutting that we are unlikely to recover? Am I allowed to have 4500 tons of negative evidence? When I began reading and thinking to prepare this small token I didn't have much of an idea where things were going to end. I'm still not sure whether I have reached an ending, and if I have, whether it is of any value. Field evidence shows us that occupation of the Fenland continued in the third and fourth century AD and that salt making continued at a time when – to judge by the Norfolk evidence – there was an expansion or shift of cultivated or enclosed land. If nothing else, this small piece of work (?guesswork) has provided another example of *the more we know, the less we understand* as my conclusions leave me having less of an idea of what the people were doing in this part of the Roman Fenland than I thought I did a year ago.

About ten years ago our paymasters told us that the Fenland Survey had been completed. Apart from this curious way of dealing with a landscape that continues to be undressed as its surface is annually lowered it is clear that there is considerable research potential in studying the facts that survey was allowed to recover.

Bibliography

Churchill, D.M., 1970, 'Post neolithic to Romano-British sedimentation in the southern Fenlands of Cambridgeshire and Norfolk' in Phillips, C.W. (ed), *The Fenland in Roman Times,* Royal Geog. Soc. Res. Ser. 5, 132-146

Darby, H.C., 1974, *The Medieval Fenland* (Cambridge)

Darby, H.C., 1983, *The Changing Fenland* (Cambridge)

Godwin, H., 1978, *Fenland: its ancient past and uncertain future* (Cambridge)

Hall, D., 1987, *The Fenland Project, Number 2: Fenland Landscapes and Settlement between Peterborough and March,* East Anglian Archaeology 35

Hall, D., 1996, *The Fenland Project, Number 10: Cambridgeshire Survey, Isle of Ely and Wisbech,* East Anglian Archaeology 79

Palmer, R., 1990, 'Bacon's Farm, Upwell, Cambridgeshire: a Roman linear 'village'' *AARGnews* 1, 24-26

Palmer, R. and Cox, C., 1993, *Uses of aerial photography in archaeological evaluations,* IFA Technical Paper 12

Silvester, R.J., 1991, *The Fenland Project, Number 4: Norfolk Survey, The Wissey Embayment and Fen Causeway,* East Anglian Archaeology 52

Waller, M., 1994, *The Fenland Project, Number 9: Flandrian Environmental Change in Fenland,* East Anglian Archaeology 70

12. RECONSTRUCTING LINCOLNSHIRE LANDSCAPES

by Tom Lane

Introduction

David Hall's contribution to the landscape archaeology of Eastern and Central England, and the Fenland in particular, is quite unlike that of anyone else. Firstly, he knows the land with an intimacy that can only come from having walked much of it. Moreover, he has walked it with enthusiasm, open-mindedness and extraordinary vision, allowing him a unique insight into the multiple landscapes of the regions. His impressive publications (listed at rear of this volume) ooze affection for the countryside in general as well as imparting his considerable wisdom of landscapes.

David is a scholar as well as an intuitive and indefatigable fieldwalker, His early labour of love, Wollaston (Hall 1977), made full use of documentary sources to complement his strikingly detailed fieldwork. The same multi-disciplinary approach has been a constant feature of David's work. Along the way this has made him the nation's acknowledged leading authority on the formation and operation of medieval fields (Hall 1982; 1995). His current work on hedgerows and woods are natural extensions to his more typical fieldwork activities.

Whether on upland or fen, David Hall's great strength is in 'landscape reconstruction' and, with this concept as an underlying framework, this paper reviews some aspects of fieldwork conducted in three different areas of Lincolnshire. The aspects chosen are selected topics which serve to demonstrate a few examples of landscape reconstruction made possible through field survey. Finally, a specific monument-type, linear boundaries, is discussed in terms of its potential for field survey. While David was not directly involved in all of the work herein described, its execution was thoroughly Hall-inspired.

Survey on the Fens

In the Fenland, the pioneering reconnaissance surveys which David devised in 1976 and subsequently honed, proved to be the framework on which the archaeology of the Fenland could be reviewed and revised radically (this vol. Chapter 1; Hall and Coles 1994). He introduced the concept of landscape reconstruction to an area once described as having *'no landscape – only land'* (Swift 1984). The *'landscape which, of all landscapes, most approximates to Nothing'* (*ibid.*, 11) was, to the contrary, shown to be *Something* and is archaeologically very special. Potential for resolving the area's long and complex natural evolution through detailed recording of sections and boreholes had long been recognised and was explored further and in detail during the Fenland Project (Waller 1994). But it was David's large-area mapping of the surface deposits, recorded in association with the more traditional forms of archaeological field evidence, which brought the Fenland Survey to life. Free of woods, pastures and, almost, of towns, the Fenland is an uninterrupted, open landscape in which regional patterns of past human activities can be traced by fieldwalking and set against changing environments, characterised by different surface sediments. Moreover, at least part of the region yields cropmarks of rare clarity (Hallam 1970; Palmer 1996), although the aerial evidence was under-emphasised during the Fenland Project until David's collaboration with Rog Palmer (Hall 1996). In this vast landscape the mapping of precise locations of ancient river channels, drainage patterns, embayments, boundaries between 'upland' and fen, and fen and marsh, were all part of David's interpretation of 'fieldwalking'. Relating these to patterns of settlement and industry over thousands of hectares was David's Fenland achievement and is well-documented elsewhere (Hall and Coles 1994; Coles and Hall 1998).

Results of the fieldwalking conducted as part of the Fenland Survey in Lincolnshire serve as examples of the possibilities of landscape reconstruction (Hayes and Lane 1992; Lane 1993). Results of follow-up excavation on certain of the sites has added a new dimension (Crowson *et al.* 2000). Detailed survey saw the discovery of numerous Roman sites and the systematic recovery of many thousands of pottery sherds. Such a detailed dataset has enabled analytical interrogations not always possible from fieldwalked collections. For instance Peter Hayes identified a preferred zone of settlement for the inhabitants of the Roman Fenland and demonstrated that this zone moved west to east over the changing landscape through time (Hayes *et al.* 1992; Hayes and Lane 1993) .

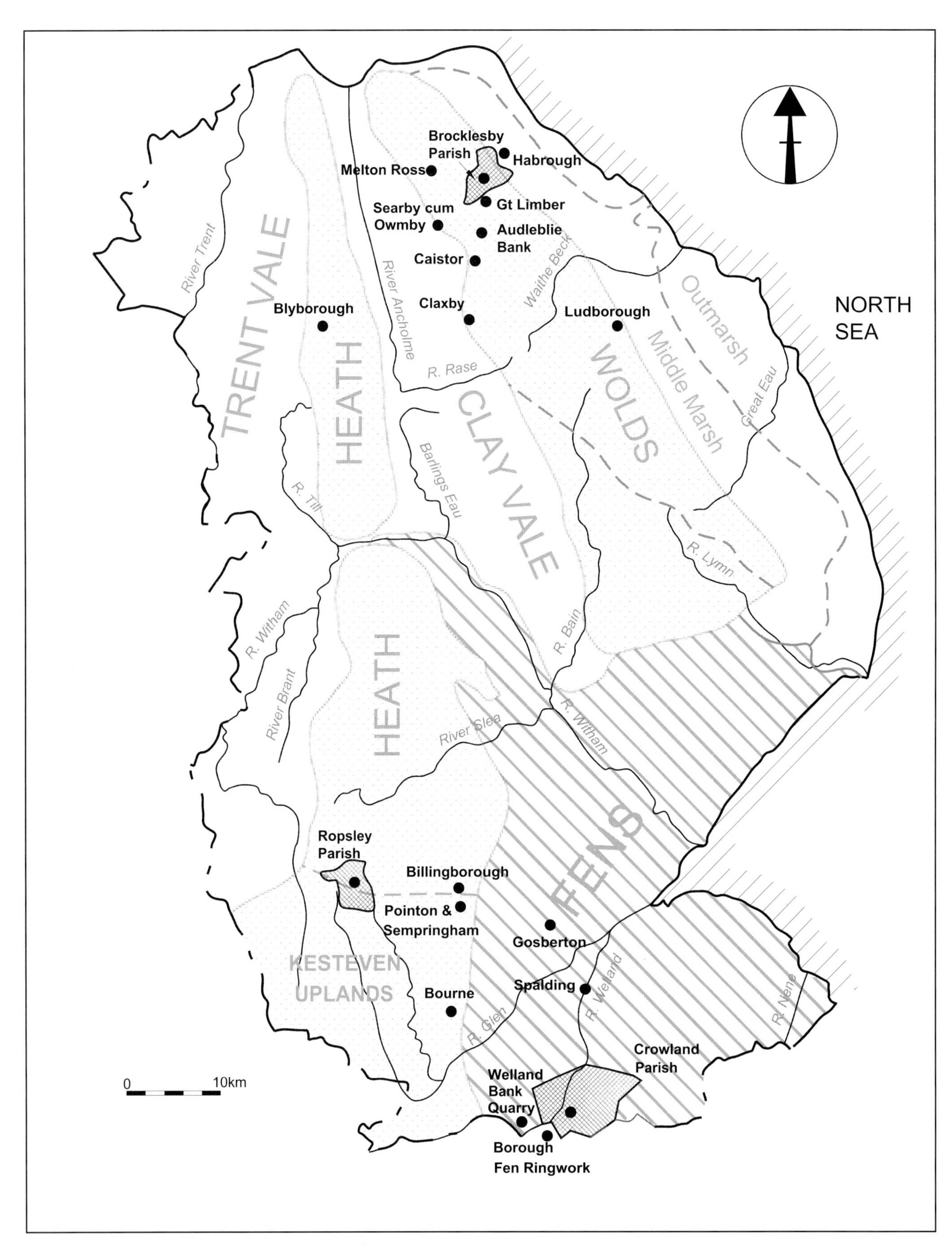

Figure 1 Lincolnshire's regions (after Robinson 1993) and places mentioned in text

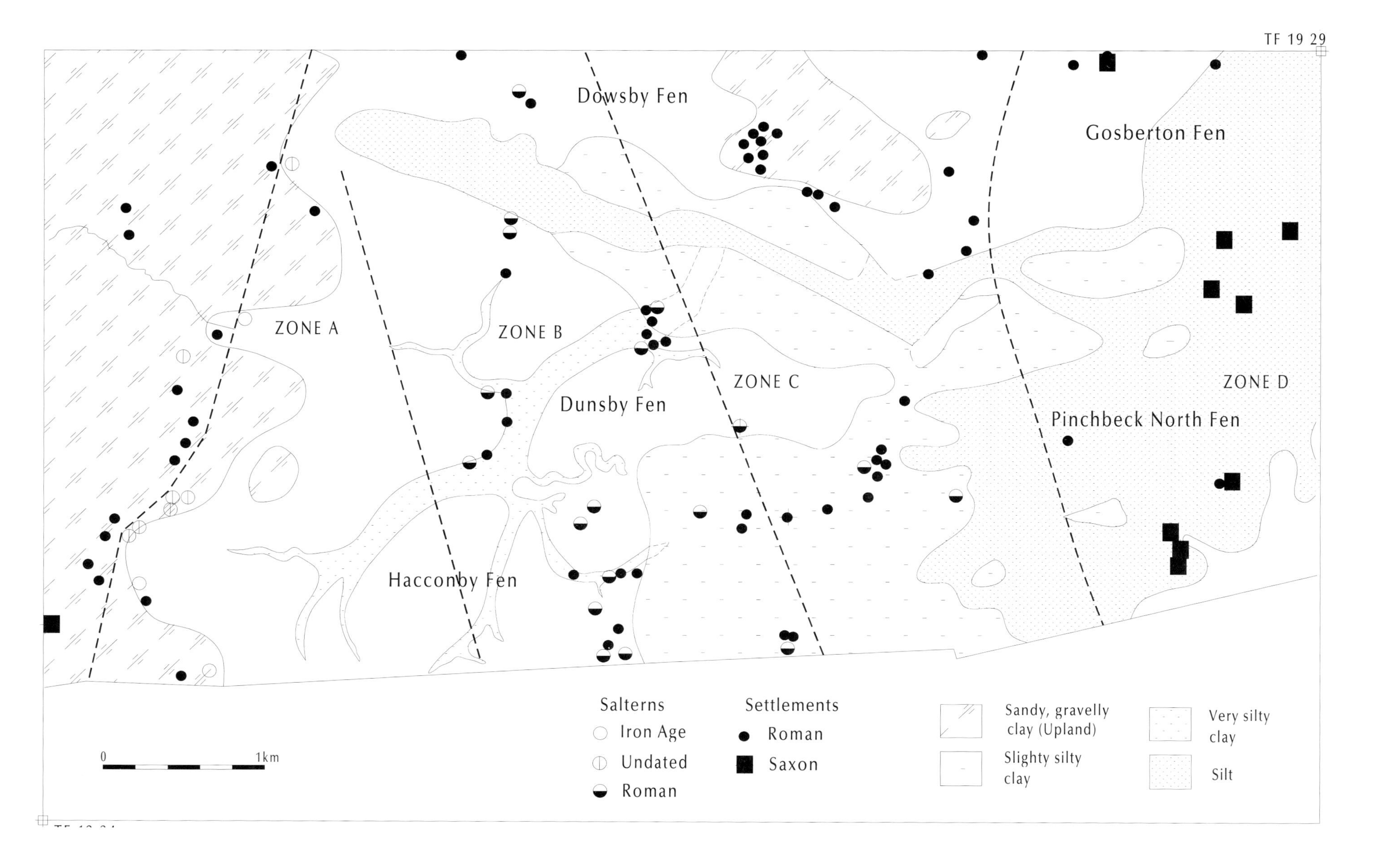

Figure 2 'Zones' in the landscape. The fen edge north of Bourne (after P. Hayes)

Roman settlement of the western fens in Lincolnshire is usually restricted to the narrow roddons, extinct tidal creeks which now protrude westward from the coarse silts into the claylands like crooked silty fingers (Hayes and Lane 1993, fig 5.2). Aside from the extinct creeks the remainder of the landscape junctions trend north-south in the area between the fen edge communities of Bourne and Billingborough (Fig. 2). Studying the locations of dated sherds of Roman pottery enabled identification of a series of broadly north-south aligned Landscape 'Zones' (four in total extending east from the fen edge to the silts) which could be equated to theoretical 'Stages' in Fenland landscape development.

Stage 1 basal peat formation on the solid geology through high groundwater levels and frequent flooding
Stage 2 accumulation of marine/brackish sediments over tens or hundreds of years
Stage 3 growth of plant communities leading to formation of higher saltmarshes. These constitute a valuable resource – rich, open, grazing land
Stage 4 formation of surface peat as freshwater-dominated environments displace the saltmarshes

In a fen margin landscape such as that north of Bourne, the Stage 3, higher saltmarsh, would move gradually west-east across the landscape through time, as the area naturally accreted. All the time it would be keeping ahead of the fen margin peats which formed on the immediate fen edge through the continued run-off of freshwater from the upland and advanced eastwards. It is believed that the 'Zones' reflect the continuing west-east translocation of that rich grazing land (and settlements) ahead of these advancing freshwater environments. Such a move saw the Stage 3 marshes in Zone B occuring in the Early Roman, Zone C in the Late Roman and Zone D by the Saxon period, as indicated by the pottery dates.

	ZONE A	ZONE B	ZONE C	ZONE D
Saxon	4	4	4	3
Late Roman	4	4	3	2
Early Roman	4	3	2	2
Pre-Roman	3	2	2	2

Table 1 Correlation of 'Stages' in Zoned Landscapes (Fig. 2) with period

Although limited in scale, excavations on three Saxon sites in Gosberton Fen corroborated Hayes' earlier model. At Third Drove, Gosberton, environmental analysis of excavated features on a site with both Roman and Early Saxon features revealed that all the Roman features had abundant evidence of a brackish/marine-dominated landscape (Stage 3) while all the Saxon features exhibited uniformly freshwater (Stage 4) indicators (Trimble 2000). The freshwater derived peatland, therefore, had pushed the Stage 3 'zone of maximum production' some 6-7km across the Fen over the course of a millennium. Such detailed minor migrations of communities through time are rarely traceable.

The ever-widening gap between the fen edge and the in-fen communities, caused by the freshwater fens, was clear from the plotting of the Saxon finds. This resulted in a marked gap between the Saxon settlers of the fen and the contemporary uplanders (Hayes 1988, fig 3). Between them lay a block of archaeologically empty land which equated to the extent of the peat at that time. It has been postulated that the 'empty' fen served as a political boundary between two historically attested tribes – the *Spaldas* and the *Bilmigas*. These tribes were recorded in a fiscal document dated to c. AD 680, which suggested a Fenland location for the former (presumably associated with Spalding) and for the Bilmigas, an upland location (around Billingborough?). The boundary between them was a physical division – the broad peat band. Having completely desiccated, this peaty physical boundary is invisible in the modern landscape, except for dark staining of the mineral soil.

Whether a specific fixed boundary within this 6-7km wide fen was ever formalised cannot be known. The later practice of intercommoning suggests a visible boundary may not have been necessary. If it was, a possible candidate could be the intriguingly-named *'Midfendyk'*, which in c.1350 was described as 'of old the division between Kesteven and Holland' but also 'so much inundated and otherwise hidden that there is complete ignorance'. Physical remains of the actual *'dyk'* itself are likely to have been removed during later construction of the Forty Foot Drain and, given the dearth of early documents and charters, it is unlikely that the evidence to support or refute this suggestion will ever become available.

Survey on the Heath

Although only *c.* 30% of the Lincolnshire Fenland was surveyed, this figure contrasts sharply with the near absence of systematic work conducted on the Heath.

Survey of one Heathland parish, Ropsley and Humby, conducted by the then Trust for Lincolnshire Archaeology, was designed to take a first look at this region. By good fortune the parish straddled the junction of the stony heath soils and the boulder clay which caps much of the limestone to the south.

Although the sample of each landscape zone is small, definite patterns emerged (Lane 1995). Firstly, the quantity of background lithics and, in particular, Bronze Age pottery, suggested strongly that the landscape on the heath had been cleared and was well settled by the early second millennium BC. To the contrary, the boulder clay produced little or nothing of any period and is likely to have remained wooded at this time and for much of the next 3500 years. However, the few lithics that were found on the boulder clay tended to be isolated single finds but of high quality. In particular, plano-convex knives were found (Lane 1995, fig 8). Did these items, which are often associated with burials, indeed have a funerary origin? Did they stem from burial sites in woodland clearings? Funerary sites were certainly present in the area with two flat cremation cemeteries of later Bronze Age date situated either side of the parish boundary in the northwest (Chowne and Lane 1987). These were located as surface pottery scatters associated with tiny cremated bone fragments. Both were restricted in area, with neither exceeding 36 m^2 when excavated. The pottery proved near identical to that scattered widely throughout the limestone soils (Lane 1995, fig 9), but no other concentrations had cremated bone fragments on the surface.

While Roman sites were relatively common on the stony heath soils at Blyborough, north of Lincoln (James Albone, *pers comm.*), the equivalent sites at Ropsley tended to be adjacent to the boundaries between clay and limestone soils, presumably near springs. Such locations would also have enabled the communities to exploit the woods and pastures on the claylands as well as the arable on the lighter soils. The majority of these sites were small in area and likely to have been minor farmsteads. Two sites had different characteristics. Straddling the eastern parish boundary, the partly excavated Roman small town better known as Sapperton (Simmons 1995), aligned on the Roman road, Long Hollow, while, to the west, a large settlement on an exposure of gravel in the boulder clay clearly had an industrial component, possibly including tile making. Fired clay, presumably hearth/oven debris, was common. Adjacent fields contained little or no background scatter and a woodland setting, with a plentiful local supply of fuel for the ovens can be suggested.

Multi-disciplinary investigation resulted in the reconstruction of the pattern of former medieval woodland in the parish and indeed some assarted areas. Fieldwalking, including checking hedgerows for former wood banks, provided the initial evidence. Fields with no medieval surface finds (these usually coincided with a lack of finds of any period) were generally concentrated on the clay soils in the south and west, where the remaining few isolated woods are situated. Some names of now arable fields betrayed a former woodland use (the rather obvious 'Hog Tree Wood', along with 'The Lounds', 'Stocking', 'Stockholms'). Documentary searches revealed the existence and sometime locations of now extinct woods, including Hog Tree Wood, Lound and Hall Woods. Air photographs revealed a ditch around Hog Tree Wood (the accompanying bank survived as a very slight rise in the arable). Finally, a hedgerow survey showed high incidences of dogwood, common in hedges that are relics of old woodland (Pollard 1973, 351). Moreover, a woodland plant, bluebell, grew below the hedges surrounding Lound.

Detailed fieldwork, hedgerow species analysis and documentary research have combined to provide a reconstruction of the medieval landscape at Ropsley and Humby. The remarkable durability of the local Middle and Later Bronze Age pottery of the Heath has also demonstrated a large presence there in the second millennium BC (Lane 1995, fig 9). This was only retrieved by detailed surface survey. Indeed, no evidence of features was recorded and not a single sherd of pottery seen during subsequent monitoring of a pipeline traversing Ropsley Heath. In this area of shallow stony soils, with little or no potential for survival of environmental evidence, further detailed survey must be undertaken, particularly if the prehistoric archaeology lies mostly in the topsoil.

Survey on the Wolds

(with Paul Cope-Faulkner)

While some previous survey has been conducted on the Wolds, the areas covered have not been substantial. In the 1980s, Patricia Phillips recognised that '...surface survey had lagged behind as a research tool' on the Wolds and led students from Sheffield University on a 400m wide by 18km long survey from Claxby to Ludborough (Phillips 1989). To the southwest of the area, the Bain valley had been surveyed by Peter Chowne (1994). In both cases, lithics proved the dominant surface find.

Towards their northern end, the Wolds are divided by the west-east aligned Kirmington Gap. Field survey was undertaken in several parishes in this region during the 1998-9 season as part of a Heritage Management Plan for a large estate (referred to below as the Brocklesby Survey). Whilst some areas surveyed were isolated and small, others were more sizeable enabling patterns to emerge. Unlike the results of Phillips' (1989) work, relatively few lithics were found. Little or no Iron Age material was forthcoming and the Roman settlements were widely scattered with pottery being low in sherd counts and generally composed exclusively of greywares. The one known exception was the Iron Age and Roman small town at Kirmington, adjacent to Humberside Airport, but which lay outside the area of the Brocklesby Survey. Its size and range of finds contrasts sharply with the scattered outlying sites discovered on the survey.

Linear Features on Wold and Fen

One aspect of the archaeology of the Wolds which differed widely from both the Fens and the Heath was the survival of earthwork banks, particularly on parish boundaries. Recent aerial survey has recorded as cropmarks a series of isolated linear ditches (presumably once having associated banks?) throughout Lincolnshire. In places, these took the form of single ditch cropmarks, while elsewhere were double and even triple ditches (Boutwood 1998). While most of the multiple linear ditches recorded by Boutwood lay to the west of the county, the boundary between Brocklesby and Habrough was recorded as an outlying and upstanding example (which has since been levelled). At the time it was believed to be the only upstanding example in Lincolnshire, although a triple ditch (known as King Lud's Entrenchments) survives in earthwork form just outside the county boundary in Leicestershire as a parish boundary between Croxton Kerrial and Sproxton (Liddle 1982, 16).

Plate 1 *Audlebie Bank*, at the boundary between Caistor and Great Limber

A number of surviving banks, many without obvious ditches were recorded during the Brocklesby Survey. Of these, the most impressive marks the division between the parishes of Great Limber and Caistor (Fig. 3). Extending through woodland for approximately 1.2km, the earthworks take various forms including single ditch with chalk bank on the northern side to double ditches with three banks (no full detailed earthwork survey has yet taken place and where it is of multiple ditch form its current woodland setting makes its precise form difficult to ascertain). Towards the eastern end the ditchline is broken by a circular mound, presumed to be a barrow. Beyond the mound the ditchline continues. For part of its length the bank(s) takes a line along the natural ridge which would, but for the current woodland, have extensive views north and south. This watershed location is reminiscent of King Lud's Entrenchments (Phillips 1934, 136) while, farther afield, the single bank and ditch known as Launditch, in Norfolk, runs for 6km along a watershed (Davies 1996, 75). Barrows as boundary features on watersheds have been cited in Yorkshire (Spratt 1981, 94).

The earliest known reference to the Great Limber/ Caistor earthworks dates from c. 1150 when *'vallum quandem que a vulgo Foxedale vocatur'* (translated as 'the ditch that was commonly called Foxdale' [Cameron 1991, 90]) indicates the earthwork's existence by that time. Later references are to *Audlebie Bank* on a map of Great Limber dating to 1676 (LAO Yarb 4/18/1). At this time there was no woodland to protect the earthwork but the area appeared to be rough grazing land with some heather. Later planting of woodland, around 1800, preserved the earthwork from wind erosion (although tree-root damage is inevitable). The monument was dismissed as a hollow way and adjacent hedge bank by an early Ordnance Survey surveyor but is more probably a rare survival of an early and likely prehistoric multiple ditch boundary.

Part of a second substantial earthwork lies at the west of nearby Hendale Wood. Again a parish boundary, this time between Great Limber and Searby cum Owmby, it lies on the probable line of High Street Roman road. It takes the form of a double bank with central depression (not ditch), although infilled side ditches could be present and undetected. Its line is a continuation of the former boundary dyke (*mère dic*), a boundary continuous for 16km and separating 13 parishes (Everson 1984).

The longest stretch of bank (but with no obvious adjacent ditch) recorded during the Brocklesby survey is the 4km length between Middlegate Lane, Melton Ross in the west and West End Road, Ulceby

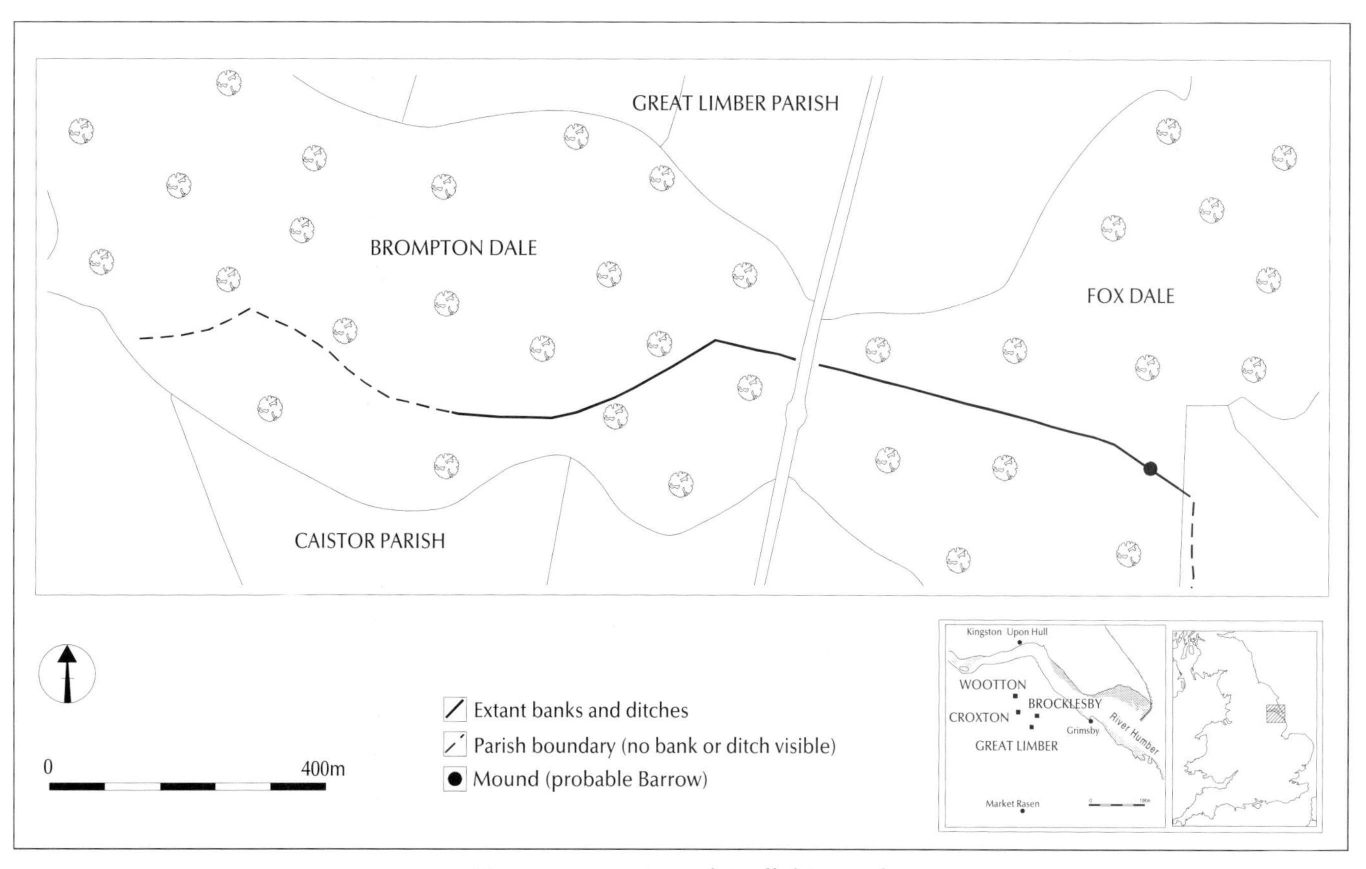

Figure 3 Location of *Audlebie Bank*

in the east. It demarcates the boundary between Croxton and Wootton parishes. The bank itself lies on the northern slope of a prominent natural dry valley and follows this position for most of the area surveyed. Over time, the bank has arrested soil slippage and fields to the north of and abutting the bank are markedly higher than those to the south. This soil movement has served to preserve the bank. However, on the lower slopes, east of the plantation, the bank is all but ploughed out and is visible on the field surface only in favourable low light or in snow. Whether by coincidence or otherwise an earthwork of probable Iron Age date which later became a Wapentake meeting place, Yarborough Camp, lies a consistent distance 2-2.5km south of and 'inside' this curving boundary; consistent enough to invite speculation on association.

A 1.5km stretch of parish boundary between Ulceby and Wootton within the survey area is marked by a single bank and passes directly through the probable barrow site of Galley Hill. Yet again, this may be an example of an ancient monument being used as a marker during laying out of a significant boundary.

Recent aerial survey in the northern Wolds region has resulted in the discovery of some 'new' single and double ditch linears (Boutwood, *pers comm.*). A number of these are situated in the immediate vicinity of *Audlebie Bank*, although none align on it. One cropmark does, however, appear to extend south from the Hendales boundary and indicates the continued line of the Roman road High Street.

Whereas a number of banks aligned on ancient or topographic features are of probable ancient (prehistoric) date, others are clearly later. Around the northern Wolds area, these later examples are much smaller than *Audlebie Bank,* being little more than 0.5m high in most cases. Some follow a 'zig-zag' pattern between pre-existing blocks of ridge and furrow, demonstrating a post-Late Saxon origin. Examples of these boundaries are found in Roxton Wood (boundary between Keelby and Brocklesby) and in woodland between Brocklesby and Kirmington. These are clearly late additions to the pattern of boundaries. That banks should be built to demarcate these later alterations is probably a reflection of an existing local tradition of embankments marking boundaries. There is reference to *'le Neudik inter Vlseeby et Broclosby'* (the new dyke/bank between Ulceby and Brocklesby) in 1312 but how long it had been new at that time is not known. In the Fenland the New Fendike is still called that, more than eight centuries after its construction.

Mention of the Fenland returns us to some previously unconsidered double and triple ditches in that area, though these are of a different nature to those cited earlier. The Royal Commission's National Mapping Programme in Lincolnshire excluded most of the Fenland and, therefore, examples from this area went unrecorded. The precinct of Crowland Abbey approximates to the modern parish boundary and encompasses some 5443ha. On at least its northern side (Queen's Bank, formerly *Asen Dike*), the precinct was marked by double or triple ditches with banks. These still survive as Scheduled earthworks between Cate's Cove and Aswick Grange and as cropmarks farther west. Where formerly embanked internal land divisions within the Precinct have now been removed, for example between the modern Postland Station and Willow Row Bank, the aerial photographic record is of three parallel ditches (Hayes and Lane 1992, 202). A similar survival of three ditches and two banks was found in a rare fragment of Fenland woodland near Dogdyke in the northern Fens. Quite why double and triple banks are required is little understood but it may well have been an effective flood protection system – if the first bank failed a second or even third would provide instant back up. Such sizeable multiple earthworks may also have made statements about status of the owners. Whilst no dating has been confirmed for the Crowland examples, they cannot pre-date the Mid-Late Saxon formation of the Abbey.

But, away from the Fens, how old are the upland Lincolnshire banks? Little in the way of dating has been forthcoming from the few sites excavated in the west of the county, although, sometimes, an Iron Age association has been inferred (Boutwood 1998, 39). Elsewhere, in Britain, later prehistoric dates are commonly assigned to linear boundaries, for example, in Yorkshire (Bevan 1997, 183), Norfolk (Davies 1996, 75), Bedfordshire (Dyer 1961) and for certain of the Cambridgeshire dykes (Malim 1996, 117). Chalk-cut boundaries as substantial (and therefore labour intensive to construct) as *Audlebie Bank* are unlikely to result from late Saxon/medieval land division or parish formalisation, unless, perhaps, instigated by religious institutions (see Crowland, above). In the case of *Audlebie Bank,* the use of the probable barrow in the layout is certainly suggestive of a prehistoric rather than late Saxon/medieval origin. Such association of barrows as components of prehistoric ditch systems is known elsewhere in the Britain, for

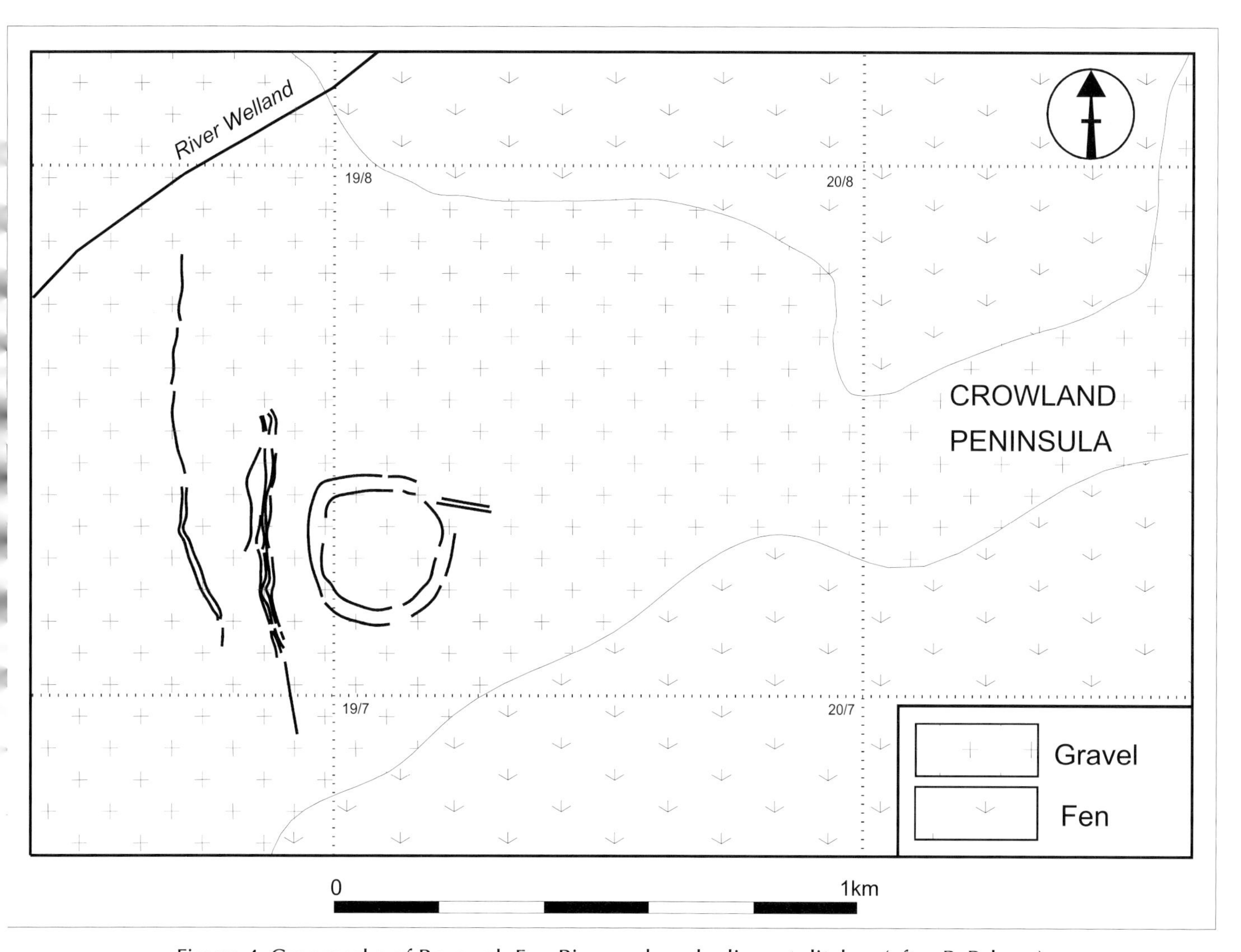

Figure 4 Cropmarks of Borough Fen Ringwork and adjacent ditches (after R. Palmer)

example in Berkshire (Bradley and Richards 1978) and Yorkshire (Bevan 1997, 183).

Just into Cambridgeshire two near parallel lengths of ditch, a double and a quadruple, occupy a strategic location which may associate them with barrows. Lying just to the west of the presumed Iron Age, but possibly Late Bronze Age, Borough Fen Ringwork, these ditches may well pre-date that monument. Alluvial soils in the floodplain of the river Welland broadly define the limit of the ditches (although the date of alluviation is unconfirmed and they may continue beneath). Both ringwork and linear ditches are sited at the narrow landward 'entrance/exit' to the Crowland peninsular which had a row of at least nine barrows along its spine with more ring ditches photographed recently by the author. The ditches and any associated banks may well have sealed access to Crowland and 'guarded' its barrowfields.

Less than a kilometre to the north, back in Lincolnshire, a linear ditch and bank of Early to Middle Bronze Age date, was part-excavated at Welland Bank Quarry (Pryor 1998a; 1998b, 118; this volume). This appeared to be of a different character and function to the upland bank and ditches. Although post-excavation anaysis is not complete it seems initially that a small braided channel of the Welland was dug out to maintain a supply of brackish water for saltmaking at Welland Bank. Spoil was placed to the south and the completed works would serve three functions – to maintain the necessary supply of brackish water, to provide a flood defence and to provide an elevated routeway. A fourth might have been to create/formalise a boundary.

While the Welland Bank earthwork appears to have been multi-functional it is presumed that the majority of Lincolnshire banks and dykes were constructed to demarcate territories of one sort or another. But why are the known lengths so relatively short? While the longest (though discontinuous) stretch of multiple ditch is some 5.7km (Boutwood 1998, 29) others are much shorter.

One length of three parallel ditches on the Fen edge gravels in Pointon and Sempringham extends for 0.6km, although hedge lines and parish boundaries suggested to Jim Pickering (1988, 42) that it may once have continued for up to 13km. It may not be coincidental that the ditches are on a similar west-east alignment to the linear Hoe Hills barrow cemetery and adjacent prehistoric stream course, which lies less than 1km to the south and forms a more traditionally 'recognisable' land division (Lane 2000; Pickering 1988, fig 14). An Iron Age and Roman settlement complex appears to overlie the Pointon and Sempringham ditches, suggesting a prehistoric date for their construction. Could it be that the ditches served some symbolic rather than functional purpose (e.g. Pollard 1996, 110)? Was the real boundary the stream? Is there any significance in the linear barrow cemetery being on one side of the stream and the ditches on the other?

How should studies of these monuments be taken forward? Fittingly for this volume and the man it honours, it would seem that field survey must now have a role to play in the investigation of linear boundaries. Aerial photography has discovered them and with spectacular images brought them to the fore, while excavation has defined profiles and generally confirmed the lack of dating evidence. It is time to build on the excellent work of Yvonne Boutwood and undertake detailed field surveys in the vicinity of the known linear boundaries. A mixture of reconnaissance and detailed fieldwalking around the known lengths might in the first instance, determine any topographical significance (e.g. watersheds, wet or dry valleys [see Boutwood 1998, fig 1]) and the presence of settlement or ritual sites overlying, underlying or associated with the linears. In the case of the cropmark sites the relationships of those cropmarks to archaeological landscapes would form part of any survey. For example, do the medieval field patterns respect the linears? If not, a pre-medieval date would seem assured. Detailed plotting of soils and geology might reveal why the ditch lengths end abruptly at specific points. Are some or all of the termini at junctions with heavy soils? Did the linears cease at existing woodland or at wide, wet valleys of now constrained rivers and streams? Were double and triple ditches confined to formerly wet areas and have a water defence function, as may have occurred at Crowland Abbey precinct, or is the purpose of the ditches more steeped in ritual and symbolism? One line of enquiry might be to seek topographic features adjacent to the cropmark ditches. The Pointon and Sempringham triple ditch (above), the St Ives pit alignments (Pollard 1996) and many of the Lincolnshire multiple ditch cropmarks align on streams. It may be worth theorising that those streams (or soil divisions, or dry valleys, or watersheds) that have adjacent, but often short lengths of ditched boundary are themselves the real boundary, rather than the ditches. That way the length of boundary could be extended by following the relevant topographic feature. Some linears may have had a function unrecognisable from the air, such as the long straggling ditch at Billingborough which is thought to have brought upland spring water to the Fen edge communities and their stock (Chowne 1988, 34), perhaps from a spring regarded as sacred?

Plate 2 Prehistoric multiple ditches near Pointon and Sempringham, Lincs

Surveys of substantial woodlands would be desirable. How many more earthworks like *Audlebie Bank* lie hidden from the aerial archaeologist's view. Foremost, the purpose of field survey would be to characterise the linears in their landscape settings and to identify the most appropriate locations where worthwhile further investigations, in particular excavation, could be targeted. This could be in wet areas where pollen and other environmental indicators might survive.

Such locations could determine whether or not the banks were hedged (stockproofed) and with what species-types. It could be where associated settlement or ritual sites would give the best chance of dating the linears. In short, the results of such work would provide context for the features by reconstructing the surrounding ancient landscapes.

Such a project would require an energetic, intuitive, visionary fieldworker – surely a job for David Hall?

Acknowledgements

David Hall has been a key inspiration in all the fieldwork as has Brian Simmons who initiated me into field survey. I thank my colleagues whose enthusiasm and ideas have rubbed off: For the Fenland, John Coles, Peter Hayes, Dale Trimble and others too numerous to list; for the northern Wolds Paul Cope-Faulkner. My thanks go to the Earl of Yarborough for permission to publish *Audlebie Banks*; to David Start and to Hilary Healey, a fount of knowledge as always; Yvonne Boutwood kindly allowed access to results of recent aerial photography; Susan Unsworth produced the illustrations.

Bibliography

Bevan, B., 1997, 'Bounding the landscape: Place and identity during the Yorkshire Wolds Iron Age' in Gwilt, A. and Haselgrove, C. (eds), *Reconstructing Iron Age Societies*, Oxbow Monograph 71, 181-91

Boutwood, Y., 1998, 'Prehistoric Linear Boundaries in Lincolnshire and its Fringes' in Bewley, R.H. (ed), *Lincolnshire's Archaeology from the Air*, Occasional Papers in Lincolnshire History and Archaeology 11, 29-46

Bradley, R. and Richards, J., 1978, 'Prehistoric Fields and Boundaries on the Berkshire Downs', in Bowen, H.C. and Fowler, P.J. (eds), *Early Land Allotment*, Brit. Arch. Rep British Series 48, 53-65

Cameron, K., 1991, *The Place names of Lincolnshire*, English Place Names Society Vol. LXIV/LXV

Chowne, P., 1988, *Aspects of Later Prehistoric settlement in Lincolnshire: A study of the western Fen margin and Bain Valley* (Unpublished Ph.D thesis, University of Nottingham)

Chowne, P., 1994, 'The Bain Valley Survey' in Parker Pearson, M and Schadla-Hall, R.T. (eds), *Looking at the Land* (Leicestershire Museums, Arts and Records Service)

Chowne, P. and Lane, T., 1987, 'Bronze Age Cremation Cemeteries at Old Somerby and Ropsley and Humby', *Lincs. Hist. and Archaeol.* Vol.22, 35-40

Coles, J. and Hall, D., 1998, *Changing Landscapes: The Ancient Fenland* (Cambridgeshire County Council/WARP)

Crowson, A., Lane, T. and Reeve, J., 2000, *Fenland Management Project Excavations 1991-1995*, Lincolnshire Archaeology and Heritage Reports Series 3

Davies, J.A., 1996, 'Where Eagles Dare: the Iron Age of Norfolk', *Proc Prehist. Soc.* 62, 63-92

Dyer, J.F., 1961, 'Dray's Ditches, Bedfordshire, and Early Iron Age territorial boundaries in the Chilterns', *Antiquaries Journal* 118, 32-43

Everson, P., 1984, 'The Pre-Conquest Estate of *Æt Bearuwe* in Lindsey', in Faull, M. (ed), *Studies in Late Anglo-Saxon Settlement* (Dept. of External Studies, Oxford), 123-27

Hall, D., 1977, *Wollaston, Portrait of a Village*. (Wollaston Society)

Hall, D., 1982, *Medieval Fields* (Shire Publications)

Hall, D., 1985, 'Survey Work in Eastern England', in Macready, S. and Thompson F.H. (eds), *Archaeological Field Survey in Britain and Abroad,* Soc. of Ants. Occ. Paper (New Series VI) 25-44

Hall, D., 1995, *The Open Fields of Northamptonshire* (Northampton Record Society Vol. 38

Hall, D., 1996, 'The Fenland Project, Number 10: Cambridgeshire Survey, Isle of Ely and Wisbech', *East Anglian Archaeology* 79

Hall, D. and Coles, J., 1994, *Fenland Survey. An essay in landscape and persistence*, English Heritage Archaeological Report 1 (London)

Hallam, S., 1970 'Settlement round the Wash' in Phillips, C.W. (ed), *The Fenland in Roman Times*, Royal Geog. Soc. Res. Ser. 5, 22-113

Hayes, P.P., 1988, 'Roman to Saxon in the south Lincolnshire Fens', *Antiquity* Vol.62, No 235, 321-6

Hayes, P.P. and Lane, T.W., 1992, *'The Fenland Project, Number 5: Lincolnshire Survey, The south-West Fens'*, East Anglian Archaeology 55

Hayes, P.P., Lane, T.W. and Samuels, J.R., 1992, 'Roman pottery and landscape archaeology in the south Lincolnshire Fens' in Hayes, P.P. and Lane, T.W., *'The Fenland Project, Number 5: Lincolnshire Survey, The south-West Fens'*, East Anglian Archaeology 55

Hayes, P.P. and Lane, T.W., 1993, 'Moving boundaries in the Fens of South Lincolnshire' in Gardiner, J. (ed), *'Flatlands and Wetlands: Current themes in East Anglian Archaeology'*, East Anglian Archaeology 50, 58-70

Lane, T.W., 1993, *'The Fenland Project, Number 8: Lincolnshire Survey, The Northern Fen-Edge'*, East Anglian Archaeology 66

Lane, T.W., 1995, *'The Archaeology and Developing Landscape of Ropsley and Humby, Lincolnshire'*, Lincolnshire Archaeology and Heritage Reports Series 2

Lane, T., 2000, 'Hoe Hills, Dowsby' in Crowson, A., Lane, T. and Reeve, J. (eds), *'Fenland Management Project Excavations 1991-1995'*, Lincolnshire Archaeology and Heritage Reports Series 3

Liddle, P., 1982 *Leicestershire Archaeology. The present state of knowledge. Vol 1 to the end of the Roman period* (Leicestershire Museums, Art Galleries and Records Service Archaeological Report No 4)

Malim, T., 1996, 'New evidence on the Cambridgeshire Dykes and Worsted Street Roman Road', *Proceedings of the Cambridge Antiquarian Society* Vol. 85, 27-122

Palmer, R., 1996, 'Air photo interpretation and the Lincolnshire Fenland', *Landscape History* Vol.18, 5-16

Phillips, C.W., 1934, 'The present state of archaeology in Lincolnshire (Part 1)', *Archaeolgical Journal* 91, 97-154

Phillips, P., 1989, 'Lincolnshire Wolds Transect Survey. Objectives and Results', in Phillips, P. (ed), *Archaeology and Landscape Studies in North Lincolnshire*, Brit. Arch. Rep. Brit. Ser. 208 (ii), 27-69

Pickering, J., 1988, 'Aerial archaeology on the Fen edge in South Lincolnshire', *Fenland Research* 5, 39-43

Pollard, E., 1973, 'Hedges. VII. Woodland relic hedges in Huntingdon and Peterborough', *J. of Ecology*, 61,343-52

Pollard, J., 1996, 'Iron Age Riverside Pit Alignments at St Ives, Cambridgeshire', *Proc. Prehist. Soc.* 62, 93-115

Pryor, F.M.M., 1998a, 'Welland Bank Quarry, South Lincolnshire', *Current Archaeology*, 160, 139-45

Pryor, F.M.M., 1998b, *Farmers in Prehistoric Britain* (Stroud, Tempus)

Robinson, D., 1993, 'Natural Regions', in Bennett, S. and Bennett, N., 1993, *An Historical Atlas of Lincolnshire* (University of Hull Press)

Spratt, D.A., 1981, 'Prehistoric boundaries on the north Yorkshire Moors', in Barker, G. (ed), *Prehistoric Communities in Northern England* (Univ. of Sheffield)

Simmons, B., 1995, 'Sapperton' in Brown, A.E. (ed), *Roman Small Towns in Eastern England and beyond,* Oxbow Monograph 52

Swift, G., 1984, *Waterland* (Picador)

Trimble, D., 2000, 'Third Drove Gosberton', in Crowson, A., Lane, T. and Reeve, J. (eds), *'Fenland Management Project Excavations 1991-1995'*, Lincolnshire Archaeology and Heritage Reports Series 3

Waller, M, 1994, *'The Fenland Project, Number 9: Flandrian Environmental Change in Fenland'*, East Anglian Archaeology 70

13. D.N. Hall – A BIBLIOGRAPHY

1966

'Sites on the North Bedfordshire and South Northamptonshire Border,' *Beds. Archaeol. J. 3*, 1-6; with N. Nickerson

1967

'Excavations at Irchester 1962-3', *Archaeol. J.* 124, 65-99; with N. Nickerson

1969

'The Earthworks of Strixton', *J. Northampton Museum* 6, 22-32

'Iron Age Pottery in North Bedfordshire and South Northamptonshire', *Beds. Archaeol. J.* 4, 1-12; with N. Nickerson

1970

'Excavations inside Newton Willows Church 1969', *J. Northampton Museum* 7, 16-36; with J. B. Hutchings

'A Circular Roman Building at Bozeat, Northamptonshire, 1964', *Beds. Archaeol. J.* 5, 57-65; with N. Nickerson

1971

'Pre-Roman Iron Age Sites at Bozeat and Strixton', *Beds. Archaeol. J.* 6, 12-22

'A Thirteenth Century Pottery Kiln Site at Harrold, Bedfordshire', *Milton Keynes J. of Archaeol. and Hist.* 1, 41-5

'Excavations inside Ravensden Church 1969', *Beds. Archaeol. J. 6*, 41-54; with J. B. Hutchings & G. J. Dring

1972

'The distribution of Archaeological Sites between the Nene and Ouse Valleys', *Beds. Archaeol. J. 7*, 1-16; with J. B. Hutchings

'An Early Iron Age site at Irthlingborough, Northamptonshire' *Beds. Archaeol. J.* 7, 17-20

'Modern Surveys of Medieval Field Systems', *Beds, Archaeol. J.* 7, 1972, 53-66

1973

'Rescue Excavations at Radwell Gravel Pits', *Beds. Archaeol. J.* 8, 67-92

'Strixton Thirteenth Century Windmill', *Beds. Archaeol. J.* 8, 108-118

1974

'Medieval Pottery from the Higham Ferrers Hundred', *J. Northampton Museum* 10, 38-58

'Rushden Church, a Reappraisal of the Architectural History', *Northamptonshire Past and Present* 5, 71-5

1975

'A group of Post-medieval Pottery from the Manor-house, Strixton Northamptonshire', *Beds. Archaeol. J.* 10, 65-70.

1976

'Little Houghton 1972, a Parish Field Survey', *Northamptonshire Past and Present* 5, 295-304

'Farndish in the counties of Bedford and Northampton or one of them' *Beds. Archaeol. J.* 11, 43-50; with J. B. Hutchings

'Wootton parish survey 1973', *Northants. Archaeol.* 11, 151-8

1977

Wollaston, Portrait of a Village (Wollaston Society)

'Excavations in Brixworth Churchyard 1971', *J. British Archaeol. Assoc.* 130, 123-32

'Radwell excavations 1974-5: the Bronze Age Ring ditches', *Beds. Archaeol. J.* 12, 1-16; with Peter Woodward

'Little Billing parish survey 1970', *Northants. Archaeol.* 12, 177-82

'The sea bank in Cambridgeshire', *Proceedings of the Cambridgeshire Antiquarian Society* 67, 67-9

1978

'Elm, a Field Survey', *Proceedings of the Cambridgeshire Antiquarian Society* 65, 21-46

'Great Billing parish survey', *Northants. Archaeol.* 13, 161-7

1979

'Brixworth, Northamptonshire, an Intensive Archaeological Survey', *J. British Archaeol. Assoc.* 122, 1-6; with Paul Martin

'New evidence of modifications of open-field systems', *Antiquity* 53, 222-224

'Great Houghton parish survey', *Northants. Archaeol.* 14, 80-88

1980

'Brixworth, Northamptonshire, New Evidence for early Prehistoric Settlement and Agriculture', *Beds. Archaeol. J.* 14, 5-14; with Paul Martin

'Thurleigh Church excavations', *Beds. Archaeol. J.* 14, 59-79; with J. B. Hutchings

'Hardingstone Parish Survey', *Northants. Archaeol.* 15, 119-32

1981

'Cambridgeshire Fenland: an intensive archaeological fieldwork survey' in Rowley, R.T. (ed), *The Evolution of Marshland Landscapes*, Oxford University Department for External Studies, 52-73

'The Changing Landscape of the Cambridgeshire Silt Fens', *Landscape History* 3, 37-49

'The Origins of Open Field Agriculture — the Archaeological Fieldwork evidence', in Rowley, R.T.. (ed), *The Origins of Open field Agriculture*, 22-38

1982

Medieval Fields, Shire Publications

'The countryside of the South-East Midlands and Cambridgeshire', in Miles, D. (ed), *The Romano-British Countryside*, British Archaeological Reports, British Series 103, 337-50

1983

'Fieldwork and field books: studies in early layout', in Roberts, B.K. and Glasscock, R.E. (eds), *Villages, Fields and Frontiers*, British Archaeological Reports, International Series 185, Oxford, 115-131

'The Fenland Project', *Antiquity* 57, 51-2; with John Coles

1984

'Fieldwork and documentary evidence for the layout and organization of early medieval estates in the English Midlands', in Biddick, K. (ed), *Archaeological approaches to Medieval Europe*, Studies in Medieval Culture, Western Michigan University, 43-68

1985

Rushden, a Duchy of Lancaster Village; with R. Harding

'Late Saxon topography and early medieval estates', in Hooke, D. (ed), *Medieval Villages*, Oxford University Committee for Archaeology, 61-9

'Survey work in Eastern England', in Macready, S. and Thompson, F.H. (eds), *Archaeological Field Survey in Britain and Abroad*, Society of Antiquaries of London Occ. Paper 6, 25-44

1986

'Recherches dans les plaines tourbeuses des fenlands dans l'est d'Angleterre (Grand Bretagne)', in Ferdiere, A. and Zadora-Roi, E. (eds), *La Prospection Archaeologique: Paysage et Peuplement*, Documents d'Archaeologie Francaise, Paris, 25-44

1987

The Fenland Project, Number 2: Fenland Landscapes and Settlement between Peterborough and March, East Anglian Archaeology 35

'Regional Fieldwork on the Wash Fenlands of England', in Coles, J.M. and Lawson, A.J. (eds), *European Wetlands in Prehistory*, Oxford, 169-80

Introduction to the Northamptonshire Domesday facsimile reproduction by Alecto Historical Editions

1988

Raunds, picturing the past; with R. Harding and C. Putt

'The late Saxon countryside — villages and their fields' in Hooke, D. (ed), *Anglo-Saxon Settlement* (Blackwells)

1989

'Field systems and township structure', in Dyer, C., Aston, M. and Austin, D. (eds), *The Rural Settlements of Medieval England*, (Blackwells)

1991

'Field surveys in Bedfordshire', *Beds. Archaeol. J.* 19, 51-56

1992

The Fenland Project, Number 6: The South-Western Cambridgeshire Fenlands, East Anglian Archaeology 56

1993

The Open Fields of Northamptonshire; the case for preservation (Northamptonshire County Council)

1994

Fenland Survey: an essay in landscape and persistence; with John Coles, English Heritage Archaeological Report 1 (London)

'Ridge and furrow in the English Midlands' in Foster, S. and Smout, T. C., *The History of soils and field systems*, 94-100 (Scottish Cultural Press)

1995

The Open Fields of Northamptonshire, Northamptonshire Record Society Vol. 38

The Wetlands of Greater Manchester, North West Wetlands Survey 2 (Lancaster); with C. E. Wells and E. Huckerby

1996

The Fenland Project, Number 10: Cambridgeshire Survey, Isle of Ely and Wisbech, East Anglian Archaeology 79

1997

'Medieval pottery from Cambridge', *Proceedings of the Cambridgeshire Antiquarian Society* 86, 153-168; with D. Edwards.

'The Fenland Project: from survey to management and beyond', *Antiquity* 71, 831-44; with John Coles

'Enclosure in Northamptonshire', *Northamptonshire Past and Present* 9, 350-367

1998

Changing Landscapes: the Ancient Fenland (Cambridgeshire County Council); with John Coles

'The pottery assemblage' in Lucas, G., 'A medieval fishery on Whittlesea Mere, Cambridgeshire', *Med. Archaeol.* 42, 26-32

1999

'The drainage of arable land in medieval England', in Williamson, T. (ed), *Water Management in the English Landscape* (Edinburgh University Press), 28-40

2000

Wollaston Notes 2000 (Wollaston Society), 2000

'Ridge and furrow survival and preservation', *Antiquity* 74, 29-30; with Rog Palmer

'The ceramic sequence' in Mortimer R., 'Village development...the Middle to Late Saxon village at...Cottenham, Cambridgeshire, *Proc. Camb. Antiq. Soc.* 89, 21-25

Three short essays; 16 'Roman salt production', 38, 'The Fenland 1066-1550' and 'Arable commons and wastes 1066-1550', in Kirby, T. and Oosthuien, S. (eds), *An Atlas of*

Cambridgeshire and Huntingdonshire History (Centre for Regional Studies, Anglia Polytechnic University)

'From aspiration to reality' in Crowson, A., Lane, T. and Reeve, J. (eds), *Fenland Management Project Excavations 1991-1995*, Lincolnshire Archaeology and Heritage Reports Series 3, 231-42; with John Coles

There are shorter articles and numerous notes in various archaeological journals, especially the Newsletter of Group 9 of the Council for British Archaeology, published by Oxford University Department for Continuing Education, which D. Hall edited for ten years, c. 1975-1985.

Editor (since 1995) of Northamptonshire Past and Present, an annual county historical journal, for the Northamptonshire Record Society.